Colorado Journeyman License Information

Electricians in Colorado are licensed by the State Electrical Board only. They need to submit the Affidavit of Experience Form to verify the experience prerequisites for the Exam and license. Applicants for a Colorado residential wireman's license need four thousand hours earned in no less than two years of electrical construction wiring experience, for lights, heat, and power.

Journeyman Electrician

Applicants for a Colorado journeyman electrician's license need eight thousand hours earned in no less than four years of electrical construction wiring experience, for lights, heat and power; with a minimum of four thousand hours earned in no less than two years of that time being commercial and/or industrial work. Verification of experience must state the hours and months of the time spent performing residential and commercial/industrial wiring.

In addition, applicants will need documentation to prove 288 hours of approved electrical education during the period of their apprenticeship (Electrical Rules and Regulations 4.4).

Note: Applicants for the journeyman examination who hold a residential wireman license must **also** be actively registered as an apprentice.

Reciprocity

Alaska, Arkansas, Idaho, Minnesota, Nebraska, North Dakota, Oregon, South Dakota, Utah, Washington, Wyoming

Contact

State Electrical Board
1580 Logan Street, Suite 550
Denver, CO 80203
Phone: (303) 894 2300
Fax: (303) 894 2310
www.colorado.gov/pacific/dora/Electrical

Applications and Forms
https://www.colorado.gov/pacific/dora/Electrical_Applications_Docs

Author: Ray Holder

Electrical Seminars, Inc.
P.O. Box 1430
Belen, NM 87002
(505)864-3554 1-800-632-7732
www.rayholderelectricalseminars.com

TABLE OF CONTENTS

INTRODUCTION

HOW TO PREPARE FOR THE EXAM

Congratulations on purchasing this book! You have taken the first step towards successfully passing your Journeyman Electrician's Licensing Exam. You have in your hands the best self-study guide available for journeyman electrician's exam preparation. This book will not make you a competent electrician, nor will it teach you the electrical trade. What it will do is give you an idea of the type of questions asked on most electrician's licensing exams and of how to answer them correctly. This book covers practically all the subjects you will likely be tested on, including: branch circuits and feeders, motors and motor controls, transformers, hazardous locations, special occupancies, conductors, box and raceway fill, services, the ever-present electrical calculations, plus much more.

This exam preparation guide is composed of multiple choice questions, since this is the format seen on most electrician's licensing exams. In this self-study guide you will find simulated exams, designed to be much like the actual test questions. These questions may require you to fill in a blank, complete a sentence, make the correct choice from a list of possible answers, or complete a mathematical calculation. These practice questions have been chosen to accurately represent the many questions the author and his student have come upon while taking numerous licensing exams in recent years.

Begin your exam preparation with two important points in mind.
 * Opportunities in life will arise - be prepared for them.
 * The more you LEARN - the more you EARN.

Attempting to take an exam without preparation is a complete waste of time. Don't make that mistake. Attend classes at your local community college. Attend seminars, electrical code updates, and company sponsored programs. Many major electrical suppliers and local unions sponsor classes of this type at no cost. Take advantage of them.

Become familiar with the National Electrical Code®; the Code has a LANGUAGE all its own. Understanding this language will help you to better interpret the NEC®. Do not become intimidated by the length of the NEC®. Become thoroughly familiar with the definitions in Chapter One; if you don't, the remainder of the NEC® will be difficult to comprehend. Remember, on the job we use different "lingo" and phrases compared to the way the NEC® is written or the way many test questions are expressed.

HOW TO STUDY

Before beginning to study, get into the right frame of mind and relax. Study in a quiet place that is conducive to learning. If such a place is not available, go to your local library. It is important that you have the right atmosphere in which to study.

It is much better to study many short lengths of time than attempt to study fewer, longer lengths of time. Try to study a little while –perhaps an hour– every evening. You will need the support and understanding of your family to set aside this much-needed time.

As you study this exam preparation book, the NEC®, and other references, always highlight the important points. This makes it easier to locate Code references when taking the exam.

Use a straight edge, such as a six-inch ruler, when using the NEC® tables and charts. A very common mistake is to get on the wrong line when using these tables: when that happens, the result is an incorrect answer.

Use tabs on the major sections of your NEC®, so they become faster and easier to locate when taking the exam. The national average allowed per question is less than three minutes. You cannot waste time.

WHAT TO STUDY
Not knowing what to study is a common reason for test-takers to be unsuccessful when attempting to pass electrical exams. Approximately forty percent of most exams are known as "core" questions. This type of question is represented in this exam preparation book.

The subject matter covered in most electrical license examinations is:

* Grounding and bonding
* Overcurrent protection
* Wiring methods and installation
* Boxes and fittings
* Services and equipment
* Motors
* Special occupancies
* Load calculations
* Lighting
* Appliances
* Box and raceway fill
* Hazardous locations

Become very familiar with questions on the above. Knowing what to study is a major step toward passing your exam.

HELPFUL HINTS ON TAKING THE EXAM

* **Complete the easy questions first.** On most tests, all questions are valued the same. If you become too frustrated on any one question, it may reflect upon your entire test.

* **Keep track of time.** Do not spend too much time on one question. If a question is difficult for you, mark the answer sheet the answer you think is correct and place a check (✓) by that question in the examination booklet. Then go on to the next question: if you have time after finishing the rest of the exam, you can go back to the questions you have checked. If you simply do not know the answer to a question, take a guess. Choose the answer that is most familiar to you. In most cases, the answer is B or C.

* **Only change answers if you know you are right.** - Usually, your first answer is your best answer.

* **Relax** - Do not get uptight and stressed out when testing.

* **Tab your Code Book.** - References are easier and faster to find.

* **Use a straightedge.** - Prevent getting on the wrong line when referring to the tables in the NEC®.

* **Get a good night's rest before the exam.** - Do not attempt to drive several hours to an exam site: be rested and alert.

* **Understand the question.** - One key word in a question can make a difference in what the question is asking. Underlining key words will help you to understand the meaning of the question.

* **Use a dependable calculator.** - Use a solar-powered calculator that has a battery back-up. Since many test sites are not well-lit, this type of calculator will prepare you for such a situation. If possible, bring along a spare calculator.

* **Show up at least 30 minutes prior to your exam time.** – Be sure to allow yourself time for traffic, etc. when planning your route to the exam location.

TYPICAL REGULATIONS AT THE PLACE OF EXAMINATION

Most licensing agencies outsource their examinations to a testing agency that is a separate entity from the licensing agency. After you get approval from the licensing agency to take the exam, contact the testing agency for their regulations. To ensure that all examinees are examined under equally favorable conditions, the following regulations and procedures are observed at most examination sites:

* Each examinee must present proper photo identification, preferably your driver's license before you will be permitted to take the examination.

* No cameras, notes, tape recorders, pagers, or cellular phones are allowed in the examination room.

* No one will be permitted to work beyond the established time limits.

* Examinees are not permitted any reference material EXCEPT the National Electrical Code®.

* Examinees will be permitted to use noiseless calculators during the examination. Calculators which provide programmable ability or pre-programmed calculators are prohibited.

* Permission of an examination proctor must be obtained before leaving the room while the examination is in progress.

* Each examinee is assigned to a seat specifically designated by name and/or number when admitted to the examination room.

TYPICAL EXAMINATION QUESTIONS

EXAMPLE 1

An equipment grounding conductor of a branch circuit shall be identified by which of the following colors?

A. gray
B. white
C. black
D. green

Here you are asked to select from the listed colors the one that is to be used to identify the equipment grounding conductor of a branch circuit. Since Section 250.119 of the NEC® requires that green or green with yellow stripes be the color of insulation used on a grounding conductor (when it is not bare), the answer is **D**.

EXAMPLE 2

An emergency electrical disconnect provided for a gasoline fuel dispensing pump must be located NOT more than _____ from the fuel dispensing device it serves.

A. 20 feet
B. 50 feet
C. 75 feet
D. 100 feet

Here the "question" is in the form of a fill-in-the-blank statement. Your task is to select the choice that best completes the statement. In this case, you should have selected **D** since Section 514.11(A) of the NEC® specifies that emergency disconnects shall be within not less than 20 ft. and NOT more than 100 ft. from the fuel dispensing devices they serve.

EXAMPLE 3

A building or other structure served shall be supplied by only one service
EXCEPT one where the capacity requirements are in excess of _____.

A. 800 amperes at a supply voltage of 1000 volts or less
B. 1000 amperes at a supply voltage of 1000 volts or less
C. 1500 amperes at a supply voltage of 1000 volts or less
D. 2000 amperes at a supply voltage of 1000 volts or less

 This "question" is in the form of a complete the statement and your task is to select the choice that best completes the statement. In this case, you are to find an exception. You have to select the condition that has to be met when supplying a building or structure by more than one service. You should have selected *D* because Section 230.2(C)(1) requires the conditions listed in *D* but does not require or permit the conditions listed in A, B, or C.

EXAMPLE 4

Disregarding exceptions, the MINIMUM size overhead service-drop conductors shall be _____ AWG copper.

A. 6
B. 8
C. 12
D. 14

 Again this "question" is in the form of fill-in-the blank statement and your task is to select the choice that best completes the statement. In this case, exceptions are not applicable. You have to select the minimum size conductor required for overhead service-drop conductors. You should have selected *B* because Section 230.23(B) specifies that the conductors shall not be smaller than 8 AWG copper.

HOW TO USE THIS BOOK

Practice exams numbers 1-12 contained in this book consist of 25 questions each. The time allotted for each of these practice exams is 75 minutes, or 3 minutes per question. After taking the first 12 exams, try the final exams. The two final exams are 80 questions in length: the allotted time for each final exam is 4 hours. Using this time limit as a standard, you should be able to complete an actual examination in the allotted time.

You will seldom find trick questions in this exam prep guide, but many will require careful reading. Certain words such as *shall*, *shall not*, *should*, and *should not*, can make a difference in the correct answer. When a question contains verbiage such as: in general; generally; the general rule is; disregarding exceptions; etc., this means exceptions are not to be taken into consideration.

To get the most out of this book you should answer every question and highlight your NEC® for future reference. If you have difficulty with a question and cannot come up with the answer that is familiar to you, put a check mark next to the question and come back to it after completing the remainder of the questions. Review your answers with the **ANSWER KEY** located in the back of this book. This will help you identify your strengths and weaknesses. When you discover you are weaker in some areas than others, you will know that further study is necessary in those areas.

Do only one practice exam contained in this book during an allotted study period. This way you do not get burned out and fatigued trying to study for too long a period of time. This also helps you develop good study habits. **GOOD LUCK!**

ABOUT THE AUTHOR

H. Ray Holder has worked in the electrical industry for over fifty years as an apprentice, journeyman, master, field engineer, estimator, business manager, contractor, inspector, consultant, and instructor.

Mr. Holder is a graduate of Texas State University and holds a Bachelor of Science Degree in Occupational Education. He also holds a lifetime teaching certificate from the Texas Education Agency, in the field of Vocational Education.

He is a certified instructor of electrical trades. His classes are presented in a simplified, easy-to-understand format for electricians.

Ray has taught over 100,000 students online, in textbooks and in the classrooms at Austin Community College, and the University of Texas at Austin, Texas, Odessa College, at Odessa, Texas, Howard College at San Angelo, Texas, Technical-Vocational Institute of Albuquerque, New Mexico, and in the public school systems in Ft. Worth and San Antonio, Texas. He is currently the Director of Education for Electrical Seminars, Inc.

Mr. Holder is a former member of the National Fire Protection Association, International Association of Electrical Inspectors, and retired member of the International Brotherhood of Electrical Workers.

USEFUL FORMULAS

To Find	Single Phase	Three Phase	Direct Current
Amperes when kVA is known	$\dfrac{kVA \times 1{,}000}{E}$	$\dfrac{kVA \times 1{,}000}{E \times 1.732}$	not applicable
Amperes when horsepower is known	$\dfrac{HP \times 746}{E \times \%Eff. \times PF.}$	$\dfrac{HP \times 746}{E \times 1.732 \times \%Eff. \times PF.}$	$\dfrac{HP \times 746}{E \times \%Eff.}$
Amperes when Kilowatts are known	$\dfrac{kW \times 1{,}000}{E \times PF.}$	$\dfrac{kW \times 1{,}000}{E \times 1.732 \times PF.}$	$\dfrac{kW \times 1{,}000}{E}$
Kilowatts	$\dfrac{I \times E \times PF.}{1{,}000}$	$\dfrac{I \times E \times 1.732 \times PF.}{1{,}000}$	$\dfrac{I \times E}{1{,}000}$
Kilovolt Amperes	$\dfrac{I \times E}{1{,}000}$	$\dfrac{I \times E \times 1.732}{1{,}000}$	not applicable
Horsepower	$\dfrac{I \times E \times \%Eff. \times PF.}{746}$	$\dfrac{I \times E \times 1.732 \times \%Eff. \times PF.}{746}$	$\dfrac{I \times E \times \%Eff.}{746}$
Watts	$E \times I \times PF.$	$E \times I \times 1.732 \times PF.$	$E \times I$

I = Amperes

E = Volt

kW = Kilowatts

kVA = Kilovolt-Amperes

HP = Horsepower

%Eff. = Percent Efficiency

PF. = Power Factor

Power – "Pie" Circle Formulas

Pie Circle

I = P/E
To Find Current

P = I x E
To Find Power

E = P/I
To Find Voltage

Ohms Law Circle Formulas

Ohms Law Circle

I=E/R
To Find Current

E=IxR
To Find Voltage

R=E/I
To Find Resistance

Power Factor Triangle Formulas

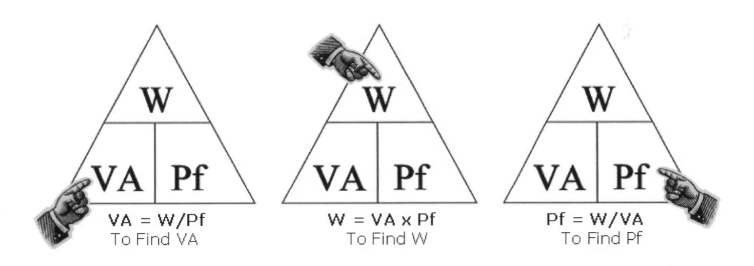

VA = W/Pf
To Find VA

W = VA x Pf
To Find W

Pf = W/VA
To Find Pf

VOLTAGE DROP FORMULAS

Formula Definitions:

VD = Volts dropped from a circuit.

2 = Multiplying factor for single-phase circuits. The 2 represents the conductor length in a single-phase circuit.

1.732 = Multiplying factor for three-phase circuits. The square root of 3 represents the conductor length in a three-phase circuit. The only difference between the single-phase and three-phase formulas is that "1.732" has replaced "2".

K = Approximate resistivity of the conductor per mil foot. A mil foot is a wire 1 foot long and one mil in diameter. The approximate K value for copper wire is **12.9** ohms and for aluminum wire is **21.2** ohms per mil foot.

I = Current or amperage draw of the load.

D = The distance from the source voltage to the load.

CM = Circular mil area of the conductor. (Chapter 9, Table 8)

*NOTE – When determining wire size, distance or current, VD is the actual volts that can be dropped from the circuit. The recommended percentage for a branch-circuit is 3%. Example: 3% of 120 volts is 3.6 volts. DO NOT enter 3% in the VD position.

To find voltage drop in a single-phase circuit.

$$VD = \frac{2 \times K \times I \times D}{CM}$$

To find wire size in a single-phase circuit.

$$CM = \frac{2 \times K \times I \times D}{VD}$$

To find distance in a single-phase circuit.

$$D = \frac{CM \times VD}{2 \times K \times I}$$

To find MAXIMUM current in amperes in a single-phase circuit.

$$I = \frac{CM \times VD}{2 \times K \times D}$$

Commonly used NEC® Tables and Articles:

Tbl. 110.26(A)(1) Working Spaces About Electrical

Equipment of 600 Volts or Less

UNIT 1

BASIC ELECTRICAL FORMULAS

Upon successfully completing this unit of study, the student will be familiar with the concepts and application of Ohm's Law, power and current formulas plus power factor.

2017

UNIT 1

BASIC ELECTRICAL FORMULAS

PIE CIRCLE FORMULAS

RELATED INFORMATION:

- [] The **PIE** formula circle illustrates the relationship between **power, current and voltage**.

- [] Power may be expressed as true power such as, **watts, kilowatts, kW** or **horsepower**; power may also be expressed in terms as apparent power such as, **volt-amps, VA, kilo volt-amps** or **kVA**.

- [] The letter "**P**" represents power.

- [] The letter "**I**" represents the intensity of current.

- [] The letter "**E**" represents voltage.

- [] The letter "**k**" is the abbreviation of kilo or one thousand (1,000).

- [] One **kW** equals 1,000 watts.

- [] One **kVA** equals 1,000 volt-amps.

- [] One **horsepower** equals 746 watts.

- [] Formulas used to determine the available power for a single-phase circuit, load or an

electrical system are:

$P = I \times E$

P = current x volts

P = volts x amps

P = VA

P = kVA

$kW = \dfrac{\text{current x volts}}{1{,}000}$

$kVA = \dfrac{\text{current x volts}}{1{,}000}$

EXAMPLE – Determine the available power, in VA, for a 100 ampere, 240 volt, single-phase circuit.

 A. 2,400 VA
 B. 24,000 VA
 C. 240,000 VA
 D. 240 VA

ANSWER – (B) 24,000 VA

 $VA = I \times E$
 VA = 100 amperes x 240 volts = 24,000 VA

EXAMPLE – Determine the apparent power, in kVA, for a 150 ampere, 120/240 Volt, single-phase electrical system.

 A. 36 kVA
 B. 3.60 kVA
 C. 360 kVA
 D. 3,600 kVA

ANSWER – (A) 36 kVA

 $kVA = \dfrac{I \times E}{1{,}000}$

 $kVA = \dfrac{150 \text{ amps x 240 volts}}{1{,}000} = \dfrac{36{,}000}{1{,}000} = 36 \text{ kVA}$

 ☐ Formulas used to determine the available power for three-phase circuits, loads or electrical systems are:

P = I x E x 1.732

P = current x volts x 1.732

P = volts x 1.732 x amps

P = VA x 1.732

$$kW = \frac{current \times volts \times 1.732}{1,000}$$

$$kVA = \frac{current \times volts \times 1.732}{1,000}$$

EXAMPLE – Determine the available power, in VA, for a 100 ampere 208Y/120 volt, three-phase circuit.

 A. 3,603 VA
 B. 36,026 VA
 C. 360,260 VA
 D. 20,800 VA

ANSWER – (B) 36,026 VA

 VA = I x E x 1.732
 VA = 100 amps x 208 volts x 1.732 = 36,026 VA

 *Note – In this situation we are to use 208 volts and multiply by 1.732 (the square root of 3), because we are to balance the load in the three current-carrying conductors.

EXAMPLE – A load that draws 50 amperes when connected to a 208Y/120 volt, three-phase source has a kW rating of _____.

 A. 18 kW
 B. 1.8 kW
 C. 180 kW
 D. 1,800 kW

ANSWER – (A) 18 kW

$$kW = \frac{current \times volts \times 1.732}{1,000}$$
$$kW = \frac{50 \times 208 \times 1.732}{} = 18,013 = 18 \ kW$$

1,000 1,000

☐ Current may be expressed in terms such as **amps**, **amperes**, **full-load current**, **FLC**, **full-load amps**, **FLA**, **load in amps** or **amperes**, **amperage**, **amperage draw** or **line load**.

☐ The letter "I" represents the intensity of the current.

☐ Formulas used to determine the current in a single-phase circuit, load or an electrical system are:

$$I = \frac{P}{E}$$

$$I = \frac{power}{voltage}$$

$$I = \frac{watts}{volts}$$

$$I = \frac{kW \times 1,000}{volts}$$

$$I = \frac{VA}{volts}$$

$$I = \frac{kVA \times 1,000}{volts}$$

EXAMPLE – Determine the current, in amperes, for a 120 volt, single-phase branch circuit that has only six (6) 100 watt incandescent luminaries (lighting fixtures) connected.

 A. 5 amperes
 B. 15 amperes
 C. 20 amperes
 D. 2 amperes

ANSWER – (A) 5 amperes

$$I = \frac{watts}{volts} \qquad I = \frac{600}{120} = 5 \text{ amperes}$$

EXAMPLE – Determine the current, in amperes, of a 2.4 kW load connected to a 240 volt, single-phase source.

A. .01 ampere
B. 1 ampere
C. 100 amperes
D. 10 amperes

ANSWER – (D) 10 amperes

$$I = \frac{2.4 \text{ kW} \times 1,000}{240} = \frac{2,400}{240} = 10 \text{ amperes}$$

☐ Formulas used to determine the current in a three (3)-phase circuit, load, or an electrical system are:

$$I = \frac{P}{E \times 1.732}$$

$$I = \frac{power}{volts \times 1.732}$$

$$I = \frac{watts}{volts \times 1.732}$$

$$I = \frac{kW \times 1,000}{volts \times 1.732}$$

$$I = \frac{VA}{volts \times 1.732}$$

$$I = \frac{kVA \times 1,000}{volts \times 1.732}$$

EXAMPLE – A 36,026 VA load connected to a 208Y/120-volt, three-phase circuit will draw _____ of current per phase.

A. 10 amperes
B. 173 amperes
C. 250 amperes
D. 100 amperes

ANSWER – (D) 100 amperes

$$I = \frac{VA}{E \times 1.732}$$
$$I = \frac{36,026 \text{ VA}}{208 \text{ volts} \times 1.732} = \frac{36,026}{360.25} = 100 \text{ amperes}$$

EXAMPLE – A balanced 60 kVA load connected to a 480Y/277-volt three-phase

electrical system will have a full-load current draw of _____ per phase.

 A. 72 amperes
 B. 125 amperes
 C. 720 amperes
 D. 80 amperes

ANSWER – (A) 72 amperes

$$I = \frac{kVA \times 1,000}{volts \times 1.732}$$

$$I = \frac{60 \ kVA \times 1,000}{480 \ volts \times 1.732} = \frac{60,000}{831.36} = 72 \ amperes$$

POWER FACTOR

RELATED INFORMATION:

- **Power factor (PF)** is the ratio between true power expressed as **watts, kilo watts** or **kW** and the apparent power expressed as **volt-amps, VA** or **kVA**.

- Power factor is expressed as a percent that does not exceed 100 percent or a decimal.

- True power, is expressed as **watts**, a unit of work, **kW** or **kilowatts**; this condition occurs in AC circuits or loads that contain only resistance. This is why electric ranges, ovens, cooktops, dryers and water heaters are all rated in **watts** or **kW**. The current and the voltage will be "in-phase", meaning that the voltage and the current will reach their peak and zero values at the same time. This is what we call unity or a power factor of 100 percent.

- True power (**watts**) equals apparent power (**VA**) in an electrical circuit or load containing only resistance.

- True power (**watts**) is less than apparent power (**VA**) in a circuit or load containing inductance or capacitance, such as motors, transformers, HID and fluorescent lighting.

- The true power (**watts**) of a single-phase circuit or load that contains inductance or capacitance can be calculated by the use of the following formula:

Watts = volts x amperes x power factor

EXAMPLE – What is the true power, in watts, of a 10 ampere load supplied with 120 volts, having a power factor of 80 percent?

A. 1,000 watts
B. 1,200 watts
C. 2,400 watts
D. 960 watts

ANSWER – (D) 960 watts

Watts = volts x amperes x power factor
Watts = 120 volts x 10 amps x .8 = 960 watts

▢ The true power (watts) of a three-phase circuit or load that contains inductance or capacitance can be calculated by the use of the following formula:

Watts = volts x 1.732 x amperes x power factor

EXAMPLE – Determine the true power (watts) of a 7.5 ampere load with a power factor of 87 percent supplied from a three-phase, 208-volt source.

A. 1,375 watts
B. 2,350 watts
C. 2,700 watts
D. 3,132 watts

ANSWER – (B) 2,350 watts

Watts = volts x 1.732 x amperes x power factor
Watts = 208 volts x 1.732 x 7.5 amps x .87 = 2,350 watts

▢ In most **ac circuits** containing inductance or capacitance a phase shift exists, the current is **"out-of-phase"** with the voltage; the current and the voltage do not reach their peak and zero values at the same time. Apparent power (VA) is usually more than the power in watts when this condition occurs. Apparent power is calculated without considering the phase shift that may be present between total voltage and current in the circuit.

▢ Formulas used to determine the power factor are:

Power factor = $\dfrac{\text{watts}}{\text{VA}}$

Power factor = $\dfrac{\text{watts}}{\text{volt amps}}$

Power factor = $\dfrac{\text{kW x 1,000}}{\text{volt amps}}$

EXAMPLE - The power factor of a 5 kW load drawing 30 amperes of current when connected to a 208-volt, single-phase source is _____.

> A. 92 percent
> B. 46 percent
> C. 80 percent
> D. 83 percent

ANSWER – (C) 80 percent

$$PF = \frac{kW \times 1{,}000}{volt \times amperes}$$

$$PF = \frac{5\ kW \times 1{,}000}{208\ volts \times 30\ amps} = \frac{5{,}000}{6{,}240} = .80\ or\ 80\%$$

☐ Formulas used to determine the current of a single-phase electrical load or system when the voltage and power factor are known are:

$$I = \frac{watts}{volts \times PF}$$

$$I = \frac{kw \times 1{,}000}{volts \times PF}$$

EXAMPLE – A 300 watt industrial type HID luminaire (lighting fixture) has a power factor of 85 percent and is connected to a 120 volt branch circuit. The luminaire will draw _____ of current.

> A. 2.94 amperes
> B. 2.50 amperes
> C. 3.25 amperes
> D. 2.13 amperes

ANSWER – (A) 2.94 amperes

$$I = \frac{watts}{volts \times PF}$$

$$I = \frac{300\ watts}{120\ volts \times .85} = \frac{300}{102} = 2.94\ amperes$$

☐ Formulas used to determine the current of a three-phase load or system when the voltage and the power factor are known are:

$$I = \frac{watts}{volts \times 1.732 \times PF}$$

$$I = \frac{kw \times 1,000}{volts \times 1.732 \times PF}$$

EXAMPLE - A 5 kW load having a power factor of 90 percent will draw _____ when connected to a 208Y/120 volt, three-phase electrical system.

 A. 37.47 amperes
 B. 13.88 amperes
 C. 17.87 amperes
 D. 15.42 amperes

ANSWER – (D) 15.42 amperes

$$I = \frac{kW \times 1,000}{volts \times 1.732 \times PF}$$

$$I = \frac{5\ kW \times 1,000}{208\ volts \times 1.732 \times .9} = \frac{5,000}{324.2} = 15.42\ amperes$$

OHM'S LAW CIRCLE FORMULAS

RELATED INFORMATION:

☐ The Ohm's Law circle formula illustrates the relationship between **voltage**, **current** and **resistance**.

☐ The letter "**E**" represents electromotive force, or voltage.

☐ The letter "**I**" represents the intensity of the current.

☐ The letter "**R**" represents the friction opposite the flow of electrons in a conductor and is known as resistance; the unit of measurement is the ohm.

□ In an alternating current circuit, factors that oppose current flow are conductor resistance, capacitive reactance, and inductive reactance. This total opposition to current flow is known as impedance and is also measured in ohms; the letter "**Z**" represents the impedance and may be substituted for the letter "**R**".

□ The formula used to determine the current flow in an electrical circuit or load when the resistance and voltage are known is:

$$I = \frac{E}{R}$$

$$I = \frac{volts}{resistance}$$

EXAMPLE – A 120 volt circuit supplies an incandescent luminaire (lighting fixture) with a resistance of 200 ohms. Determine the current flow, in amperes, of the circuit.

 A. 6.00 amperes
 B. 0.60 amperes
 C. 3.00 amperes
 D. 1.60 amperes

ANSWER – (B) 0.60 amperes

$$I = \frac{volts}{resistance} = \frac{120 \ volts}{200 \ ohms} = 0.60 \ amperes$$

□ The formula used to determine the voltage or voltage drop in an electrical circuit when the current and resistance are known is:

$$E = I \times R$$

E = current x resistance

EXAMPLE – Determine the voltage drop of two size 10 AWG copper conductors that supply a 16 ampere load located 100 feet from the voltage source. Given: The total resistance of the two conductors is 0.25 ohms.

 A. 2.00 volts
 B. 0.40 volts
 C. 4.00 volts
 D. 40.00 volts

ANSWER – (C) 4.00 volts

$$E = I \times R$$
E = 16 amperes x .25 ohms = 4 volts

The formula used to determine the resistance in an electrical circuit or load when the voltage and current are known is:

$$R = \frac{E}{I}$$

$$R = \frac{voltage}{current}$$

EXAMPLE – Determine the resistance of the heating elements of an electric baseboard heater that draws 8 amperes when supplied from a 120 volt source.

 A. 0.07 ohms
 B. 960 ohms
 C. 15 ohms
 D. 150 ohms

ANSWER – (C) 15 ohms

$$R = \frac{volts}{current} = \frac{120 \text{ volts}}{8 \text{ amperes}} = 15 \text{ ohms}$$

UNIT 1
SELF-ASSESSMENT QUIZ

1. One kVA is equal to _____.

 A. 100 VA
 B. 1,000 volts
 C. 1,000 VA
 D. 10,000 VA

2. 5,000 watts is equal to _____.

 A. 500 kW
 B. 5 kW
 C. 0.50 kW
 D. 50 kW

3. Where a 120-volt microwave oven is rated 1,200 watts, how much current, in amperes, will the microwave oven draw?

 A. 0.10 amperes
 B. 5 amperes
 C. 10 amperes
 D. 15 amperes

4. When an electric hair dryer draws six (6) amperes when connected to a 120 volt source, the rating of the hair dryer is _____ .

 A. 720 watts
 B. 750 watts
 C. 20 watts
 D. 200 watts

5. When a 240-volt, single-phase branch circuit has a current flow of 20 amperes, what is the resistance, in ohms, of this branch circuit?

A. 3 ohms
B. 6 ohms
C. 9 ohms
D. 12 ohms

6. When a 2 kW electric baseboard heater is connected to a 240-volt, single-phase circuit, the current flow in the circuit is _____.

 A. 4.15 amperes
 B. 8.33 amperes
 C. 12.50 amperes
 D. 16.66 amperes

7. Determine the power consumed, in VA, by a lighting load that operates at 115 volts, draws eight amperes and has a power factor of 80 percent.

 A. 1,150 VA
 B. 960 VA
 C. 920 VA
 D. 736 VA

8. A 150 ampere rated, 120/240-volt, single-phase residential service will have a volt-ampere rating of _____.

 A. 180,000 VA
 B. 90,000 VA
 C. 36,000 VA
 D. 72,000 VA

9. A 15 kW, 208-volt, single-phase heat pump will have a full-load current rating of _____.

 A. 72 amperes
 B. 46 amperes
 C. 66 amperes
 D. 33 amperes

10. What is the power factor of a 6,500 watt load that draws 33 amperes of current when connected to a 240-volt, single-phase source?

 A. 1.21 percent
 B. 82.0 percent

C. 68.0 percent
D. 1.04 percent

11. Given: An electric baseboard heater has a total resistance of 22 ohms and is supplied with a 240-volt, single-phase power source. Determine the current.

 A. 10.9 amperes
 B. 21.8 amperes
 C. 0.09 amperes
 D. 1.01 amperes

12. The power factor of a 5 kW load drawing 30 amperes of current when connected to a 208-volt, single-phase source is _____.

 A. 92 percent
 B. 46 percent
 C. 80 percent
 D. 83 percent

13. A 200 ampere rated, 208Y/120-volt, three-phase, 4-wire commercial service will have a VA rating of _____.

 A. 360 VA
 B. 43,231 VA
 C. 41,600 VA
 D. 72,051 VA

14. Ohm's Law is a relationship between _____.

 A. current, voltage and amperes
 B. current, voltage and power
 C. voltage, current and resistance
 D. voltage, power and resistance

15. What is the rated secondary current of a 600 VA, single-phase transformer at unity power factor, that has a 200-volt input and a 15-volt secondary?

 A. 10 amperes
 B. 20 amperes
 C. 13 amperes
 D. 40 amperes

16. Determine the line current, in amperes, on a balanced three-phase electrical system with a load of 25 kVA per phase and a line voltage of 208Y/120-volts. Total power is 75 kVA.

 A. 87 amperes
 B. 144 amperes
 C. 208 amperes
 D. 360 amperes

17. If an industrial type HID luminaire (lighting fixture), rated at 300 watts, is connected to a 120-volt branch circuit and is drawing three amperes of current, the luminaire has a power factor of _____.

 A. 83 percent
 B. 93 percent
 C. 1.2 percent
 D. 79 percent

18. 5 horsepower is equal to _____.

 A. 5 kW
 B. 3,730 watts
 C. 5,000 watts
 D. 5 kVA

19. When eight (8) 400 watt metal halide luminaries (lighting fixtures), each have a power factor of .86, are connected to a 277-volt, single-phase lighting branch circuit, the full-load current (FLC) of the luminaires will be _____.

 A. 11.55 amperes
 B. 5.54 amperes
 C. 13.43 amperes
 D. 6.68 amperes

20. When a 400 ampere rated commercial service is supplied with a 480Y/277 volt, three-phase, 4-wire electrical system, the service has a rating of _____.

 A. 144.10 kVA
 B. 110.80 kVA
 C. 192.00 kVA
 D. 332.50 kVA

NOTES

PRACTICAL CALCULATIONS FOR ELECTRICIANS
UNIT 1
SELF-ASSESSMENT QUIZ
ANSWER KEY

ANSWER	REFERENCE

1. C Trade Knowledge

$1 \text{ kVA} \times 1,000 = 1,000 \text{ VA}$

2. B Trade Knowledge

$\dfrac{5,000}{1,000} = 5 \text{ kW}$

3. C Current Formula

$I = \dfrac{1,200 \text{ watts}}{120 \text{ volts}} = 10 \text{ amperes}$

4. A Power Formula

$P = 6 \text{ amperes} \times 120 \text{ volts} = 720 \text{ watts}$

5. D Ohm's Law

$R = \dfrac{240 \text{ volts}}{20 \text{ amps}} = 12 \text{ ohms resistance}$

6. B Current Formula

$I = \dfrac{2 \text{ kW} \times 1,000}{240 \text{ volts}} = \dfrac{2,000}{240} = 8.33 \text{ amperes}$

7. D Power Formula

P= 8 amperes x 115 volts x .8 (pf) = 736 VA

8. C Power Formula

P = 240 volts x 150 amperes = 36,000 VA

9. A Current Formula

$$I = \frac{15 \text{ kW x 1,000}}{208 \text{ volts}} = \frac{15,000}{208} = 72 \text{ amperes}$$

10. B Power Factor Formula

$$PF = \frac{6,500 \text{ watts}}{240 \text{ volts x 33 amps}} = \frac{6,500 \text{ watts}}{7,920 \text{ VA}} = .82 = 82\%$$

11. A Ohm's Law

$$I = \frac{240 \text{ volts}}{22 \text{ ohms}} = 10.90 \text{ amperes}$$

12. C Power Factor Formula

$$PF = \frac{5 \text{ kW x 1,000}}{208 \text{ volts x 30 amps}} = \frac{5,000 \text{ watts}}{6,240 \text{ VA}} = .80 = 80\%$$

13. D Power Formula, 3-phase

VA = 208 volts x 1.732 x 200 amps =72,051 VA

14. C Ohm's Law

$$\frac{\text{volts}}{\text{current x resistance}} \qquad \frac{E}{I \times R}$$

15. D Current Formula

$$I = \frac{600 \text{ VA}}{15 \text{ volts}} = 40 \text{ amperes}$$

*NOTE – The VA rating of the transformer is the same on both the primary and on the secondary.

16. C Current Formula, 3-phase

$$I = \frac{75,000 \text{ VA}}{208 \text{ volts x } 1.732} = \frac{75,000}{360.25} = 208.30 \text{ amperes}$$

17. A Power Factor Formula

$$PF = \frac{300 \text{ watts}}{120 \text{ volts x 3 amps}} = \frac{300}{360} = .83 \text{ (83\%)}$$

18. B General Knowledge

5 HP x 746 watts = 3,730 watts

19. C Current Formula

$$I = \frac{400 \text{ watts}}{277 \text{ volts x } .86} = \frac{400}{238.22} = 1.679 \text{ amperes}$$

1.679 amperes x 8 (luminaires) = 13.43 amperes

20. D Power Formula, 3-phase

$$P = \frac{400A \text{ x } 480V \text{ x } 1.732}{1,000} = \frac{332,544 \text{ VA}}{1,000} = 332.5 \text{ kVA}$$

UNIT 2

BRANCH CIRCUITS

Upon successfully completing this unit of study, the student will be familiar with the concept of sizing, rating and overcurrent protection of branch circuits as well as calculating the number required.

$$\text{\# of CIRCUITS} = \frac{\text{LOAD VA}}{\text{CIRCUIT VA}}$$

UNIT 2

BRANCH CIRCUITS

RELATED INFORMATION:

- The definition of a **branch circuit** is the circuit conductors between the final overcurrent device (circuit breaker or fuse) protecting the circuit and the outlet(s). **[Article 100]** In other words, that portion of a wiring system that is beyond the final overcurrent device protecting the circuit and the outlet(s).

- The rating of a **branch circuit** is determined by the maximum ampere rating of the overcurrent protective device (circuit breaker or fuse) and **NOT** by the size of the conductors used for the branch-circuit. **[210.3]**

- In general, branch-circuit conductors shall have an allowable ampacity (current-carrying capacity) of **NOT** less than **125%** of the **continuous** load, plus **100%** of the **non-continuous** load to be served. **[210.19(A)(1)(a)]**

EXAMPLE – When a single branch-circuit serves a continuous load of 20 amperes and a non-continuous load of 10 amperes, the branch-circuit conductors are required to have an allowable current-carrying capacity of at least _____.

 A. 30.00 amperes
 B. 37.50 amperes
 C. 35.00 amperes
 D. 32.50 amperes

ANSWER – (C) 35.00 amperes

 20 amperes x 1.25 = 25 amperes
 10 amperes x 1.00 = 10 amperes
 TOTAL = 35 amperes

- The definition of a **continuous** load is a load where the maximum current is expected to continue for **3 hours** or more. **[Article 100]**

- Examples of **continuous** loads are lighting loads for commercial and industrial occupancies that are expected to be operated for at least three (3) hours.

☐ Examples of **non-continuous** loads are general-purpose receptacle outlets provided for commercial, industrial, and residential occupancies and general-purpose lighting loads for residential occupancies.

☐ In general, overcurrent devices protecting branch-circuits shall have a rating of not less than **125%** of the **continuous** load to be served plus **100%** of the **non-continuous** load to be served. **[210.20(A)]** In other words, overcurrent devices protecting branch circuits are not to be loaded more than **80%** of their rated value when protecting **continuous** loads.

EXAMPLE - When a 100 ampere rated circuit breaker is used to protect a branch circuit serving a continuous load, the load shall not exceed _____.

 A. 80 amperes
 B. 100 amperes
 C. 125 amperes
 D. 115 amperes

ANSWER – (A) 80 amperes

 100 amperes x .80 = 80 amperes

☐ Note the exception to **210.20(A)**. If the overcurrent device protecting the circuit is **listed** for **continuous operation**, it shall be permitted to have a rating of **100%** of the continuous load(s) to be served. **Be advised**, circuit breakers are **NOT** listed for continuous operation, unless they have a rating of at least **400 amperes** or more.

☐ In general, branch-circuit loads shall be calculated as shown in **220.12**, **220.14**, and **220.16** **[220.10]**

☐ In general, lighting loads are to be supplied by 15-and 20-ampere rated branch-circuits. **[210.23(A)]**

☐ Lighting loads for specific occupancies shall be based on the unit load per square foot depending on the type of occupancy as given on **Table 220.12**. **[220.12]**

Table 220.12 General Lighting Loads by Occupancy

Type of Occupancy	UNIT LOAD	
	Volt-Amperes per Square Meter	Volt-Amperes per Square Foot
Armories and auditoriums	11	1
Banks	39[b]	3½[b]
Barber shops and beauty parlors	33	3
Churches	11	1
Clubs	22	2
Court rooms	22	2
Dwelling units[a]	33	3
Garages – commercial (storage)	6	½
Hospitals	22	2
Hotels and motels, including apartment houses without provision for cooking by tenants[a]	22	2
Industrial commercial (loft) buildings	22	2
Lodge rooms	17	1½
Office buildings	39[b]	3½[b]
Restaurants	22	2
Schools	33	3
Stores	33	3
Warehouses (storage)	3	¼
In any of the preceding occupancies except one-family dwellings and individual dwelling units of two-family and multifamily dwellings:		
Assembly halls and auditoriums	11	1
Halls, corridors, closets, stairways	6	½
Storage spaces	3	¼

[a]See 220.14(J) [b]See 220.14(K)

⬜ General lighting loads are to be calculated from the outside dimensions of the building. **[220.12]**

⬜ To determine the area, in square feet, of a building, simply multiply the length of the building times the width of the building.

EXAMPLE - A building has outside dimensions of 100 feet in length and 75 feet in width. The building has a total area of _____.

 A. 750 square feet
 B. 175 square feet
 C. 7,500 square feet
 D. 1,750 square feet

ANSWER - (C) 7,500 sq. ft.

 100 ft. x 75 ft. = 7,500 sq. ft.

⬜ When calculating the area, in square feet, of a multi-story building, multiply the length of the building by the width of the building by the number of stories.

EXAMPLE - A three (3) story building having outside dimensions of 100 feet by 75 feet has a total area of _____.

 A. 2,225 square feet
 B. 7,500 square feet
 C. 15,000 square feet
 D. 22,500 square feet

ANSWER - (D) 22,500 sq. ft.

 100 ft. x 75 ft. x 3 (stories) = 22,500 sq. ft.

⬜ When calculating lighting loads for **dwelling units** do **NOT** include open porches, garages or unfinished spaces not adaptable for future use. **[220.12]**

⬜ Remember, in general, lighting loads for habitable spaces of dwelling units and guest rooms of hotels and motels are **not considered** as continuous use. But lighting loads of commercial and industrial occupancies **are considered** as continuous use.

⬜ The formula used to determine the minimum number of general lighting branch-circuits required for a dwelling unit is:

Number of Circuits = $\dfrac{\text{load VA}}{\text{circuit VA}}$

EXAMPLE – A dwelling unit having 2,000 sq. ft. of habitable space is required to have at least _____ 15-ampere, 120-volt general-purpose lighting branch-circuits.

 A. two
 B. three
 C. four
 D. five

ANSWER - (C) four

$$\dfrac{2,000 \text{ sq. ft. x 3 VA}}{120 \text{ volts x 15 amperes}} = \dfrac{6,000 \text{ VA}}{1,800 \text{ VA}} = 3.3 = 4 \text{ circuits}$$

☐ When calculating branch-circuits, when your calculation is more than a whole number, ex. 3.3, you must go to the next whole number. In other words, you cannot install part of a circuit or circuit breaker.

☐ Multifamily apartment dwellings without provisions for cooking by tenants are to be calculated at the same value, **2 VA** per square foot, as hotels and motels when determining the minimum of general lighting branch-circuits required for the living units. **[Table 220.12]**

EXAMPLE - A multifamily condo, without cooking facilities provided for the tenants, having 12,000 sq. ft. of living area, is required to have at least _____ 20 ampere, 120-volt general lighting branch-circuits, or at least _____ 15 ampere, 120-volt general lighting branch-circuits.

 A. ten – ten
 B. fourteen – fourteen
 C. ten – thirteen
 D. ten – fourteen

ANSWER – (D) ten – fourteen

$$\dfrac{12,000 \text{ sq. ft. x 2 VA}}{120 \text{ volts x } \mathbf{20} \text{ amperes}} = \dfrac{24,000 \text{ VA}}{2,400 \text{ VA}} = 10 \text{ circuits}$$

$$\dfrac{12,000 \text{ sq. ft. x 2 VA}}{120 \text{ volts x } \mathbf{15} \text{ amperes}} = \dfrac{24,000 \text{ VA}}{1,800 \text{ VA}} = 13.3 = 14 \text{ circuits}$$

☐ A formula used to determine the minimum number of required general lighting branch-circuits for an office building, store, bank, restaurant, etc. is :

$$\text{Number of Circuits} = \frac{\text{load VA x } \textbf{125\%}}{\text{circuit VA}}$$

EXAMPLE - A 10,000 sq. ft. restaurant is required to be provided with at least _____ 20-ampere, 120-volt general lighting branch-circuits.

 A. eight
 B. nine
 C. ten
 D. eleven

ANSWER - (D) eleven

$$\frac{10{,}000 \times 2 \text{ VA} \times \textbf{125\%}}{120 \text{ volts} \times 20 \text{ amps}} = \frac{25{,}000 \text{ VA}}{2{,}400 \text{ VA}} = 10.4 = 11 \text{ circuits}$$

☐ Because the circuit breakers protecting the branch-circuits are not permitted to be loaded to more than **80 percent** of their rated value, **[210.20(A)]** we can also use this formula:

$$\text{number of circuits} = \frac{\text{load VA}}{\text{circuit VA x } \textbf{80\%}}$$

$$\text{number of circuits} = \frac{10{,}000 \times 2 \text{ VA}}{120 \times 20 \times \textbf{80\%}} = \frac{20{,}000 \text{ VA}}{1{,}920 \text{ VA}} = 10.4 = 11 \text{ circuits}$$

☐ Notice that **Table 220.12** reflects minimum requirements for general lighting loads. Many commercial, particularly mercantile, occupancies have luminaries (lighting fixtures) installed for display, specialty, enhancement or accent lighting in addition to the general lighting. These loads are required to be included when calculating lighting loads.

EXAMPLE - A 15,000 sq. ft. retail store has 10,000 VA of accent lighting in addition to the general lighting. How many 120-volt, 20-ampere branch-circuits are required for the accent and general lighting loads?

 A. 30
 B. 24
 C. 36
 D. 32

ANSWER - (A) 30 circuits

$$\text{General ltg. circuits} = \frac{15,000 \times 3 \text{ VA}}{120 \times 20 \times 80\%} = \frac{45,000}{1,920} = 23.4 = 24$$

$$\text{Accent ltg. circuits} = \frac{10,000 \text{ VA}}{120 \times 20 \times 80\%} = \frac{10,000}{1,920} = 5.2 = 6$$

24 + 6 = 30 circuits total

☐ When reviewing **Table 220.12** notice the subscript **(b)** opposite of banks and office buildings which refers you to **220.14(K)**. This article indicates when the number of general-purpose receptacle outlets to be installed in the building has not yet been determined, **one VA** per square foot is to be added to the calculation for the outlets. The NEC® initiated this requirement because it is common practice for banks and office buildings to have future tenant spaces and the actual number of general-purpose receptacle outlets to be installed have not been determined prior to complete construction of the building.

☐ For non-dwelling units, receptacle outlets are to be calculated at a value of not less than **180 volt-amperes** for each single or duplex receptacle. **[220.14(I)]** In banks and office buildings, the receptacle loads are to be calculated to be the larger of (1) the calculated load from **220.14(I)** or
(2) one VA per square ft. **[220.14(K)]**

☐ The formula used to determine the maximum number of receptacle outlets permitted on a branch-circuit is:

$$\text{Number of Receptacles} = \frac{\text{circuit VA}}{180 \text{ VA}}$$

EXAMPLE - No more than _____ duplex receptacle outlets installed in a commercial establishment may be supplied from a single 20-ampere rated, 120-volt branch-circuit.

 A. ten
 B. twelve
 C. thirteen
 D. fourteen

ANSWER - (C) thirteen

$$\frac{120 \text{ volts} \times 20 \text{ amperes}}{180} = \frac{2,400}{180} = 13.3 = 13 \text{ receptacles}$$

180 VA 180

☐ When determining the minimum number of required branch-circuits for general-purpose receptacle outlets when the specific number of receptacle outlets to be installed in a commercial building is known, this formula may be used:

number of circuits = $\frac{\text{180 VA x number of receptacles}}{\text{circuit VA}}$

EXAMPLE - You are to install one hundred (100) duplex receptacle outlets in an existing office building. How many 20-ampere, 120-volt, branch-circuits will need to be added to supply the additional receptacles?

 A. twelve
 B. ten
 C. seven
 D. eight

ANSWER - (D) eight

$$\frac{\text{180 VA x 100}}{\text{120 volts x 20 amps}} = \frac{18{,}000}{2{,}400} = 7.5 = 8 \text{ circuits}$$

☐ Section
☐ **220.14(G)** indicates two methods are permitted when calculating branch-circuits for show window lighting.
(1) 180 VA per receptacle outlet in compliance with **210.62**, which
requires one receptacle per twelve linear feet of the show window.
(2) 200 volt-amps per linear foot of the show window.

The linear foot calculation method is the most commonly used method. The following formula may be used:

number of circuits = $\frac{\text{200 VA x linear ft. x } \textbf{125\%}}{\text{circuit VA}}$

EXAMPLE - A retail department store is to have seventy five (75) continuous linear feet of show window space. Using the linear foot method of calculation, how many 20-ampere, 120-volt, branch-circuits must be provided for the show window lighting?

 A. eight
 B. seven
 C. six
 D. five

ANSWER - (A) eight

$$\frac{\text{200 VA x 75 ft. x } \textbf{125\%}}{\text{20 amps x 120 volts}} = \frac{18{,}750}{2{,}400} = 7.8 = 8 \text{ circuits}$$

☐ When calculating the number of required branch-circuits for multioutlet assemblies installed in commercial, industrial and educational locations, the calculation is to be based on the use of the supplied cord-connected equipment that is expected to be used at the same time. **[220.14(H)]**

☐ When calculating the required branch-circuits for fixed multioutlet assemblies where the cord-connected appliances are **unlikely** to be used simultaneously, you can use the following formula:

number of circuits = $\dfrac{(\text{linear ft.}/5) \times 180\ VA}{\text{circuit VA}}$

EXAMPLE - A small cabinet makers shop is to install fifty (50) feet of multioutlet assembly where the appliances to be used are unlikely to be operated simultaneously. Where 20-ampere, 120-volt branch-circuits are used to supply the assembly, what is the minimum required?

 A. one
 B. two
 C. three
 D. four

ANSWER - (A) one

$$\frac{(50/5) \times 180}{120\text{ volts} \times 20\text{ amps}} = \frac{(10) \times 180}{2,400} = \frac{1,800}{2,400} = .75 \text{ or } 1 \text{ circuit}$$

☐ When calculating the branch-circuits required for fixed multioutlet assemblies where the cord-connected appliances are **likely** to be used simultaneously, the following formula may be used:

number of circuits = $\dfrac{\text{linear ft.} \times 180\ VA}{\text{circuit VA}}$

EXAMPLE - Seventy five (75) feet of fixed multioutlet assembly is to be wall-mounted in a retail outlet displaying television sets where most of the TV sets are operating simultaneously. How many 20-ampere, 120-volt branch-circuits are needed to supply this installation?

A. two
B. five
C. six
D. seven

ANSWER - (C) six

$$\frac{75 \text{ ft.} \times 180 \text{ VA}}{120 \text{ volts} \times 20 \text{ amps}} = \frac{13,500}{2,400} = 5.6 = 6 \text{ circuits}$$

☐ The definition of an individual branch-circuit is a branch-circuit that supplies only one utilization equipment. Examples of individual branch circuits would be branch-circuits supplying electric water heaters, dryers, ranges, cooktops, air conditioners, etc. **[Article 100]**

☐ For **other than** individual branch-circuits the rating of the circuits shall be 15, 20, 30, 40 and 50 amperes. **[210.3] Individual** branch circuits may also have ratings of the same size, in addition they may have ratings of 25, 35, 45 and 60 amperes or more. See **Table 240.6(A)** for the standard size ampere ratings of fuses and circuit breakers.

☐ When selecting ampere ratings of overcurrent protective devices, if the conductors being protected are **NOT** part of a multi-outlet branch circuit supplying receptacles for cord-and-plug-connected portable loads and the ampacity of the conductors do not correspond with the standard ampere rating of a fuse or circuit breaker and the next higher standard rating selected does **not exceed 800 amperes**, the next higher standard overcurrent device shall be permitted to be used. **[240.4(B)(1),(2)&(3)]**

☐ When selecting overcurrent protective devices where the overcurrent device is rated **over 800 amperes**, if the ampacity of the conductors do not correspond with the standard rating of a fuse or a circuit breaker you must go **down** to the next standard size fuse or circuit breaker. **[240.4(C)]**

☐ The overcurrent protection for small conductors, sizes 14 AWG through 10 AWG, shall be as listed in **240.4(D)**. Do not get overcurrent confused with ampacity.

☐ When sizing branch-circuits and overcurrent protection for appliances such as water heaters and cooktops, they are to be sized per **Article 422**. Branch-circuits for household cooking appliances shall be permitted to be in accordance with **Table 220.55**, which will be discussed later. **[422.10(A)]**

☐ Fixed storage-type water heaters with a capacity of 120 gallons or less shall be considered a continuous load when sizing branch-circuits. **[422.13]**

EXAMPLE - The branch-circuit conductors supplying a 5 kW, 240-volt, single-phase water heater, are required to have an ampacity of at least _____.

 A. 15.0 amperes
 B. 20.8 amperes
 C. 26.0 amperes
 D. 31.2 amperes

ANSWER - (C) 26.0 amperes

$$I = \frac{5\ kW \times 1,000}{240\ volts} = \frac{5,000}{240} = 20.8 \times \textbf{125\%} = 26.04\ amperes$$

 *NOTE - To solve this problem you should refer to **422.13** and **422.10(A)**.

EXAMPLE - The MAXIMUM size circuit breaker that may be used to protect a 5 kW, 240-volt, single-phase electric water heater has a rating of _____.

 A. 20 amperes
 B. 25 amperes
 C. 30 amperes
 D. 35 amperes

ANSWER - (D) 35 amperes

$$I = \frac{5,000}{240} = 20.8\ amps \times 150\% = 31.2\ amperes$$

 *NOTE - The next standard size circuit breaker has a rating of 35 amperes. To solve this problem you should refer to **422.11(E)(3)** and **240.6(A)**.

☐ When sizing branch-circuits and overcurrent protection for fixed electric space-heating equipment, they are to be sized in compliance with **Article 424**.

☐ Fixed electric space-heating equipment shall be considered as **continuous loads**. **[424.3(B)]**

EXAMPLE - The branch-circuit conductors supplying a 15 kW, 240 volt, single-phase fixed
electric space-heater, are required to have an ampacity of at least _____.

 A. 42 amperes
 B. 52 amperes
 C. 63 amperes
 D. 78 amperes

ANSWER - (D) 78 amperes

$$I = \frac{15 \times 1{,}000}{240} = \frac{15{,}000}{240} = 62.5 \times \mathbf{125\%} = 78 \text{ amperes}$$

 ☐ The following formula may be used to determine the minimum number of a required
branch-circuits to supply fixed electric space-heating equipment:

$$\text{number of circuits} = \frac{\text{load VA} \times \mathbf{125\%}}{\text{circuit VA}}$$

EXAMPLE - What is the minimum number of 20-ampere, 240-volt branch-circuits required for
twelve (12) baseboard heaters, each rated 1,250 watts at 240-volts, single-phase?

 A. three
 B. four
 C. six
 D. eight

ANSWER – (B) four

$$\frac{1{,}250 \times 12 \times \mathbf{125\%}}{240 \text{ volts} \times 20 \text{ amps}} = \frac{18{,}750}{4{,}800} = 3.9 = 4 \text{ circuits}$$

UNIT 2
SELF-ASSESSMENT QUIZ

1. A continuous load is a load where the maximum current is expected to continue for _____ or more.

 A. 15 minutes
 B. one hour
 C. two hours
 D. three hours

2. Disregarding exceptions, branch-circuit conductors serving continuous loads are required to have an allowable ampacity of at LEAST _____ of the load(s) to be served.

 A. 80 percent
 B. 100 percent
 C. 125 percent
 D. 150 percent

3. A six (6) story office building having outside dimensions of 100 feet by 150 feet, has a total area of _____ .

 A. 10,000 sq. ft.
 B. 15,000 sq. ft.
 C. 90,000 sq. ft.
 D. 60,000 sq. ft.

4. Of the following listed, which one is NOT a standard rating for a circuit breaker?

 A. 50 amperes
 B. 75 amperes
 C. 90 amperes
 D. 110 amperes

5. In general, regardless of the conductor insulation, size 10 AWG copper conductors shall have overcurrent protection rated at NOT more than _____ .

 A. 30 amperes

B. 25 amperes
C. 35 amperes
D. 20 amperes

6. The MINIMUM number of 120-volt, 15-ampere, general lighting branch-circuits required for a dwelling with 70 feet by 30 feet of livable space is _____.

 A. two
 B. three
 C. four
 D. five

7. When calculating the minimum number of required branch-circuits for general- purpose receptacles in a dwelling, how many VA per square foot is to be used for the calculation?

 A. none
 B. one VA
 C. two VA
 D. three VA

8. For other than dwelling units, receptacle outlets are to be calculated at a value of NOT less than _____ for each single or duplex receptacle.

 A. 100 VA
 B. 120 VA
 C. 150 VA
 D. 180 VA

9. What is the MAXIMUM continuous load, in VA, that a 240-volt, single-phase branch-circuit may be protected with a 20-ampere rated circuit breaker?

 A. 2,400 VA
 B. 2,850 VA
 C. 3,840 VA
 D. 4,800 VA

10. Determine the MINIMUM number of 15-ampere, 120-volt general lighting branch-circuits required for a dwelling having 2,600 sq. ft. of habitable space, a garage that measures 20 feet by 30 feet, and a 1,300 sq. ft. basement that is adaptable for future use.

 A. eight
 B. seven

C. six
D. five

11. A 240-volt, single-phase, 3,600 watt electric water heater is to be installed in a residential garage. What is the MAXIMUM size circuit breaker permitted for overcurrent protection for the water heater?

A. 15 amperes
B. 20 amperes
C. 30 amperes
D. 25 amperes

12. A multifamily apartment complex, with cooking facilities provided for the tenants, having 16,000 sq. ft. of living area, is required to have at LEAST _____ 20-ampere, 120-volt general lighting branch-circuits.

A. 18
B. 27
C. 20
D. 14

13. A 6,000 sq. ft. bank is required to be provided with at LEAST _____ 20-ampere, 120-volt general lighting branch-circuits.

A. 8
B. 9
C. 10
D. 11

14. For a retail store, determine the MAXIMUM number of 120-volt fluorescent luminaries (lighting fixtures), each drawing 1.6 amperes, may be supplied from a 20-ampere rated, 120-volt lighting branch-circuit.

A. ten
B. eight
C. thirteen
D. nine

15. For a commercial building, NO more than _____ single or duplex receptacles may be supplied from a 15-ampere, 120-volt branch-circuit.

A. ten
B. eleven
C. twelve
D. thirteen

16. Two hundred (200) feet of fixed multioutlet assembly is to be wall-mounted in a computer classroom where most of the computers are to be operating simultaneously. Determine the MINIMUM number of 20-ampere, 120-volt branch-circuits required to supply the multioutlet assembly.

 A. twelve
 B. fifteen
 C. thirteen
 D. eleven

17. The branch-circuit conductors supplying a 30 gallon fixed storage-type water heater, are required to have an ampacity of at LEAST _____ of the marked nameplate rating of the appliance.

 A. 80 percent
 B. 100 percent
 C. 125 percent
 D. 150 percent

18. Given: You are to install one hundred (100), 277-volt fluorescent luminaries (lighting fixtures) in a tenant space of a retail outlet mall. The lighting fixtures have a current rating of 0.75 amperes each. Determine the MINIMUM number of 20-ampere, 277-volt branch-circuits required to supply the luminaries.

 A. four
 B. seven
 C. six
 D. five

19. A branch-circuit is to supply a continuous load of 160 amperes. The branch circuit conductors are required to have an ampacity (current-carrying capacity) of at LEAST _____.

 A. 160 amperes
 B. 200 amperes
 C. 150 amperes
 D. 128 amperes

20. The MAXIMUM ampere rating for a circuit breaker protecting a residential central space electric heating unit rated at 18 kW at 240-volts, single-phase, is _____.

 A. 75 amperes
 B. 80 amperes
 C. 90 amperes
 D. 100 amperes

NOTES

PRACTICAL CALCULATIONS FOR ELECTRICIANS
UNIT 2
SELF-ASSESSMENT QUIZ
ANSWER KEY

ANSWER	**REFERENCE**	**NEC PG. #**
1. D	Article 100 - Definitions	pg. 35
2. C	210.19(A)(1)(a)	pg. 62
3. C	General Knowledge	

100 ft. x 150 ft. x 6 stories = 90,000 sq. ft.

4. B	Table 240.6(A)	pg. 95
5. A	240.4(D)(7)	pg. 94
6. C	Table 220.12	pg. 71

70 ft. x 30 ft. = 2,100 sq. ft. x 3 VA = 6,300 VA

$$\text{number of circuits} = \frac{6,300 \text{ VA}}{120 \text{ volts x 15 amps}} = 3.5 = 4 \text{ circuits}$$

7. A	220.14(J)	pg. 71
8. D	220.14(I)	pg. 71
9. C	210.20(A)	pg. 62

240 volts x 20 amperes x 80% = 3,840 VA

10. B	220.12 Table 220.12	pg. 70 pg. 71

2,600 sq. ft. + 1,300 sq. ft. = 3,900 sq. ft. total

$$\frac{3,900 \text{ sq. ft. x 3 VA}}{120 \text{ volts x 15 amps}} = \frac{11,700 \text{ VA (load)}}{1,800 \text{ VA (circuit)}} = 6.5 = 7 \text{ circuits}$$

11. D 422.11(E)(3) pg. 277
 Current Formula
 Table 240.6(A) pg. 95

 $I = \dfrac{3,600 \text{ VA}}{240 \text{ volts}}$ = 15 amps x 150% = 22.5 amperes

 *NOTE- The **next** size circuit breaker has a rating of 25 amperes.

12. C Table 220.12 pg. 71

 $\dfrac{16,000 \text{ sq. ft. x 3 VA}}{120 \text{ volts x 20 amps}} = \dfrac{48,000 \text{ VA (load)}}{2,400 \text{ VA (circuit)}}$ = 20 circuits

 *NOTE- Apartments **with** cooking facilities are considered dwelling units.

13. D Table 220.12 pg. 71
 210.19(A)(1)(a) pg. 62

 $\dfrac{6,000 \text{ x 3.5 VA x \textbf{125\%}}}{120 \text{ volts x 20 amps}} = \dfrac{26,250 \text{ VA (load)}}{2,400 \text{ VA (circuit)}}$ = 10.9 = 11 circuits

14. A 220.18(B) pg. 72
 210.20(A) pg. 62

 $\dfrac{120 \text{ volts x 20 amps x \textbf{80\%}}}{120 \text{ volts x 1.6 amps}} = \dfrac{1,920 \text{ VA (circuit)}}{192 \text{ VA (fixture)}}$ = 10 luminaires

15. A 220.14(I) pg. 71

 $\dfrac{120 \text{ volts x 15 amps}}{180 \text{ VA}} = \dfrac{1,800 \text{ VA (circuit)}}{180 \text{ VA (recpt.)}}$ = 10 receptacles

16. B 220.14(H)(2) pg. 71

 $\dfrac{200 \text{ ft. x 180 VA}}{120 \text{ volts x 20 amps}} = \dfrac{36,000 \text{ VA (load)}}{2,400 \text{ VA (circuit)}}$ = 15 circuits

17. C 422.13 pg. 277
 422.10(A) pg. 276

18. D 220.18(B) pg. 72

$$\frac{100 \times 277 \text{ V} \times .75 \text{ A}}{277 \text{ V} \times 20 \text{ A} \times \textbf{80\%}} = \frac{20{,}775 \text{ VA}}{4{,}432 \text{ VA}} \begin{array}{l}\text{(load)}\\\text{(circuit)}\end{array} = 4.6 = 5 \text{ circuits}$$

19. B 210.19(A)(1)(a) pg. 62

160 amps x **125%** = 200 amperes

20. D Current Formula
 424.3(B) pg. 280
 210.20(A) pg. 62
 240.4(B)(1),(2)&(3) pg. 94
 Table 240.6(A) pg. 95

$$I = \frac{18 \times 1{,}000}{240 \text{ volts}} = \frac{18{,}000}{240} = 75 \text{ amps} \times 125\% = 93.73 \text{ amperes}$$

*NOTE- The **next** standard size circuit breaker has a rating of 100 amperes.

UNIT 3

COOKING EQUIPMENT & APPLIANCE DEMAND LOADS

Upon successfully completing this study unit, the student will be familiar with the concept of calculating demand loads for household cooking equipment and appliances.

Unit 3

COOKING EQUIPMENT & APPLIANCE DEMAND LOADS

RELATED INFORMATION:

☐ The definition of **demand factor** is the ratio of the maximum demand of a system, or part of a system, to the total connected load of a system or the part of the system under consideration. **[Article 100]**

☐ The **demand load** of an electrical system or an electrical appliance is the MAXIMUM load of the system or appliance that may be required at a given time. In other words, **demand factors** are applied because all of the electrical loads are not used at the same time; all of the luminaires (lighting fixtures) will not be on at the same time, neither will all the receptacle outlets and appliances be fully loaded at the same time.

☐ A good example of this concept would be an electric range having a **connected load** rating of **12 kW**. The range-top has four heating elements, the oven has one heating element, another heating element is required for the broiler, and accessories such as timers and lights are included in the total connected load. Therefore, we can apply **demand factors** as shown in **Table 220.55** which reflects a **demand load** of **8 kW**, because we would not be using all of the heating elements and the accessories at their **MAXIMUM** value at any given time.

☐ **Table 220.55** and its related notes are to be used to apply **demand factors** for household electric ranges, wall-mounted ovens, counter-mounted cooking units, and other household cooking appliances over **1¾ kW** rating. This table is to be used when applying **demand factors** when sizing services, feeders and branch circuits for dwelling units and instructional programs for educational institutions.

Table 220.55 Demand Factors and Loads for Household Electric Ranges, Wall-Mounted Ovens, Counter-Mounted Cooking Units, and Other Household Cooking Appliances over 1¾ kW Rating (Column C to be used in all cases except as otherwise permitted in Note 3).

Demand Factor (Percent) (See Notes)

Number of Appliances	Column A (Less than 3½ kW Rating)	Column B (3½ kW to 8¾ kW Rating)	Column C Maximum Demand (kW) (See Notes) (Not over 12 kW Rating)
1	80	80	8
2	75	65	11
3	70	55	14
4	66	50	17
5	62	45	20
6	59	43	21
7	56	40	22
8	53	36	23
9	51	35	24
10	49	34	25
11	47	32	26
12	45	32	27
13	43	32	28
14	41	32	29
15	40	32	30
16	39	28	31
17	38	28	32
18	37	28	33
19	36	28	34
20	35	28	35
21	34	26	36
22	33	26	37
23	32	26	38
24	31	26	39
25	30	26	40
26-30	30	24	15 kW + 1 kW for each range
31-40	30	22	
41-50	30	20	25 kW + ¾ kW for each range
51-60	30	18	
61 and over	30	16	

1. Over 12 kW through 27 kW ranges all of same rating. For ranges individually rated more than 12 kW but not more than 27 kW, the maximum demand in Column C shall be increased 5 percent for each additional kilowatt of rating or major fraction thereof by which the rating of individual ranges exceeds 12 kW.

2. Over 8¾ kW through 27 kW ranges of unequal ratings. For ranges individually rated more than 8¾ kW and of different ratings, but none exceeding 27 kW, an average value of rating shall be calculated by adding together the ratings of all ranges to obtain the total connected load (using 12 kW for any range rated less than 12 kW) and dividing by the total number of ranges. Then the maximum demand in Column C shall be increased 5 percent for each kilowatt or major fraction thereof by which this average value exceeds 12 kW.

3. Over 1¾ kW through 8¾ kW. In lieu of the method provided in Column C, it shall be permissible to add the nameplate ratings of all household cooking appliances rated more than 1¾ kW but not more than 8¾ kW and multiply the sum by the demand factors specified in Column A and Column B for the given number of appliances. Where the rating of cooking appliances falls under both Column A and Column B, the demand factors for each column shall be applied to the appliances for that column, and the results added together.

4. Branch-Circuit Load. It shall be permissible to calculate the branch-circuit load for one range in accordance with Table 220.55. The branch-circuit load for one wall-mounted oven or one counter-mounted cooking unit shall be the nameplate rating of the appliance. The branch-circuit load for a counter-mounted cooking unit and not more than two wall-mounted ovens, all supplied from a single branch circuit and located in the same room, shall be calculated by adding the nameplate rating of the individual appliances and treating this total as equivalent to one range.

5. This table also applies to household cooking appliances rated over 1¾ kW and used in instructional programs.

☐ Take notice that household electric ranges having a rating of **8.75 kW** or **more** are required to be supplied by at least a **40 ampere** rated branch circuit.

[210.19(A)(3)] Also, **note 4** to **Table 220.55** states the branch circuit load for **one** wall-mounted oven or **one** counter-mounted cooking unit shall be the **nameplate rating** of the appliance. Therefore, demand factors are **not** to be applied when sizing branch circuits for these single cooking units.

☐ **Table 220.55** is separated into four columns. The first column shows the number of appliances. **Column A** is to be used when determining demand factors of cooking equipment of **less than 3½ kW rating** and is expressed in **percent**. **Column B** is used for equipment rated **3½ to 8¾ kW** and is also expressed in **percent**. **Column C** lists applicable demand factors for equipment rated **not over 12 kW** and is expressed in **kW**. When applying demand factors be sure you are in the correct column and on the right line, because the maximum demand changes in relationship with the number of appliances.

☐ As per **note 3**, When the rating of cooking appliances fall under **both** Column A and B, the demand factors for each column shall be applied for that column and the results added together.

EXAMPLE – A small residential duplex has a 3 kW counter-mounted cooktop and a 4 kW wall-mounted oven installed in each unit. Determine the demand load, in kW, to be added to the ungrounded service-entrance conductors for the cooking equipment.

 A. 9.7 kW
 B. 14.0 kW
 C. 11.2 kW
 D. 10.5 kW

ANSWER - (A) 9.7 kW

 Col. A – 3 kW + 3 kW = 6 kW x **75%** = 4.5 kW
 Col. B – 4 kW + 4 kW = 8 kW x **65%** = 5.2 kW
 TOTAL = 9.7 kW demand

☐ When a single range having a rating of **3½ kW to 8¾ kW** is used as cooking equipment for households, we may use the demand factors shown in **Column B** when sizing branch-circuits, (**note 4**) feeders and service-entrance conductors.

EXAMPLE – What is the demand load, in kW, for the branch-circuit conductors supplying an 8 kW residential electric range?

 A. 8.0 kW
 B. 6.4 kW
 C. 6.0 kW

D. 7.2 kW

ANSWER – (B) 6.4 kW

8 kW x 80% = 6.4 kW demand load

☐ Column C is to be used when applying demand factors for electric ranges of **not over 12 kW** rating.

EXAMPLE - Determine the demand load, in kW, to be added to the ungrounded service-entrance conductors for a 9.6 kW residential electric range.

A. 9.6 kW
B. 8.0 kW
C. 10.0 kW
D. 12.0 kW

ANSWER - (B) 8.0 kW

Column C of Table 220.55 shows a demand of **8 kW** for one range not over 12 kW rating.

☐ When we have multiple ranges of **equal ratings** up to **12 kW** we are to also use **Column C**.

EXAMPLE - A ten (10) unit apartment complex is to have a 10 kW electric range installed in each unit. When sizing the ungrounded service-entrance conductors, the total demand load for the multiple ranges is _____.

A. 30 kW
B. 80 kW
C. 25 kW
D. 100 kW

ANSWER - (C) 25 kW

Column C of Table 220.55 shows a demand of 25 kW for ten ranges of not over 12 kW rating.

☐ When applying maximum demand factors for ranges all of the **same rating over 12 kW through 27 kW**, we are to apply **note 1 and Column C** of **Table 220.55**, which states we are to increase the Column C demand value by **5%** for each kW that exceeds 12 kW.

EXAMPLE - What is the branch-circuit demand load, in amperes, for one 16 kW, 240 volt, single-phase residential electric range?

 A. 33 amperes
 B. 50 amperes
 C. 40 amperes
 D. 67 amperes

ANSWER – (C) 40 amperes

 16 kW – 12 kW = 4 kW x 5% = 20% increase in Column C
 Col. C demand (1 range) = 8 kW x 120% = 9.6 kW demand

$$I = \frac{9.6 \text{ kW x } 1,000}{240 \text{ volts}} = \frac{9,600}{240} = 40 \text{ amperes}$$

☐ When applying demand factors for **multiple ranges**, all having the **same** nameplate rating of **more than 12 kW**, but **not more than 27 kW**, we are to also apply **note 1 and Column C** of **Table 220.55**.

EXAMPLE - A four (4) unit residential town house has a 14 kW electric range installed in each unit. What is the demand load for the ranges, in kW, to be added to the ungrounded service-entrance conductors when sizing the service?

 A. 56.0 kW
 B. 44.8 kW
 C. 28.0 kW
 D. 18.7 kW

ANSWER - (D) 18.7 kW

 14 kW – 12 kW = 2 kW x 5% = 10% increase in Column C
 Col. C demand (4 ranges) = 17 kW x 110% = 18.7 kW

☐ When applying maximum demand factors of ranges having **unequal ratings of 8¾ kW through 27 kW** we are to apply **note 2 and Column C** of **Table 220.55**.

EXAMPLE - The vocational education department of a high school is to have three (3) electric ranges installed in a classroom; one 10 kW, one 11 kW and one 12 kW. The ranges are to be supplied by a 208 volt, single-phase feeder from a sub-panel. What is the demand load, in amperes, on the ungrounded feeder conductors?

 A. 58 amperes

B. 67 amperes
C. 136 amperes
D. 142 amperes

ANSWER - (B) 67 amperes

In this situation you simply refer to Column C, which shows demand of 14 kW for three ranges, because not any of the ranges have a nameplate rating above 12 kW.

$$I = \frac{14 \text{ kW x } 1{,}000}{208 \text{ volts}} = \frac{14{,}000}{208} = 67.3 \text{ amperes}$$

☐ When calculating demand factors for ranges of **unequal ratings** of **8¾ through 27 kW**, when the nameplate rating of any **range less than 12 kW** you are to use **12 kW** as a **minimum** and add the ratings together and divide by the number of ranges to obtain the average, then apply the same steps as per **note 1**. **[Note 2, Table 220.55]**

EXAMPLE - Refer to the previous example. Another classroom in the high school is to install two electric ranges, one 16 kW and one 11 kW. Determine the demand load, in amperes, on the 208 volt, single-phase ungrounded feeder conductors.

A. 67 amperes
B. 76 amperes
C. 58 amperes
D. 63 amperes

ANSWER – (C) 58 amperes

$$12 \text{ kW (minimum) + 16 kW} = \frac{28 \text{ kW}}{2 \text{ (ranges)}} = 14 \text{ kW average}$$

14 kW – 12 kW = 2 kW x **5%** = **10%** increase in Column C
Col. C demand (2 ranges) = 11 kW x **110%** = 12.1 kW demand

$$I = \frac{12.1 \text{ kW x } 1{,}000}{208 \text{ volts}} = \frac{12{,}100}{208} = 58 \text{ amperes}$$

☐ **Note 4** of **Table 220.55** addresses **branch-circuits**; it states it is permissible to calculate the branch-circuit load for one range in accordance with **Table 220.55**, as we have shown. As mentioned before, the branch-circuit load for **one wall-mounted oven** or **one counter-mounted cooking unit** shall be the **nameplate rating** of the appliance. When sizing branch-circuit loads for a **single branch-circuit** supplying a counter-mounted cooking unit and not more than two (2) wall-mounted ovens, it is permissible to add the nameplate ratings of the appliances

together and treat the result as one range.

EXAMPLE - A 240-volt, single-phase branch-circuit (home run) is to supply one (1) 6 kW rated counter-mounted cooking unit and two (2) wall-mounted 4 kW rated ovens in a residential kitchen. What is the demand load, in amperes, on the branch-circuit for the appliances?

 A. 22 amperes
 B. 27 amperes
 C. 33 amperes
 D. 37 amperes

ANSWER - (D) 37 amperes

 6 kW + 4 kW + 4 kW = 14 kW connected load
 14 kW – 12 kW = 2 kW x 5% = **10%** increase in Column C
 Col. C demand (1 range) = 8 kW x 110% = 8.8 kW demand load

$$I = \frac{8.8 \text{ kW x } 1{,}000}{240 \text{ volts}} = \frac{8{,}800}{240} = 36.6 \text{ amperes}$$

 ☐ **Section 220.61(B)(1)** permits an additional demand factor of **70 percent** for the **neutral** (grounded) conductor, for a feeder or service supplying household electric ranges, wall-mounted ovens, counter mounted cooking units, and electric dryers after apply the applicable demand factors of **Table 220.55** for ranges and **Table 220.54** for dryers.

EXAMPLE - A four (4) unit apartment house is to have a 10.5 kW electric range installed in each unit. Determine the demand load, in kW, on the grounded (neutral) service-entrance conductor for the ranges.

 A. 11.9 kW
 B. 13.6 kW
 C. 17.0 kW
 D. 10.4 kW

ANSWER - (A) 11.9 kW

 Column C shows a demand of 17 kW for the demand on the ungrounded conductors for the four (4) electric ranges.

 17 kW x **70%** = 11.9 kW neutral demand

☐ In a residential occupancy, a **75%** demand factor is permitted to be applied when **four(4) or more** fastened in place appliances such as water heaters, trash compactors, garage door openers, dishwashers, garbage disposers, sump pumps, attic fans, etc., are supplied from the same feeder or service. **[220.53]** **Note** this section does not apply to ranges, clothes dryers, space-heating and air-conditioning equipment.

EXAMPLE - A one-family dwelling unit is to have the following fastened in place appliances installed:

one – 1,200 VA dishwasher
one – 4,000 VA water heater
one – 1,150 VA garbage disposer
one - 700 VA attic fan
one – 1,920 VA garage door opener

The demand load, in VA, on the ungrounded service-entrance conductors for the listed appliances is _____.

A. 7,728 VA
B. 6,728 VA
C. 6,276 VA
D. 8,970 VA

ANSWER - (B) 6,728 VA

1,200 VA dishwasher
4,000 VA water heater
1,150 VA garbage disposer
 700 VA attic fan
1,920 VA garage door opener
8,970 VA connected load x **75%** = 6,728 VA demand

☐ In residential occupancies, demand factors may also be applied to electric clothes dryers; the use of demand factors in **Table 220.54** shall be permitted when sizing feeders and service entrance conductors. Each dryer shall be calculated at a **minimum of 5,000 watts (volt-amperes)** or the nameplate rating, whichever is larger. **[220.54]**

EXAMPLE - An eight (8) unit multifamily dwelling is to have the following electric clothes dryers installed in the laundry rooms of the tenants:

two – 4.5 kW rated
two – 5.5 kW rated

two – 6.0 kW rated
two – 6.5 kW rated

The demand load, in kW, to be added to the ungrounded feeder conductors for the listed electric dryers is _____.

 A. 27.0 kW
 B. 27.6 kW
 C. 34.5 kW
 D. 33.8 kW

ANSWER - (B) 27.6 kW

 two dryers @ 5.0 kW (minimum) = 10 kW
 two dryers @ 5.5 kW = 11 kW
 two dryers @ 6.0 kW = 12 kW
 two dryers @ 6.5 kW = <u>13 kW</u>
 connected load = 46 kW x **60%** = 27.6 kW

 ☐ An additional demand factor of **70 percent** is permitted for the **neutral** (grounded conductor) for a feeder or service supplying electric clothes dryers for dwelling units. **[220.61(B)(1)]**

EXAMPLE - Refer to the previous example. The demand, in kW, on the grounded (neutral) conductor of the feeder conductors is _____.

 A. 32.20 kW
 B. 27.60 kW
 C. 19.32 kW
 D. 18.90 kW

ANSWER - (C) 19.32 kW

 27.6 kW (demand) load x **70%** (neutral demand) = 19.32 kW

 ☐ For commercial cooking related equipment, branch-circuits and overcurrent protection are sized according to the nameplate rating on the appliance. When sizing feeder and service conductors we may apply demand factors in accordance with **Table 220.56**. These demand factors shall not apply to space heating, ventilating or air-conditioning equipment. However, the feeder or service demand load is **not** permitted to be less than the sum of the **largest two** kitchen equipment loads. **[220.56]**

EXAMPLE - A feeder is to supply the following cooking related equipment in the kitchen of a restaurant:

 oven - 10 kW
 booster heater - 15 kW

dishwasher - 2 kW
garbage disposal - 1 kW
water heater - 6 kW
steamer - 4 kW

What is the demand load on the ungrounded feeder conductors for the appliances?

A. 38.0 kW
B. 24.7 kW
C. 26.6 kW
D. 25.0 kW

ANSWER - (D) 25.0 kW

oven - 10 kW
booster heater - 15 kW
dishwasher - 2 kW
garbage disposal - 1 kW
water heater - 6 kW
steamer - 4 kW
 Total = 38 kW (connected load)
 X **65%** (demand)
 = 24.7 kW **demand load**

But, the **two largest** loads are rated 10 kW and 15 kW which
totals **25 kW**.

UNIT 3
SELF-ASSESSMENT QUIZ

1. What is the demand load, in kW, on the ungrounded service-entrance (line) conductors of a residence for one 8.5 kW rated electric range?

 A. 6.8 kW
 B. 8.0 kW
 C. 8.5 kW
 D. 10.6 kW

2. The demand factor for six (6) residential electric clothes dryers installed in a multifamily dwelling unit is _____.

 A. 70 percent
 B. 80 percent
 C. 60 percent
 D. 75 percent

3. A single-family dwelling has three (3) ovens, one rated 6 kW, one rated 8 kW and one rated 3.5 kW. The kitchen also has a counter-mounted cooktop rated at 6 kW and a broiler rated at 3.5 kW. The feeder demand will be _____ on the ungrounded (line) conductors for the cooking equipment.

 A. 12.2 kW
 B. 18.6 kW
 C. 27.3 kW
 D. 30.1 kW

4. It shall be permissible to apply a demand factor of _____ to the nameplate rating of four (4) or more fastened in place storage-type electric water heaters in a multifamily dwelling, when calculating the demand load on the service entrance or feeder conductors.

 A. 50 percent
 B. 75 percent
 C. 80 percent
 D. 90 percent

5. When doing residential service and feeder calculations, electric clothes dryers are to be calculated at a MINIMUM of _____ watts (VA) or the nameplate rating, whichever is larger.

 A. 3,000
 B. 4,500
 C. 5,000
 D. 6,000

6. For residential electric ranges rated at 8.75 kW or more, the MINIMUM branch circuit rating shall be at LEAST _____.

 A. 30 amperes
 B. 40 amperes
 C. 50 amperes
 D. 60 amperes

7. Determine the demand load, in VA, on the service-entrance (line) conductors of a one-family dwelling when the house has the following fastened in place electric appliances:

 water heater - 4,800 VA
 dishwasher - 1,200 VA
 garbage disposal - 1,150 VA
 trash compactor - 800 VA
 attic fan - 1,200 VA

 A. 6,863 VA
 B. 9,150 VA
 C. 8,579 VA
 D. 11,438 VA

8. What is the branch-circuit demand load, in amperes, for one (1) 240-volt, single-phase, 6 kW wall-mounted oven located in a dwelling unit?

 A. 40 amperes
 B. 30 amperes
 C. 25 amperes
 D. 20 amperes

9. When doing dwelling unit service and feeder calculations, when a residence has an electric clothes dryer rated at 240-volts, 30 amperes, the demand load, in VA, to be applied to the ungrounded (line) conductors is _____.

 A. 3,500 VA
 B. 5,000 VA
 C. 6,000 VA

D. 7,200 VA

10. Determine the demand load, in kW, to be added to the grounded (neutral) service-entrance conductor for one 10.5 kW residential electric range.

 A. 5.6 kW
 B. 8.0 kW
 C. 10.5 kW
 D. 12.0 kW

11. An 18 kW residential electric range has a demand load of _____ on the ungrounded (line) feeder and service-entrance conductors.

 A. 12.0 kW
 B. 10.4 kW
 C. 14.4 kW
 D. 12.6 kW

12. When sizing a branch-circuit for a 5 kW, 240-volt, single-phase commercial booster heater installed in the kitchen of a restaurant, the branch-circuit conductors are required to have the ability to carry at LEAST _____.

 A. 30 amperes
 B. 35 amperes
 C. 21 amperes
 D. 25 amperes

13. A twelve (12) unit multifamily apartment complex is to have a 9 kW electric range installed in each unit. When sizing the ungrounded (line) service-entrance conductors, the total demand load for the multiple ranges is _____.

 A. 99 kW
 B. 30 kW
 C. 36 kW
 D. 27 kW

14. A residential branch circuit is to supply two (2) wall-mounted ovens rated at 4.5 kW each and one (1) counter-mounted cooktop rated at 6 kW. The appliances are rated 240-volts, single-phase. The demand load on the branch-circuit conductors is _____.

 A. 32.4 amperes
 B. 38.3 amperes
 C. 42.1 amperes
 D. 43.8 amperes

15. The demand factor of an electrical system is the ratio of the maximum demand for a system to _____.

 A. the total connected load of the system.
 B. 125% of the total connected load of the system.
 C. 125% of the total connected continuous load of the system.
 D. 80% of the total connected non-continuous load plus 125% of the total connected continuous load of the system.

16. What is the service demand load, in kW, for six (6) storage type electric water heaters rated at 5 kW each, installed in a multifamily dwelling unit?

 A. 30.0 kW
 B. 24.0 kW
 C. 22.5 kW
 D. 26.0 kW

17. For dwelling units, the feeder and service neutral demand load for electric clothes dryers shall be calculated at _____ of the demand load as determined by Table 220.54.

 A. 100 percent
 B. 75 percent
 C. 80 percent
 D. 70 percent

18. What is the branch-circuit demand load, in amperes, for one 13.5 kW rated, 240-volt, single-phase residential electric range?

 A. 33 amperes
 B. 37 amperes
 C. 50 amperes
 D. 58 amperes

19. What is the demand load, in kW, for the feeder and service conductors for the following commercial kitchen equipment installed in a restaurant?

water heater	- 6.0 kW
dishwasher	- 2.0 kW
booster heater	- 7.5 kW
oven	- 6.0 kW
waste disposal	- 1.5 kW
mixer	- 2.5 kW

 A. 13 kW
 B. 17 kW

C. 26 kW
D. 19 kW

20. What is the demand load, in kW, on the grounded (neutral) service-entrance conductor for a multifamily dwelling when six (6) household electric ranges, each having a 9.5 kW rating, are installed?

 A. 15 kW
 B. 21 kW
 C. 26 kW
 D. 34 kW

NOTES

PRACTICAL CALCULATIONS FOR ELECTRICIANS
UNIT 3
SELF-ASSESSMENT QUIZ
ANSWER KEY

ANSWER		REFERENCE	NEC PG. #
1.	A	Table 220.55, Column B	pg. 74

8.5 kW x 80% = 6.8 kW demand

| 2. | D | Table 220.54 | pg. 73 |
| 3. | A | Table 220.55 & Note 3 | pg. 74 |

Use Column B – 5 appliances = 45% demand
6 kW + 8 kW + 3.5 kW + 6 kW + 3.5 kW = 27 kW connected load
27 kW x 45% = 12.15 kW demand load

4.	B	220.53	pg. 73
5.	C	220.54	pg. 73
6.	B	210.19(A)(3)	pg. 62
7.	A	220.53	pg. 73

4,800 VA – water heater
1,200 VA – dishwasher
1,150 VA – garbage disposal
 800 VA – trash compactor
<u>1,200 VA</u> – attic fan
9,150 VA connected load x 75% demand = 6,863 VA demand load

| 8. | C | Note 4 to Table 220.55
Single-phase current formula
$I = P \div E$ | pg. 74 |

$$I = \frac{6 \text{ kW} \times 1{,}000}{240 \text{ volts}} = \frac{6{,}000}{240} = 25 \text{ amperes}$$

9. D 220.54 pg. 73
 Power Formula
 VA = E x I

 VA = 240 volts x 30 amperes = 7,200 VA

10. A Table 220.55, Column C pg. 74
 220.61(B)(1) pg. 75

 Column C demand (1 range) = 8 kW x 70% = 5.6 kW

11. B Table 220.55, Column C pg. 74
 Note 1 to Table 220.55

 18 kW – 12 kW = 6 kW x 5% = 30% increase in Column C
 Column C demand (1 range) = 8 kW x 130% = 10.4 kW demand

12. C 220.56 pg. 73
 Single-phase current formula
 I = watts ÷ volts

 $I = \dfrac{5 \text{ kW} \times 1{,}000}{240 \text{ volts}} = \dfrac{5{,}000}{240} = 20.8 \text{ amperes}$

13. D Table 220.55, Column C pg. 74

14. B Table 220.55, Note 4 pg. 74
 Single-phase current formula
 I = watts ÷ volts

 6 kW + 4.5 kW + 4.5 kW = 15 kW connected load
 Treat as one range
 15 kW – 12 kW = 3 kW x 5% = 15% increase in Column C
 Column C demand (1 range) = 8 kW x 115% = 9.2 kW demand load

 $I = \dfrac{9.2 \text{ kW} \times 1{,}000}{240 \text{ volts}} = \dfrac{9{,}200}{240} = 38.3 \text{ amperes}$

15. A Article 100 - Definitions pg. 35

16. C 220.53 pg. 73

 6 water heaters x 5 kW = 30 kW connected load
 30 kW x 75% (demand factor) = 22.5 kW demand load

17. D 220.61(B)(1) pg. 75

18. B Table 220.55, Notes 1 & 4 pg. 74
Single-phase current formula
$I = $ power $\div$ volts

13.5 kW (rounded up) = 14 kW
14 kW – 12 kW = 2 kW x 5% = 10% increase in Column C
Column C demand (1 range) = 8 kW x 110% = 8.8 kW demand

$$I = \frac{8.8 \text{ kW x } 1{,}000}{240 \text{ volts}} = \frac{8{,}800}{240} = 36.6 \text{ amperes}$$

19. B 220.56 pg. 73
Table 220.56 pg. 75

6.0 kW – water heater
2.0 kW – dishwasher
7.5 kW – booster heater
6.0 kW – oven
1.5 kW – waste disposal
2.5 kW – mixer
25.5 kW connected load x 65% demand = 16.5 kW demand load

20. A Table 220.55, Column C pg. 74
220.61(B)(1) pg. 75

21 kW demand (6 ranges) in Column C
21 kW x 70% (neutral demand) = 15 kW demand load

UNIT 4

CONDUCTOR AMPACITY AND SIZING

Upon successfully completing this unit of study, the student will be familiar with the concept of determining the ampacity of conductors, application of ampacity correction factors, proper sizing, and insulation ratings of conductors.

$$\text{Required Ampacity} = \frac{\textbf{Load}}{\textbf{Correction Factors}}$$

UNIT 4

CONDUCTOR AMPACITY AND SIZING

RELATED INFORMATION:

☐ The definition of **ampacity** is the maximum current, in amperes, that a conductor can carry continuously under the conditions of use **without exceeding** its temperature rating. **[Article 100]** To get a better understanding of **ampacity**, perhaps we might consider it as **current-carrying capacity**, or the maximum amperage a conductor can carry without damaging the conductor and/or its insulation.

☐ When determining the ampacity of a conductor, or sizing a conductor, there are several factors needed to be taken into consideration; the ambient temperature, the type and temperature rating of the conductor insulation, the number of current-carrying conductors contained in the raceway or cable, the temperature rating of the terminations, characteristics of the load to be served, the environment the conductor will be subject to and voltage drop, which will be discussed later.

☐ **Table 310.104 (A)** lists the various types of insulated conductors, rated 600 volts, that includes maximum operating temperatures, application provisions and insulation characteristics. Some conductors are dual rated in regard to the location in which they are installed. For example, type **THHW** is rated **75 deg. C** for wet locations and **90 deg. C** for dry locations.

☐ **Table 310.15(B)(16)** lists the ampacity values for copper, aluminum or copper clad aluminum conductors, up to 2000 volts, with temperature ratings of 60 deg. C through 90 deg. C. This table is based on **not more than three** current-carrying conductors in a raceway, cable or directly buried in the earth at an ambient temperature (temperature surrounding the wire) of **30 deg. C or 86 deg. F**.

Table 310.15(B)(16) (formerly Table 310.16) Allowable Ampacities of Insulated Conductors Rated Up to and Including 2000 Volts, 60°C Through 90°C (140°F Through 194°F), Not More Than Three Current-Carrying Conductors in Raceway, Cable or Earth (Directly Buried), Based on Ambient Temperature of 30°C (86°F)*

Size AWG or kcmil	Temperature Rating of Conductor (See Table 310.104(A)						Size AWG or kcmil
	60°C (140°F)	75°C(167°F)	90°C(194°F)	60°C(140°F)	75°C (167°F)	90° (194°F)	
	Types TW, UF	Types RHW, THHW,THW THWN,XHHW, USE, ZW	Types TBS, SA, SIS, FEP, FEPB, MI, RHH, RHW-2, THHN, THHW, THW-2, THWN-2, USE-2, XHH, XHHW, XHHW-2, ZW-2	Types TW, UF	Types RHW, THHW,THW THWN, XHHW, USE	Types TBS, SA, SIS, THHN, THHW, THW-2, THWN-2, RHH, RHW-2, USE-2, XHH, XHHW, XHHW-2, ZW-2	
	COPPER			ALUMINUM OR COPPER-CLAD ALUMINUM			
18	-	-	14	-	-	-	-
16	-	-	18	-	-	-	-
14**	15	20	25	-	-	-	-
12**	20	25	30	15	20	25	12**
10**	30	35	40	25	30	35	10**
8	40	50	55	35	40	45	8
6	55	65	75	40	50	55	6
4	70	85	95	55	65	75	4
3	85	100	115	65	75	85	3
2	95	115	130	75	90	100	2
1	110	130	145	85	100	115	1
1/0	125	150	170	100	120	135	1/0
2/0	145	175	195	115	135	150	2/0
3/0	165	200	225	130	155	175	3/0
4/0	195	230	260	150	180	205	4/0
250	215	255	290	170	205	230	250
300	240	285	320	195	230	260	300
350	260	310	350	210	250	280	350
400	280	335	380	225	270	305	400
500	320	380	430	260	310	350	500
600	350	420	475	285	340	385	600
700	385	460	520	315	375	425	700
750	400	475	535	320	385	435	750
800	410	490	555	330	395	445	800
900	435	520	585	355	425	480	900
1000	455	545	615	375	445	500	1000
1250	495	590	665	405	485	545	1250
1500	525	625	705	435	520	585	1500
1750	545	650	735	455	545	615	1750
2000	555	665	750	470	560	630	2000

* Refer to 310.15(B)(2) for the ampacity correction factors where the ambient temperature is other than 30°C (86°F).
*Refer to 240.4(D) for conductor overcurrent protection limitations.

☐ The body of **Table 310.15(B)(16)** lists ampacities of conductors used in areas where the ambient temperature is 30 deg. C or 86 deg. F, this is called **normal operating temperature**. The left half of the table is for **copper** conductors and the right half of the table is for **aluminum or copper clad aluminum** conductors.

☐ The temperature rating of a conductor is the maximum temperature, at any location along its length, that the conductor can withstand over a prolonged period of time without serious damage occurring. **[310.15(A)(3), INF. Note #1]**

☐ When conductors are subject to ambient temperatures above 86 deg. F, the resistance of the conductors are also increased proportionately. The greater the elevated ambient temperature, the greater the resistance. When the **resistance** of a conductor **increases** the **ampacity** of the conductor **decreases**. When this condition occurs, you must apply the appropriate temperature correction factors given in **Table 310.15(B)(2)(a).**

Table 310.15(B)(2)(a) Ambient Temperature Correction Factors Based on 30°C (86°F)				
For ambient temperatures other than 30°C (86°F), multiply the allowable ampacities specified in the ampacity table by the appropriate correction factor shown below.				
Ambient Temp. (°C)	Temperature Rating of Conductor			Ambient Temp. (°F)
	60° C	75°C	90° C	
10 or less	1.29	1.20	1.15	50 or less
11-15	1.22	1.15	1.12	51-59
16-20	1.15	1.11	1.08	60-68
21-25	1.08	1.05	1.04	69-77
26-30	1.00	1.00	1.00	78-86
31-35	0.91	0.94	0.96	87-95
36-40	0.82	0.88	0.91	96-104
41-45	0.71	0.82	0.87	105-113
46-50	0.58	0.75	0.82	114-122
51-55	0.41	0.67	0.76	123-131
56-60	-	0.58	0.71	132-140
61-65	-	0.47	0.65	141-149
66-70	-	0.33	0.58	150-158
71-75	-	-	0.50	159-167
76-80	-	-	0.41	168-176
81-85	-	-	0.29	177-185

EXAMPLE - When a size 3 AWG copper conductor, with THW insulation, is installed in an area where the ambient temperature is 114 deg. F, the wire has an allowable ampacity of _____.

 A. 100 amperes
 B. 75 amperes
 C. 82 amperes
 D. 58 amperes

ANSWER - (B) 75 amperes

 100 amperes x .75 = 75 amperes

 To solve this problem, first we locate the wire size on the left side of **Table 310.15(B)(16)** and look to the right under the copper THW column, with a temperature rating of 75°C, and note the ampacity of the wire is 100 amperes at normal operating temperature. Then, we apply the values as shown in **Table 310.15(B)(2)(a).** Look to the right side of the table where the ambient temperature is shown as **°F** and find the ambient temperature. Next, we follow that line to the left where the line intersects with the **75° C column** (temperature rating of conductor) to find our correction factor of **.75**, or 75%. Finally, to find the allowable ampacity of the conductor, multiply the two values together.

EXAMPLE - When a size 1/0 AWG THWN aluminum conductor is installed in an ambient temperature of 45 deg. C, the conductor has an allowable ampacity of _____.

 A. 100 amperes
 B. 90 amperes
 C. 98 amperes
 D. 104 amperes

ANSWER - (C) 98 amperes

 1/0 THWN aluminum ampacity before derating = 120 amperes
 120 amps x .82 (correction factor) = 98.4 amperes

We use the same steps as before. First, we find the wire size which has an ampacity of 120 amperes. **[Tbl. 310.15(B)(16)]** Then, we find the ambient temperature, this time on the left portion of **Table 310.15(B)(2)(a)**, and go to the right under the THWN aluminum column (temperature rating of conductor) to find the correction factor of **.82**. Next, multiply the two values together.

☐ The temperature correction factors on **Table 310.15(B)(2)(a)** are to be applied when sizing conductors for a given load located in an area with an elevated ambient temperature. The following formula should be used:

Required ampacity = $\underline{\hspace{1cm}\text{load}\hspace{1cm}}$
$\hspace{3cm}$ correction factor

EXAMPLE - Where a 100 ampere load is to be supplied with THWN copper conductors in an area where the ambient temperature will reach 110 deg. F, size _____ THWN conductors are required to serve the load.

 A. 1 AWG
 B. 2 AWG
 C. 3 AWG
 D. 1/0 AWG

ANSWER - (A) 1 AWG

$$\text{required ampacity} = \frac{100 \text{ amps}}{.82} = 122 \text{ amperes}$$

Table 310.15(B)(16) indicates size 1 AWG copper conductors with an ampacity of 130 amperes, should be selected. To cross reference:

130 amperes x .82 (correction factor) = 107 amperes

☐ Conductors are to be sized in accordance with the lowest temperature rating of the terminal, device or conductor of the circuit. **[110.14(C)]** In other words, conductors must be sized to the **lowest temperature rating** of the wire, circuit breaker, terminal or device.

☐ Conductors with temperature ratings higher than that of the terminations are permitted to be used for ampacity adjustment and/or correction. **[110.14(C)]** Today, most terminations are rated at **60 deg. C or 75 deg. C**. This permits us to use THHN conductors for derating purposes, but the conductor size is based on the lower terminal rating of the circuit breaker, equipment or device, not the 90 deg. C rating of the conductor insulation.

EXAMPLE - The load on a size 6 AWG THHN copper conductor is limited to _____ where connected to a circuit breaker with a termination rated at 60° C.

 A. 75 amperes
 B. 65 amperes
 C. 60 amperes
 D. 55 amperes

ANSWER - (D) 55 amperes

 Table 310.15(B)(16) lists the ampacity of size 6 AWG, copper, 60° C rated conductors to be 55 amperes.

EXAMPLE - The load, in amperes, on a size 6 AWG THHN copper conductor is permitted to be no more than _____ where connected to a fusible disconnect switch with terminals rated at 75 deg. C.

 A. 75 amperes
 B. 65 amperes
 C. 60 amperes
 D. 55 amperes

ANSWER - (B) 65 amperes

 Table 310.15(B)(16) lists the ampacity of size 6 AWG copper 75 deg. C rated conductors to be 65 amperes.

☐ Many circuit breakers and disconnect switches now have dual ratings marked **60/75 deg. C**. Under this condition, for 60 deg. C conductors, derating and ampacity values are to be based on the 60 deg. C terminal ratings; 75 deg. C and 90 deg. C conductors derating and ampacity values may be based on either the 60 deg. C or 75 deg. C terminal ratings.

☐ Many conductors now are dual rated such as **THWN/THHN**. The ampacity rating is based on the THWN, 75 deg. C values, but the derating factor(s) may be based on the THHN 90 deg. C values.

☐ The allowable **ampacity** of **Types NM**, **NMC** and **NMS** cable shall be in accordance with the **60 deg. C** conductor temperature rating. The **90 deg. C** rating shall be permitted to be used for **ampacity derating** purposes, provided the final ampacity does not exceed that for a 60 deg. C rated conductor. **[334.80]**

EXAMPLE - A size 12/2 AWG w/ground copper NM cable is to be installed in an attic of a
 dwelling where the ambient temperature is 125 deg. F. Determine the ampacity of
 the cable.

 A. 22.8 amperes
 B. 14.5 amperes
 C. 24.6 amperes
 D. 17.4 amperes

ANSWER - (A) 22.8 amperes

 Ampacity of 12 AWG at 90 deg. C before derating = 30 amperes
 30 amperes x .76 (temperature correction) = 22.8 amperes

 Under this condition, the ampacity of 22.8 amperes is NOT
 permitted, because this value is more than the 20 ampere rating of
 the 12 AWG conductors at the 60 deg. C temperature rating.

EXAMPLE - A size 10/3 AWG w/ground copper NM cable is to be installed in the crawl space of a
 dwelling where the ambient temperature is 100 deg. F. Determine the ampacity of
 the cable.

 A. 24.6 amperes
 B. 36.4 amperes
 C. 32.3 amperes
 D. 30.0 amperes

ANSWER - (D) 30.0 amperes

 Ampacity of 10 AWG at 90 deg. C before derating = 40 amperes
 40 amperes x .91 (temp. correction) = 36.4 amperes

 Under this condition the ampacity of 36.4 amperes is also NOT permitted,
 because this value is more than the 30 ampere rating of 10 AWG conductors
 at the 60 deg. C rating.

 When there are more than three (3) current-carrying conductors in a raceway or
cable, the ability of the conductors to dissipate heat is reduced. Therefore, when this
condition exists in a raceway or cable longer than 24 inches the allowable ampacity of
each conductor shall be reduced as shown in **Table 310.15(B)(3)(a)**.

EXAMPLE - What is the allowable ampacity of a size 1/0 AWG THW copper conductor installed
 in a conduit longer than 24 inches, when there are three (3) other current-carrying
 conductors contained in the same pipe?

 A. 150 amperes
 B. 120 amperes
 C. 105 amperes

D. 140 amperes

ANSWER - (B) 120 amperes

 150 amperes x .8 (adjustment factor) = 120 amperes

 First, find the ampacity of the conductor, before derating, as shown in **Table 310.15(B)(16).** Then, apply the appropriate adjustment factor as shown in **Table 310.15(B)(3)(a).**

☐ When there are four (4) or more current-carrying conductors in a raceway or cable, longer than 24 inches, installed in an area with an elevated temperature, **both** the temperature correction and the adjustment factor for the number of current-carrying conductors must be applied.

EXAMPLE - Determine the allowable ampacity of a size 2 AWG THWN aluminum conductor installed in a 20 foot long conduit with seven (7) other current-carrying conductors of the same size and insulation, where the ambient temperature is 99 deg. F.

 A. 59 amperes
 B. 71 amperes
 C. 55 amperes
 D. 63 amperes

ANSWER - (C) 55 amperes

 Size 2 AWG THWN AL ampacity before derating = 90 amperes
 90 amperes x .88 (temp. correction) x .7 (adj. factor) = 55 amps

 First, find the ampacity of the conductor as shown in **Table 310.15(B)(16)** before derating. Then, apply the temperature correction factor. **[Table 310.15(B)(2)(a)]** Next, apply the adjustment factor for the multiple current-carrying conductors as shown in **Table 310.15(B)(3)(a),** and multiply the three values together.

☐ When sizing conductors for a given load in an area with an elevated ambient temperature, installed in a raceway or cable more than 24 inches in length, the following formula may be used when there are more than three current-carrying conductors in the raceway or cable.

 Required ampacity = $\dfrac{\text{Load}}{\text{temp. correction x adj. factor}}$

EXAMPLE - A 100 ampere load is located in an environment where the temperature reaches 115 deg. F, and is to be supplied with four (4) 75 deg. C rated copper current-carrying conductors. Determine the proper size wire to serve the load. All terminations are rated at 75 deg. C.

A. 1/0 AWG
B. 2/0 AWG
C. 1 AWG
D. 3 AWG

ANSWER - (B) 2/0 AWG

$$\text{ampacity} = \frac{100 \text{ amperes (load)}}{.76 \text{ (temp.) x .8 (adj.)}} = \frac{100}{0.6} = 167 \text{ amperes}$$

*NOTE – Size 2/0 AWG copper conductors rated at 75 deg. C
with an ampacity of 175 amperes are required.

When considering current-carrying conductors, the neutral conductor is **not counted** when the neutral carries only the **unbalanced current** of the circuit; for example, 120/240-volt single-phase systems. **[310.15(B)(5)(a)]** The neutral does carry current, but is not required to be counted.

☐ The neutral **is considered** a current-carrying conductor on a 4-wire, 3-phase wye circuit where the major portion of the load consists of **nonlinear loads**. **[310.15(B)(5)(c)]** Examples of nonlinear loads are high intensity discharge (HID) lighting and fluorescent lighting, information technology equipment, computers, and data processing equipment.

☐ As per Section **310.15(B)(7)** for sizing **120/240-volt**, **3-wire**, **single-phase** service and feeder conductors rated 100 through 400 amperes, for one-family dwelling units and individual units of a multi-family dwelling, they are permitted to have an ampacity not less than 83 percent of the service or feeder rating.

EXAMPLE - A one-family dwelling is supplied with a 120/240-volt, single-phase electrical system from the local utility company and has a demand load of 200 amperes. What is the MINIMUM size THWN/THHN aluminum service-entrance conductors required?

A. 250 kcmil
B. 4/0 AWG
C. 3/0 AWG
D. 2/0 AWG

ANSWER - (B) 4/0 AWG

200 amperes x .83 = 166 amperes

Size 4/0 AWG THWN/THHN aluminum service-entrance conductors with an ampacity of 180 amperes should be selected from **Table 310.15(B)(16).**

☐ When single-insulated conductors are installed in free air, they can dissipate the heat caused by the current flowing in the conductors more readily than when installed in raceways. The conductors have a greater allowable ampacity therefore, **Table 310.15(B)(17)** may be applied in the same manner as previously referenced in this unit.

EXAMPLE - When ambient temperature is not a consideration, when installed in free air, a size 6 AWG THWN copper conductor has a MAXIMUM allowable ampacity of _____.

 A. 65 amperes
 B. 75 amperes
 C. 105 amperes
 D. 95 amperes

ANSWER - (D) 95 amperes

 Table 310.15(B)(17) shows size 6 AWG THWN copper conductors to have an allowable ampacity of 95 amperes.

UNIT 4
SELF-ASSESSMENT QUIZ

1. A conduit having a length of fifty (50) feet contains nine (9) conductors. Six (6) of the conductors are considered to be current-carrying. What is the derating factor that must be applied to the ampacity of the current-carrying conductors?

 A. 80 percent
 B. 70 percent
 C. 60 percent
 D. 50 percent

2. Type XHHW insulated conductors may be used in _____.

 A. dry locations only
 B. wet locations only
 C. dry or damp locations only
 D. dry, damp or wet locations

3. A twenty five (25) feet run of electrical metallic tubing encloses three (3) current-carrying size 2 AWG THW copper conductors in an area where the ambient temperature is 125 deg. F. The correction factor that must be applied for the elevated ambient temperature is _____.

 A. 0.67
 B. 0.82
 C. 0.75
 D. 0.76

4. What is the MINIMUM size copper SE cable with Type XHHW insulation that may be used as ungrounded service-entrance conductors for a 150-ampere, 120/240 volt, single-phase residential service?

 A. 1/0 AWG

B. 1 AWG
C. 2 AWG
D. 3 AWG

5. When ambient temperature is not a factor, a size 8 AWG single copper conductor with Type
 FEPB insulation, installed in free air, will have a MAXIMUM allowable ampacity of _____.

 A. 80 amperes
 B. 55 amperes
 C. 45 amperes
 D. 83 amperes

6. What is the MAXIMUM allowable ampacity of a size 8 AWG THWN copper conductor
 installed in a conduit with two (2) other current-carrying conductors where the ambient
 temperature is 86 deg. F?

 A. 40 amperes
 B. 45 amperes
 C. 50 amperes
 D. 55 amperes

7. Three (3) size 1/0 AWG THW copper current-carrying conductors are contained within a
 raceway where the ambient temperature is 120 deg. F. What is the allowable ampacity of
 the individual conductors?

 A. 113 amperes
 B. 130 amperes
 C. 146 amperes
 D. 150 amperes

8. Determine the MAXIMUM allowable current-carrying capacity of a size 4 AWG copper
 conductor with THWN insulation installed in a conduit ten (10) feet in length with five (5)
 other current-carrying conductors.

 A. 60 amperes
 B. 52 amperes
 C. 85 amperes
 D. 68 amperes

9. You are to serve a 240-volt, single-phase, 3-wire, 200-ampere non-continuous load in an area where the expected ambient temperature is 110 deg. F. Using 75 deg. C rated aluminum conductors and considering terminations are rated at 75 deg. C, determine the MINIMUM size conductors required to supply the load.

 A. 250 kcmil
 B. 300 kcmil
 C. 350 kcmil
 D. 400 kcmil

10. When a 60 deg. C rated size 6 AWG copper conductor is terminated on a circuit breaker having a marked temperature rating of 60/75 deg. C, the conductor has an allowable ampacity of _____.

 A. 40 amperes
 B. 55 amperes
 C. 50 amperes
 D. 65 amperes

11. The allowable ampacity of a size 3/0 AWG THHN copper conductor installed in an environment with an ambient temperature of 50 deg. C is _____.

 A. 225 amperes
 B. 200 amperes
 C. 164 amperes
 D. 185 amperes

12. The allowable ampacity of size 2 AWG copper conductors with a dual rated insulation of THWN/THHN enclosed in a rigid metal conduct (RMC) when installed in a wet location is _____.

 A. 115 amperes
 B. 130 amperes
 C. 95 amperes
 D. 100 amperes

13. After all demand factors have been taken into consideration for a one-family dwelling, the demand load is determined to be 45,000 VA. The house is to be supplied with a 120/240-volt, single-phase underground installed electrical system. What MINIMUM size USE cable with aluminum conductors is required for the underground supplied service?

 A. 2/0 AWG
 B. 3/0 AWG
 C. 4/0 AWG
 D. 250 kcmil

14. Adjustment factors for ambient temperature correction and more than three (3) current-carrying conductors in a raceway, shall not apply to conductors rated 0 to 2000 volts, in a raceway having a length NOT exceeding _____.

 A. 48 inches
 B. 36 inches
 C. 30 inches
 D. 24 inches

15. What MINIMUM size THHN copper conductors are required for a 240-volt, single-phase, 70 ampere branch circuit if the temperature on the circuit breaker and the equipment are listed for 75 deg. C when the demand load is 65 amperes?

 A. 10 AWG
 B. 8 AWG
 C. 6 AWG
 D. 4 AWG

16. The ampacity of eight (8) current-carrying size 10 AWG THW copper conductors enclosed in an electrical metallic tubing (EMT) 18 inches long is _____.

 A. 30 amperes
 B. 35 amperes
 C. 28 amperes
 D. 24 amperes

17. Under which, if any, of the following conditions is the neutral NOT to be counted as a current-carrying conductor?

 I. When it is only carrying the unbalanced current of a single-phase system.
 II. When it is the neutral of a 3-phase, wye connected system where the major portion of the load consists of nonlinear loads.

 A. I only
 B. II only
 C. both I and II
 D. neither I nor II

18. A conductor with _____ insulation has a different ampacity and temperature rating when

used in a wet location compared to when used in a dry location.

 A. THWN
 B. THHN
 C. THW
 D. XHHW

19. A 3-phase, 4-wire, 208Y/120-volt feeder is to supply a panelboard of a department store with a 104 ampere continuous fluorescent lighting load. Where using 75 deg. C rated aluminum feeder conductors, determine the MINIMUM size required.

 A. 250 kcmil
 B. 4/0 AWG
 C. 3/0 AWG
 D. 2/0 AWG

20. Eight (8) 75 deg. C rated current-carrying branch circuit conductors are to be installed in a common raceway having a length of fifty (50) feet where located in an attic having an ambient temperature of 100 deg. F. Each conductor is to supply a continuous lighting load of 15 amperes and terminate on a 75 deg. C circuit breaker. Each conductor is required to have an ampacity of at least _____.

 A. 21.3 amperes
 B. 26.8 amperes
 C. 30.4 amperes
 D. 32.6 amperes

NOTES

PRACTICAL CALCULATIONS FOR ELECTRICIANS
UNIT 4
SELF-ASSESSMENT QUIZ
ANSWER KEY

ANSWER		REFERENCE	NEC PG. #
1.	A	Table 310.15(B)(3)(a)	pg. 148
2.	D	Table 310.104(A)	pg. 168
3.	A	Table 310.15(B)(2)(a)	pg. 147
4.	B	310.15(B)(7)(1)	pg. 149
		Table 310.15(B)(16)	pg. 150

150 amperes x 83% = 124.5 amperes

Size 1 AWG XHHW copper conductors with an ampacity of 130 amperes should be selected from the 75°C column of Table 310.15(B)(16).

5.	A	Table 310.15(B)(17)	pg. 151
6.	C	Table 310.15(B)(16)	pg. 150
7.	A	Table 310.15(B)(16)	pg. 150
		Table 310.15(B)(2)(a)	pg. 147

Size 1/0 AWG THW ampacity (before derating) = 150 amperes
150 amperes x .75 (temperature correction) = 112.5 amperes

8.	D	Table 310.15(B)(16)	pg. 150
		Table 310.15(B)(3)(a)	pg. 148

Size 4 AWG THWN ampacity (before derating) = 85 amperes
85 amperes x .8 (adjustment factor) = 68 amperes

9.	C	Table 310.15(B)(16)	pg. 150
		Table 310.15(B)(2)(a)	pg. 147

$$\text{Required ampacity} = \frac{200 \text{ amperes}}{.82 \text{ (temp. correction)}} = 243.9 \text{ amperes}$$

Table 310.15(B)(16) requires size 350 kcmil aluminum conductors rated for 75 deg. C with an ampacity of 250 amperes.

10.	B	Table 310.15(B)(16)	pg. 150

11. D Table 310.15(B)(16) pg. 150
 Table 310.15(B)(2)(a) pg. 147

 3/0 AWG THHN ampacity (before adjusting) = 225 amperes
 225 amperes x .82 (temperature correction) = 184.5 amperes

12. A Table 310.104(A) pg. 167
 Table 310.15(B)(16) pg. 150

13. C Single-Phase Current Formula
 310.15(B)(7)(1) pg. 149
 Table 310.15(B)(16) pg. 150

$I = \dfrac{P}{E}$ $I = \dfrac{45{,}000 \text{ VA}}{240 \text{ volts}}$ = 187.5 amperes x 83% = 155.625 amperes

Table 310.15(B)(16) requires a size 4/0 AWG aluminum USE cable.

14. D 310.15(B)(3)(a)(2) pg. 147

15. C 110.14(C) pg. 45
 Table 310.15(B)(16) pg. 150
 240.4(B)(2) pg. 94

16. B 310.15(B)(3)(a)(2) pg. 147
 Table 310.15(B)(16) pg. 150

17. A 310.15(B)(5)(a)&(b) pg. 148

18. D Table 310.104(A) pg. 168

19. B 310.15(B)(5)(c) pg. 148
 215.2(A)(1)(a) pg. 67
 Table 310.15(B)(3)(a) pg. 148
 Table 310.15(B)(16) pg. 150

Required ampacity = $\dfrac{104 \text{ amperes x } 125\%}{.8 \text{ (adjustment factor)}}$ = $\dfrac{130}{.8}$ = 162.5 amperes

20. C 210.19(A)(1)(a) pg. 62
 Table 310.15(B)(2)(a) pg. 147
 Table 310.15(B)(3)(a) pg. 148
 Table 310.15(B)(16) pg. 150

Required ampacity = $\dfrac{15 \text{ amps x } 125\%}{.7 \text{ (adj. factor) x } .88 \text{ (temp. cor.)}}$ = $\dfrac{18.75}{.616}$ = 30.4 amperes

UNIT 5

BOX AND RACEWAY SIZING

Upon successfully completing this unit of study the student will be familiar with the concept of properly sizing electrical boxes and raceways.

Number of Wires Permitted =

$$\frac{\textbf{Allowable Fill}}{\textbf{Wire Size}}$$

UNIT 5

BOX AND RACEWAY SIZING

Outlet and Device Box Sizing

RELATED INFORMATION:

 ☐ Device and junction boxes are required to be of a sufficient size to house conductors and/or devices, clamps and support fittings without damaging the conductor's insulation. Therefore, when sizing boxes, conductors, clamps and support fittings are required to be counted in order to select the proper size box. **[314.16]**

 ☐ To properly size outlet boxes you must count the conductors within the box correctly. **Section 314.16(B)(1)** is to be used as a guideline to count the conductors as follows:

 1) Conductors that originate outside the box or that are spliced within the box are counted **one** for each conductor.

 2) Conductors unbroken within the box, less than 12 inches in length, that pass through the box without splicing or terminating are counted **one** for each conductor.

 3) Conductors 12 inches or longer that are looped and unbroken are counted as **two** for a single conductor.

 4) Conductors that originate within the box and do not leave the box such as, bonding jumpers and pigtails are **not counted**.

 5) Conductors from a domed luminaire (fixture) that terminate within the box are **not counted**.

 ☐ When sizing device and junction boxes, the insulation of the conductors are not required to be taken into consideration. The volume required for the individual conductors is expressed in **cubic inches** and/or **cubic centimeters**, no matter what the insulation characteristics of the conductor(s) is/are.

 ☐ To determine the volume, in cubic inches, of a box simply multiply the length times the width times the depth of the box.

EXAMPLE - A box that measures 6 inches x 6 inches and is 4 inches deep has a volume of _____.

 A. 96 cubic inches

B. 144 cubic inches
C. 24 cubic inches
D. 36 cubic inches

ANSWER - (B) 144 cubic inches

6 in. x 6 in. x 4 in. = 144 cubic inches

☐ **Table 314.16(A)** may be used to determine the **MINIMUM** size outlet box required for a given number of conductors, or when determining the **MAXIMUM** number of conductors permitted in an outlet box when all of the conductors in the box are of the **same size**.

EXAMPLE - Determine the MAXIMUM number of size 12 AWG THWN conductors permitted in a 4 x 1½ in. square box.

A. seven
B. eight
C. nine
D. ten

ANSWER - (C) nine

The right hand side of **Table 314.16(B)** under the **12** column shows nine conductors permitted in the box.

EXAMPLE - Of the following listed, which one of the boxes is the MINIMUM required to house three (3) size 12 AWG THWN/THHN conductors and three (3) size 12 AWG THW conductors?

A. 4 x 1½ in. octagon
B. 4 x 2¼ in. octagon
C. 4 x 1½ in. square
D. 4 x 2¼ in. square

ANSWER - (A) 4 x 1½ in. octagon

Table 314.16(B) permits six (6) size 12 AWG conductors in a 4 x 1½ in. octagon box.

☐ **Table 314.16(A)** shall apply where no fittings or devices, such as cable clamps, luminaire studs, hickeys, receptacles, switches or dimmers, are enclosed in the box. **Table 314.16(A)** does not take into consideration the fill requirements for these fittings or devices; where one or more of these items are contained in the box, the number of conductors permitted as shown in the table shall be reduced as follows:

Copyright© 2017

1) **cable clamps** – One or more internal cable clamps present in the box are counted as **one** conductor, based on the **largest** conductor in the box. **[314.16(B)(2)]**

2) **support fittings** – One or more luminaire (fixture) studs and/or hickeys in the box are counted as **one** conductor for each type of fitting, based on the **largest** conductor in the box. **[314.16(B)(3)]**

3) **devices** – For each yoke or strap containing one or more device present in the box, they are to be counted as **two wires**, based on the **largest** conductor connected to the device. **[314.16(B)(4)]**

4) **equipment grounding conductors** – One or more equipment grounding conductors or bonding jumpers contained in a box are to be counted as **one** conductor, based on the **largest** equipment grounding conductor or bonding jumper in the box. **[314.16(B)(5)]** Where an **additional set** of isolated equipment grounding conductors are in the box, they are to be counted as **one** conductor, based on the **largest** equipment grounding conductor in the additional set.

☐ When doing box fill calculations we must take into consideration the volume taken up by all conductors, fittings and devices contained in the box to properly size the box.

EXAMPLE - A device box contains two (2) internal clamps, two (2) equipment grounding conductors, one (1) bonding jumper and one (1) duplex receptacle. The number of conductors permitted in the box is to be reduced by _____ conductors.

 A. three
 B. four
 C. five
 D. six

ANSWER - (B) four

clamps	= 1 wire
receptacle	= 2 wires
equip. grounding & bonding wires	= 1 wire
TOTAL	= 4 wires

☐ When calculating the proper size outlet box to be used when the conductors are of different sizes, you are to determine the volume of the conductors, in cubic inches, by applying **Table 314.16(B)**, and then size the box by using **Table 314.16(A)**.

EXAMPLE - Determine which one of the following listed outlet boxes is the MINIMUM size required to enclose the following conductors:

- six (6) size 12 AWG conductors
- two (2) size 14 AWG conductors
- one (1) size 14 AWG equipment grounding conductors

 A. 4 x 1½ in. octagon
 B. 4 x 1½ in. square
 C. 4 x 2¼ in. square
 D. 4¼ x 1½ in. square

ANSWER - (B) 4 x 1½ in. square

 Size 12 AWG = 2.25 cu. in. x 6 = 13.5 cubic inches
 Size 14 AWG = 2.00 cu. in. x 2 = 4.0 cubic inches
 Size 14 AWG Equip. grounding x 1 = 2.0 cubic inches
 19.5 cubic inches

 Table 314.16(A) requires a 4 x 1½ inch square box having a volume of 21 cubic inches.

Junction and Pull Box Sizing

RELATED INFORMATION:

 ☐ **Section 314.16** states when boxes enclosing conductors of size **4 AWG or larger** are used as pull or junction boxes, they are to comply with the provisions of **314.28**. Under this condition, pull and junction boxes are to be sized by the raceways entering the box(es) and not by the size of the conductors contained in the box.

 ☐ In straight pulls, the length of the box shall not be less than **eight times** the trade diameter of the largest raceway entering the box. **[314.28(A)(1)]**

EXAMPLE - Determine the MINIMUM length of a pull box that has a trade size 3½ inch conduit entering at each end, and containing conductors of size 250 kcmil, when a straight pull of the conductors is to be made.

 A. 21 inches
 B. 24 inches
 C. 28 inches
 D. 32 inches

ANSWER - (C) 28 inches

3.5 in. (conduit) x 8 = 28 inches

☐ Where splices, angle or U-pulls are made, the distance between each raceway entry inside the box and opposite wall of the box shall not be less than **six (6) times** the trade size of the raceway in a row. **[314.28(A)(2)]** Then, you are to add the sum of the trade size diameter of any additional raceways entering the box. In other words, for angle or U-pulls, the proper size junction box can be determined by multiplying the largest raceway by six (6) and add any additional conduits.

EXAMPLE - A junction box is to be installed where the conductors are larger than size 4 AWG and an angle (90 deg.) pull of the conductors is to be made. Two (2) trade size 3 inch conduits are to enter the box from the top and two (2) trade size 3 inch conduits are to enter the box from the side. Determine the MINIMUM size pull box required.

 A. 36 in. x 36 in.
 B. 27 in. x 27 in.
 C. 24 in. x 24 in.
 D. 21 in. x 21 in.

ANSWER - (D) 21 in. x 21 in.

 Top to bottom – 3 in. (largest conduit) x 6 = 18 in. + 3 in. = 21 in.
 Side to side – 3 in. (largest conduit) x 6 = 18 in. + 3 in. = 21 in.

EXAMPLE - A pull box has one (1) trade size 2 inch conduit and one (1) trade size 1½ inch conduit entering the top and two (2) trade size 2 inch conduits on the left side. Where conductors are larger than 4 AWG and an angle (90 deg.) pull of the conductors is to be made, determine the MINIMUM distance required from the top wall to the bottom wall.

 A. 13½ inches
 B. 11 inches
 C. 12 inches
 D. 16 inches

ANSWER - (A) 13½ inches

 2 in. (largest conduit) x 6 = 12 + 1½ in. = 13½ inches

Conduit and Tubing Sizing

RELATED INFORMATION:

- ☐ When electrical conduit or tubing enclose conductors of the same size, with the same type of insulation, when the conduit or tubing is more than 24 inches in length, application of **Annex C**, **Tables C.1 through C.13(A)** is permitted to be used when determining the MAXIMUM number of conductors permitted. **[Chapter 9, Table 1]** This is the fastest and easiest method of determining the MAXIMUM number of conductors allowed in a standard trade size conduit or tubing.

- ☐ Located at the first part of **Annex C** there is a listing of the various types of standard electrical conduits. Use this table to find the particular type of conduit you are going to use when determining conduit fill.

EXAMPLE - Determine the MINIMUM trade size electrical metallic tubing (EMT), more than 24 inches in length, permitted to enclose twelve (12) size 10 AWG THWN conductors.

 A. 3/4 in.
 B. 1 in.
 C. 1¼ in.
 D. 1½ in.

ANSWER - (B) 1 inch

 First locate **Table C.1** of **Annex C**. Next, refer to the type of insulation **(THWN)** of the conductors. Then, locate the wire size **(10 AWG)**, and you will find for twelve (12) size 10 AWG THWN conductors a trade size 1 inch EMT is required.

EXAMPLE - A trade size 1½ inch Schedule 40 PVC conduit, 25 feet in length, is permitted to enclose no more than _____ size 2 AWG XHHW compact aluminum conductors.

 A. six
 B. seven
 C. eight
 D. ten

ANSWER - (C) eight
 First, locate **Table C.11(A)** of **Annex C**. Next, find the insulation type **(XHHW)** of the conductors. Then, locate the conduit size **(1½ in.)** and conductor size **(2 AWG)**, and

you will find a trade size 1½ inch Schedule 40 PVC is
permitted to enclose eight (8) size 2 AWG XHHW compact
aluminum conductors.

☐ When conduit or tubing enclose conductors of different sizes and/or insulations,
Chapter 9, **Tables 4, 5 and 5A**, with their related notes, are to be applied to
determine the proper fill.

☐ **Table 1** of **Chapter 9** shows the permitted fill, in percent of conduit and tubing,
when one, two or over two conductors are installed; for example, when more than
two (2) conductors are installed in a conduit or tubing they shall be permitted to be
filled to **40 percent** of their cross-sectional area.

☐ Where conduit or tubing nipples have a MAXIMUM length not to exceed 24 inches
between boxes and enclosures, the nipples shall be permitted to be filled to **60
percent** of their total cross-sectional area.
 [Chapter 9, Note 4]

☐ **Table 4, Chapter 9** list the various types of conduit and tubing. Each type of
conduit or tubing is shown as a separate table. At the top of each table is shown the
internal diameter and the percent of fill. Under the percent of fill heading you will
find the allowable fill of each size conduit or tubing expressed in square inches and
millimeters. On the left side of the table the trade size and metric designator of the
conduit or tubing are listed. To find the allowable fill of a specific conduit or tubing
simply locate the conduit or tubing size and extend to the right under the proper
percent of fill heading.

EXAMPLE - When more than two (2) conductors are installed in a trade size 2 inch electrical
metallic tubing (EMT) longer than 24 inches, the EMT has an allowable fill of _____.

 A. 2.013 square inches
 B. 1.778 square inches
 C. 1.040 square inches
 D. 1.342 square inches

ANSWER - (D) 1.342 square inches

 Under this condition the 2 in. EMT is permitted to have an allowable
 fill of 40 percent. **[Table 4, Chapter 9]**

EXAMPLE - When four (4) current-carrying conductors are installed in a trade size 2 inch
electrical metallic tubing (EMT) nipple 18 inches long, the EMT has a MAXIMUM
allowable fill of _____.

 A. 2.013 square inches
 B. 1.778 square inches
 C. 1.040 square inches
 D. 1.342 square inches

ANSWER - (A) 2.013 square inches

Under this condition the 2 in. EMT is permitted to have an allowable fill of 60 percent. **[Table 4, Chapter 9]**

☐ **Table 5**, **Chapter 9** shows the various sizes and insulations of conductors expressed in millimeters and square inches in accordance with appropriate diameter and area. In most cases we relate to the **approximate area** in **square inches** on the right side of the table.

EXAMPLE - A size 8 AWG THWN copper conductor has an approximate area of _____.

A. 0.0437 square inches
B. 0.0366 square inches
C. 0.0835 square inches
D. 0.2160 square inches

ANSWER - (B) 0.0366 square inches

First, we locate the insulation **(THWN)** of the conductor.
Then, the size **(8 AWG)**, and look to the extreme right side of the table to find the approximate area in square inches.
[Table 5, Chapter 9]

☐ **Table 5A**, **Chapter 9** shows the various sizes and insulations of **compact aluminum conductors** expressed in millimeters and square inches with approximate diameter and area, much like **Table 5 of Chapter 9**. This table is structured different than **Table 5** but, is easier to use because there is only four (4) types of conductor insulations listed. Again refer to the approximate area in square inches of the conductor when calculating raceway fill.

EXAMPLE - What is the area, in square inches, of a size 3/0 AWG XHHW compact aluminum conductor.

A. 0.590 square inches
B. 0.2733 square inches
C. 0.2290 square inches
D. 0.1885 square inches

ANSWER - (C) 0.2290 square inches

First, from **Table 5A of Chapter 9**, locate the insulation **(XHHW)** of the conductor.
Then, locate the wire size, **(3/0 AWG)**, and look under the **in.²** heading to find the area.

☐ Where equipment grounding or bonding conductors are installed in conduit or tubing, they shall be included when calculating the permitted fill. **[Chapter 9, Note 3]** If insulated, use the **Table 5** to find the approximate area; if bare find the area in square inches from **Table 8 of Chapter 9**, look under the heading of **in²**.

EXAMPLE - A size 8 AWG solid bare equipment grounding conductor has an area of _____.

 A. 0.128 square inches
 B. 0.146 square inches
 C. 0.017 square inches
 D. 0.013 square inches

ANSWER - (D) 0.013 square inches

First, locate the wire size and stranding properties from **Table 8 of Chapter 9**.
Next, extend to the right under the **in.²** heading to find the area.

☐ Conduits or tubing enclosing different size conductors and/or conductors having different insulations are sized by locating the area, in square inches, of each conductor per **Table 5**, **Table 5A** or **Table 8** and multiplying by the number of conductors. This total is used to select the proper size raceway using **Table 4** in **Chapter 9**.

EXAMPLE - Determine the MINIMUM trade size intermediate metal conduit (IMC) permitted to enclose three (3) size 8 AWG XHHW copper branch-circuit conductors and six (6) size 12 AWG THWN copper control-circuit conductors. The IMC is to be fifty (50) feet in length.

 A. 1/2 in.
 B. 3/4 in.
 C. 1 in.
 D. 1¼ in.

ANSWER - (B) 3/4 in.

 8 XHHW = .0437 sq. in. x 3 conductors = .1311 square inches
 12 THWN = .0133 sq. in. x 6 conductors = .0798 square inches
 TOTAL = .2109 square inches

A trade size 3/4 in. IMC having an allowable fill @ 40% of 0.235 square inches is the MINIMUM required.

EXAMPLE - Determine the MINIMUM trade size, one (1) foot long, rigid metal conduit (RMC) to enclose the following listed copper conductors.

- four (4) – 3/0 AWG THWN
- four (4) – 4/0 AWG THHN

 A. 3 in.
 B. 2 in.
 C. 3½ in.
 D. 2½ in.

ANSWER - (D) 2½ inches

 3/0 THWN = .2679 x 4 conductors = 1.0716 square inches
 4/0 THHN = .3237 x 4 conductors = <u>1.2948 square inches</u>
 TOTAL = 2.3664 square inches

A trade size 2½ in. RMC nipple having an allowable fill @ 60% of 2.919 square inches is the MINIMUM required.

☐ When determining the number of conductors, all of the same size, permitted in a conduit or tubing 24 inches or less in length, simply divide the allowable fill area of the conduit or tubing by the area of one (1) conductor.

EXAMPLE - Determine the MAXIMUM number of size 2/0 AWG THHN copper conductors permitted to be installed in a trade size 2 in. electrical metallic tubing (EMT) 18 inches long.

 A. seven
 B. eight
 C. nine
 D. ten

ANSWER - (C) nine

 <u>2.013 sq. in.</u> (allowable fill) = 9.05 or 9 wires
 .2223 sq. in. (area of wire)

☐ When calculating the MAXIMUM number of conductors, all of the same size, permitted in a conduit or tubing, when the calculation results in a decimal of **0.8** or larger, an

additional wire of the same size may be installed. **[Chapter 9, Note 7]**

EXAMPLE - Determine the MAXIMUM number of size 1/0 AWG THWN copper
conductors permitted to be installed in a trade size 1¼ in. rigid metal
conduit (RMC) nipple.

 A. four
 B. five
 C. six
 D. seven

ANSWER - (B) five

$$\frac{0.916 \text{ sq. in. (allowable fill)}}{.1855 \text{ sq. in. (area of wire)}} = 4.9 \text{ or } 5 \text{ wires}$$

Wireway and Gutter Sizing

RELATED INFORMATION:

 ☐ When calculating the number of conductors, all of the same size, permitted in a metal
or nonmetallic wireway, or an auxiliary gutter, the fill shall not exceed **20 percent** of
the interior cross-sectional area of the wireway or gutter where splices or taps are not
made. **[366.22(A)&(B)]**, **[376.22(A)]** and **[378.22]** Use the same steps as
before; first, find the allowable fill and divide by the area of one (1) conductor.
Disregard the length of the wireway or gutter.

EXAMPLE - Determine the MAXIMUM number of size 4/0 AWG XHHW copper conductors
permitted to be installed in a 4 in. x 4 in. metal wireway.

 A. ten
 B. eleven
 C. twenty
 D. sixteen

ANSWER - (A) ten

4 in. x 4 in. = 16 sq. in. x 20% = 3.2 sq. in. permitted fill

$$\frac{3.2 \text{ sq. in. (permitted fill)}}{.3197 \text{ sq. in. (area of wire)}} = 10 \text{ wires}$$

 ☐ When conductors are of different sizes and/or insulations, **wireways** and **gutters**
can be properly sized by dividing the total area, in square inches, of the conductors
by the **20 percent** permitted fill area, where splices or taps are not made. Or find

the area, in square inches, of a specific wireway or gutter and multiply by **20 percent** to find the allowable fill. Using this method you may have to try more than one size gutter or wireway to find the proper size.

EXAMPLE - A wireway is to contain the following listed conductors.

- three – size 250 kcmil THHN compact aluminum
- three – size 4/0 AWG THHN compact aluminum
- three – size 1/0 AWG THHN compact aluminum

Which one of the following listed wireways is the MINIMUM size required to house the conductors?

A. 4 in. x 4 in.
B. 6 in. x 6 in.
C. 8 in. x 8 in.
D. 12 in. x 12 in.

ANSWER - (A) 4 in. x 4 in.

First, go to **Table 5A of Chapter 9** to determine the area of the conductors.

250 kcmil THHN compact AL = .3525 sq. in. x 3 = 1.0575 sq. in.
4/0 AWG THHN compact AL = .2780 sq. in. x 3 = 0.8340 sq. in.
1/0 AWG THHN compact AL = .1590 sq. in. x 3 = 0.4770 sq. in.
TOTAL = 2.3685 sq. in.

2.3685 (area of wires) = 11.8425 sq. in. required area
 20% (permitted fill)
A 4 in. x 4 in. wireway with an area of 16 square inches is required.

To cross-check:
4 in. x 4 in. = 16 sq. in. x 20% = 3.2 square inches allowable fill
This wireway having an allowable fill of 3.2 square inches may contain the conductors having an area of 2.3685 square inches.

UNIT 5
SELF-ASSESSMENT QUIZ

1. A 4 in. x 1½ in. octagon junction box with a flat blank cover may contain no more than _____ size 14 AWG conductors.

 A. six
 B. seven
 C. nine
 D. ten

2. A luminaire stud in a ceiling-mounted outlet box is considered an equivalent of _____ conductor(s).

 A. one
 B. two
 C. three
 D. none of these

3. When determining box fill, size 12 AWG THHN conductors are to be calculated at _____ for each conductor housed in the box.

 A. 1.75 cubic inches
 B. 2.00 cubic inches
 C. 2.25 cubic inches
 D. 2.50 cubic inches

4. For the purpose of determining conductor fill in a device box, a three-way switch is counted as equal to _____ conductor(s), based on the largest conductor connected to the switch.

 A. zero
 B. one
 C. two
 D. three

5. How many size 12/2 AWG with ground, nonmetallic sheathed cable(s) (NM) is/are permitted to be installed in a device box having a total volume of 18 cubic inches where a duplex receptacle outlet is in the box?

 A. one
 B. two
 C. three
 D. four

6. Determine the MINIMUM size trade size, fifty (50) foot long, intermediate metal conduit (IMC) permitted to enclose four (4), size 8 AWG THWN copper branch circuit conductors.

A. ½ inch
B. ¾ inch
C. 1 inch
D. 1¼ inches

7. A two-gang device box is to contain two (2) size 12/2 AWG with ground nonmetallic sheathed (NM) cables connected to a duplex receptacle and two (2), size 14/2 AWG with ground NM cables connected to a single-pole switch. The device box will contain four (4) internal clamps. The two-gang box is required to have a volume of at least _____.

 A. 36 cubic inches
 B. 34 cubic inches
 C. 30 cubic inches
 D. 28 cubic inches

8. A single-gang FS box is permitted to contain no more than _____ size 14 AWG THHN conductors.

 A. six
 B. seven
 C. eight
 D. nine

9. Two (2) size 12 AWG conductors are looped inside a junction box so that there is more than 12 inches of free conductor. The conductors are not spliced and do not terminate on devices. What volume, in cubic inches, must be counted for the looped conductors?

 A. 2.25 cubic inches
 B. 3.75 cubic inches
 C. 4.50 cubic inches
 D. 9.00 cubic inches

10. When a pull-box is to contain conductors of size 4 AWG or larger and a straight pull of the conductors is to be made, the length of the box shall not be less than _____ times the trade size of the largest raceway entering the box.

 A. six
 B. four
 C. eight
 D. none of these

11. Where a conduit or tubing more than 24 inches in length, contains more than two (2) conductors, the conduit or tubing is permitted an allowable fill of _____ of its cross-sectional area.

 A. 40 percent
 B. 60 percent
 C. 53 percent

D. 75 percent

12. Where a conduit having a length of 24 inches or less is installed between a panelboard and a wireway, the conduit is permitted to be filled to no more than _____ of its cross-sectional area.

 A. 40 percent
 B. 60 percent
 C. 53 percent
 D. 75 percent

13. For the purpose of determining conductor fill in conduit, what is the total area, in square inches (in.²), of four (4) size 4/0 AWG THWN and three (3) size 3/0 AWG THWN copper conductors?

 A. 2.0985 square inches
 B. 1.8081 square inches
 C. 2.3664 square inches
 D. 2.4223 square inches

14. Determine the MAXIMUM number of size 300 kcmil RHW copper conductors, without outer coverings, permitted to be installed in an 18 inch long, trade size 4 inch, electrical metallic tubing (EMT) nipple.

 A. fourteen
 B. fifteen
 C. sixteen
 D. seventeen

15. A junction box is to be installed where size 4/0 AWG THWN conductors enclosed in trade size 2½ in. electrical metallic tubing (EMT) are to be spliced. One EMT enters the box from the top and one EMT enters the box from the side. The NEC® mandates a distance of not less than _____ be maintained between the conduits inside the box.

 A. 20 inches
 B. 12 inches
 C. 18 inches
 D. 15 inches

16. A pull box is to be installed where the conductors are larger than size 4 AWG and an angle (90°) pull of the conductors is to be made. Two (2) trade size 3 inch conduits are to enter the box from the top and one (1) trade size 3 inch conduit and one (1) trade size 2½ inch conduit are to enter the box from the side. The pull box is required to have dimensions of at LEAST _____.

 A. 21 in. x 21 in.
 B. 21 in. x 20½ in.

C. 18 in. x 18 in.
D. 24 in. x 24 in.

17. A fifty (50) ft. run of Schedule 40 PVC conduit is to contain the following copper conductors:

- four (4) size 1 AWG XHHW
- one (1) size 6 AWG bare

Determine the MINIMUM trade size PVC required per the NEC®.

A. 2 inches
B. 1½ inches
C. 1¼ inches
D. 1 inch

18. The fill shall not exceed _____ of the interior of the cross-sectional area of a metal wireway where splices or taps are not made.

A. 20 percent
B. 40 percent
C. 53 percent
D. 75 percent

19. Determine the MAXIMUM number of size 250 kcmil XHHW compact aluminum conductors permitted to be installed in a 4 in. x 4 in. six (6) ft. long metal wireway.

A. twenty
B. ten
C. eight
D. nine

20. A metal wireway is to contain the following listed copper conductors:

- eight (8) - size 500 kcmil THWN
- twenty-four (24) - size 2 AWG THWN

Which one of the following listed wireways is the MINIMUM size to house the conductors?

A. 10 in. x 10 in.
B. 6 in. x 6 in.
C. 8 in. x 8 in.
D. 12 in. x 12 in.

NOTES

PRACTICAL CALCULATIONS FOR ELECTRICIANS
UNIT 5
SELF-ASSESSMENT QUIZ
ANSWER KEY

ANSWER		REFERENCE	NEC PG. #
1.	B	Table 314.16(A)	pg. 176
2.	A	314.16(B)(3)	pg. 176
3.	C	Table 314.16(B)	pg. 176
4.	C	314.16(B)(4)	pg. 176
5.	B	314.16(B)(4) Table 314.16(B)	pg. 176 pg. 176

$$\frac{18 \text{ cu. in. (box)}}{2.25 \text{ cu. in. (\#12 wire)}} = 8 \text{ wires (allowable fill)}$$

8 wires (allowable fill) – 2 (device) = 6 wires may be added

#12/2 with ground NM cable = 3 wires per cable

$$\frac{6 \text{ wires (allowed)}}{3 \text{ wires (per cable)}} = 2 \text{ cables are permitted}$$

6.	B	ANNEX C, Table C.4	pg. 732
7.	C	314.16(B)(1),(2),(4)&(5) Table 314.16(B)	pg. 175 & 176 pg. 176

```
size 14/2    = 2.00 cu. in. x 4 =  8.00
size 12/2    = 2.25 cu. in. x 4 =  9.00
equip. grnd. = 2.25 cu. in. x 1 =  2.25
clamps       = 2.25 cu. in. x 1 =  2.25
receptacle   = 2.25 cu. in. x 2 =  4.50
switch       = 2.00 cu. in. x 2 =  4.00
              TOTAL = 30.00 cubic inches
```

*NOTE – One or more clamps are counted as equal to the largest wire in the box per 314.16(B)(2). One or more equipment grounding conductors are counted as equal to the largest equipment grounding conductor in the box per 314.16(B)(5). Devices are counted as equal to two (2) conductors, based on the largest wire connected to the device per 314.16(B)(4).

8.	A	Table 314.16(A)	pg. 176

9. D 314.16(B)(1) pg. 175
 Table 314.16(B) pg. 176

 2.25 cu. in. x 4 wires = 9.00 cubic inches

10. C 314.28(A)(1) pg. 180

11. A Chapter 9, Table 1 pg. 679

12. B Chapter 9, Note 4 to Tables pg. 679

13. A Chapter 9, Table 5 pg. 685

 4/0 THWN - .3237 sq. in. x 4 wires = 1.2948 sq. in.
 3/0 THWN - .2679 sq. in. x 3 wires = 0.8037 sq. in.
 TOTAL = 2.0985 sq. in.

14. C Chapter 9, Table 4 pg. 680
 Chapter 9, Table 5 pg. 685

 Allowable fill of 4 in. EMT @ 60% = 8.852 square inches
 Area of 300 kcmil RHW w/o covering = .5281 square inches

$$\text{number of wires} = \frac{8.852 \ (\text{allowable fill})}{.5281 \ (\text{one wire})} = 16.76 = 16 \ \text{wires}$$

15. D 314.28(A)(2) pg. 180

 2.5 in. (conduit) x 6 = 15 inches

16. B 314.28(A)(2) pg. 180

 Top to bottom – 3 in. (largest conduit) x 6 = 18 in. + 3 in. = 21 inches
 Side to side – 3 in. (largest conduit) x 6 = 18 in. + 2½ in. = 20½ inches

17. B Chapter 9, Table 5 pg. 687
 Chapter 9, Table 8 pg. 689
 Chapter 9, Table 4 pg. 683

 size 1 AWG XHHW = .1534 sq. in. x 4 wires = .6136 sq. in.
 size 6 AWG bare = .0270 sq. in.
 .6406 sq. in.

 *NOTE – A trade size 1½ in. Schedule 40 PVC with an allowable fill of .794 sq.
 in. should be selected.

18. A 376.22(A) pg. 220

19. D 376.22(A) pg. 220
 Chapter 9, Table 5A pg. 688

4 in. x 4 in. = 16 sq. in. x 20% = 3.2 sq. in. permitted fill

number of wires = 3.2 sq. in. (permitted fill) = 9.3 = 9 wires
 .3421 sq. in. (one wire)

20. C Chapter 9, Table 5 pg. 685
 376.22(A) pg. 220

500 kcmil THWN = .7073 sq. in. x 8 wires = 5.6584 sq. in.
2 AWG THWN = .1158 sq. in. x 24 wires = 2.7792 sq. in.
 TOTAL = 8.4376 sq. in.

required area = 8.4376 sq. in. (wire) = 42.188 sq. in.
 20% (permitted fill)

*NOTE – An 8 in. x 8 in. wireway with an area of 64 square inches is required.

UNIT 6

VOLTAGE DROP CALCULATIONS

Upon successfully completing this unit of study the student will be familiar with the concept of calculating voltage drop in conductors, causes of voltage drop, as well as the means to prevent excessive voltage drop in three-phase and single-phase circuits.

$$VD = \frac{2 \times K \times I \times D}{CM}$$

UNIT 6

VOLTAGE DROP CALCULATIONS

RELATED INFORMATION:

☐ The conductors of an electrical system should be of sufficient size so that the voltage drop is not excessive. Typical results of excessive voltage drop are as follows:

1) luminaires (lighting fixtures) dimming when appliances or motors are turned on,
2) overheating of motors and appliances,
3) shortened life span of appliances such as computers, TVs, refrigerators and freezers,
4) nuisance tripping of circuit breakers,
5) delayed starting of high-intensity discharge lighting.

☐ The loss of voltage, known as voltage drop, is apparent in all electrical circuits due to the resistance of the circuit conductors. This loss of voltage varies with conductor material, conductor size, conductor length, ambient temperature and intensity of the current.

☐ The NEC® recommends the MAXIMUM voltage drop to be limited to 3 percent at the farthest outlet for branch circuits and 5 percent on both feeder and branch circuits to the farthest outlet. **[210.19(A)(1) IN#4]** and **[215.2(A)(3) IN#2]** In practical work, many engineers try to limit the voltage drop for lighting and power branch circuits to 2 percent and 4 percent for feeders.

☐ **The smaller the wire size, the greater the resistance** because, the small cross-sectional area of the conductor restricts the flow of electrons; thus, the greater the voltage drop. **The larger the wire size, the less the resistance** because, the larger cross-sectional area of the conductor permits the electrons to flow more freely; thus, the less voltage drop. So, the most practical way to limit voltage drop is increase the wire size. Although not always practical, voltage drop may be decreased by:

1) increasing the voltage, which reduces the intensity of the current,
2) change the conductor material say, from aluminum to copper which reduces the resistance,
3) move the load closer to its source voltage, which reduces the conductor

resistance.

⬜ A useful and common formula that may be used to determine the voltage drop in a single-phase circuit is:

$$VD = \frac{2 \times K \times I \times D}{CM}$$

Formula Definitions:

VD – Volts dropped from a circuit.

2 – Multiplying factor for single-phase circuits. The **2** represents the conductor length in a single-phase circuit.

K - Approximate resistivity of the conductor per mil foot at an operating temperature of 75°C/167°F. A mil foot is a wire one (1) foot long and one (1) mil in diameter. The approximate **K** value (constant) for copper wire is **12.9 ohms** and for aluminum wire is **21.2 ohms**.

I - Current or amperage draw of the load at 100 percent.

D - The distance, in feet, from the source voltage to the load.

CM - The area of the conductor expressed in **circular mils**, which can be found in **Chapter 9, Table 8**, which lists wire sizes from 18 AWG through 2,000 kcmil. For example, a size 10 AWG conductor has a cross-sectional area of 10,380 circular mils. For conductors of size 250 kcmil through size 2,000 kcmil, the cross-sectional area in circular mils can be determined by adding three (3) zeros to the kcmil size. For example, a size 300 kcmil conductor has a cross-sectional area of 300,000 circular mils.

EXAMPLE - A 120-volt, single-phase branch circuit, using size 12 AWG copper conductors, is supplying a 15 ampere load located sixty (60) feet from the panelboard. Determine the approximate voltage drop. (K = 12.9)

 A. 2 volts
 B. 4 volts
 C. 6 volts
 D. 8 volts

ANSWER - (B) 4 volts

 CM = 6,530 (12 AWG)
 K = 12.9 ohms (copper)

I = 15 amperes
D = 60 feet

$$VD = \frac{2 \times 12.9 \times 15 \times 60}{6,530} = \frac{23,220}{6,530} = 3.55 \text{ volts}$$

☐ A useful and common formula that may be used to determine the voltage drop in a **three-phase** circuit is:

$$VD = \frac{1.732 \times K \times I \times D}{CM}$$

☐ The multiplying factor for **three-phase** circuits is **1.732**. The square root of 3 represents the conductor length in a three-phase circuit. The only difference between the single-phase and the three-phase formulas is that "**1.732**" has replaced "2".

EXAMPLE - A 208Y/120-volt, three-phase feeder, using size 4 AWG aluminum conductors is to supply an 80 ampere load located one hundred (100) feet from the switchboard. Determine the approximate voltage drop.
(K = 21.2)

 A. 9.3 volts
 B. 5.0 volts
 C. 7.0 volts
 D. 9.0 volts

ANSWER - (C) 7.0 volts

 CM = 41,740 (4 AWG)
 K = 21.2 ohms (aluminum)
 I = 80 amperes
 D = 100 feet

$$VD = \frac{1.732 \times 21.2 \times 80 \times 100}{41,740} = \frac{293,747}{41,740} = 7.0 \text{ volts}$$

☐ As stated before, the size of the conductor affects voltage drop because of the resistance variables. Conductors are to be sized to prevent excessive voltage drop. A useful formula that may be used to size the conductors and prevent excessive voltage drop in a single-phase circuit is:

$$CM = \frac{2 \times K \times I \times D}{VD}$$

☐ When determining wire size, VD is the actual volts allowed to be dropped from the circuit. For example, the recommended voltage drop in a 240 volt, single-phase

branch circuit is 3 percent; 3 percent of 240 volts is 7.2 volts. DO NOT enter 3 percent in the VD position in the formula, enter the value of the actual voltage permitted to be lost or dropped.

EXAMPLE - A 240-volt, single-phase, 52 ampere load is located two-hundred (200) feet from the panelboard. What MINIMUM size copper branch circuit conductors should be used to supply this load when voltage drop is to be limited to 3 percent? (K = 12.9)

 A. 8 AWG
 B. 6 AWG
 C. 4 AWG
 D. 2 AWG

ANSWER - (C) 4 AWG

$$VD = 240 \times 0.03 = 7.2 \text{ volts}$$
$$K = 12.9 \text{ ohms (copper)}$$
$$I = 52 \text{ amperes}$$
$$D = 200 \text{ feet}$$

$$CM = \frac{2 \times 12.9 \times 52 \times 200}{7.2} = \frac{268,320}{7.2} = 37,267 \text{ CM}$$

In this situation, a size 4 AWG conductor with a circular mil area (CMA) of 41,740 CM is required because, a size 6 AWG conductor with a CMA of 26,240 CM would not limit the voltage drop to 3 percent.

A useful formula that may be used to size conductors in a three-phase circuit to prevent excessive voltage drop is:

$$CM = \frac{1.732 \times K \times I \times D}{VD}$$

EXAMPLE - A 208Y/120-volt, 3-phase, 150 ampere load is located two hundred and fifty (250) feet from the main distribution switchboard. What MINIMUM size copper feeder conductors are required to supply the load when voltage drop is to be limited to 3 percent? (K = 12.9)

 A. 4/0 AWG
 B. 1/0 AWG
 C. 2/0 AWG
 D. 3/0 AWG

ANSWER - (D) 3/0 AWG

VD = 208 x 0.03 = 6.24 volts
K = 12.9 ohms (copper)
I = 150 amperes
D = 250 feet

$$CM = \frac{1.732 \times 12.9 \times 150 \times 250}{6.24} = \frac{83,786}{6.24} = 134,272 \text{ CM}$$

A size 3/0 AWG conductor with a CMA of 167,800 CM is required to limit the voltage drop to 6.24 volts.

☐ Voltage drop can be limited in a circuit by limiting the length of the circuit conductors. The following formula can be used to determine the approximate distance circuit conductors may be installed to prevent excessive voltage drop in a single-phase circuit.

$$D = \frac{CM \times VD}{2 \times K \times I}$$

EXAMPLE - What is the approximate MAXIMUM distance a 120-volt, single-phase, 1,800 VA load, supplied with size 12 AWG copper branch circuit conductors can be located from the panelboard, when the permitted voltage drop is to be not more than three percent?

A. 60 feet
B. 75 feet
C. 90 feet
D. 120 feet

ANSWER - (A) 60 feet

CM = 6,530 (12 AWG)
VD = 120 volts x .03 = 3.6 volts
K = 12.9 ohms
$$I = \frac{VA}{volts} = \frac{1,800 \text{ VA}}{120 \text{ volts}} = 15 \text{ amperes}$$

$$D = \frac{6,530 \times 3.6}{2 \times 12.9 \times 15} = \frac{23,508}{387} = 60.7 \text{ feet}$$

☐ When determining the approximate distance circuit conductors may be installed in three-phase circuits to prevent excessive voltage drop, the following formula can be

used:

$$D = \frac{CM \times VD}{1.732 \times K \times I}$$

EXAMPLE - A transformer having a 208Y/120-volt, 3-phase secondary is to supply a panelboard with a 130 ampere demand load. The feeder conductors are size 1/0 AWG THWN copper. What is the MAXIMUM approximate distance the panelboard can be located from the transformer so that the voltage drop does not exceed three percent?

 A. 125 feet
 B. 65 feet
 C. 225 feet
 D. 200 feet

ANSWER - (C) 225 feet

 CM = 105,600 (1/0 AWG)
 VD = 208 volts x .03 = 6.24 volts
 K = 12.9 ohms
 I = 130 amperes

$$D = \frac{105,600 \times 6.24}{1.732 \times 12.9 \times 130} = \frac{658,944}{2,905} = 227 \text{ feet}$$

Another way of limiting voltage drop is to limit the intensity of the current on the conductors. Perhaps, you may have an existing installation and if additional loads are added, this may cause excessive voltage drop on the feeder conductors. The following formula can be used to determine the MAXIMUM load permitted when limiting voltage drop on single-phase circuits:

$$I = \frac{CM \times VD}{2 \times K \times D}$$

EXAMPLE - A 240-volt, single-phase feeder with size 2/0 AWG THWN aluminum conductors is supplying an existing panelboard located 260 feet from the main switchboard. What is the MAXIMUM load that can be placed on the panelboard so that the voltage drop is limited to three percent?

 A. 143 amperes
 B. 175 amperes
 C. 122 amperes
 D. 87 amperes

ANSWER - (D) 87 amperes

 CM = 133,100 CM (2/0 AWG)
 VD = 240 volts x .03 = 7.2 volts

K = 21.2 ohms (aluminum)
D = 260 feet

$$I = \frac{133,100 \times 7.2}{2 \times 21.2 \times 260} = \frac{958,320}{11,024} = 86.9 \text{ amperes}$$

☐ The following formula can be used to determine the MAXIMUM load permitted when limiting the voltage drop on three-phase circuits:

$$I = \frac{CM \times VD}{1.732 \times K \times D}$$

EXAMPLE - An existing 208Y/120-volt, three-phase, 4-wire, panelboard is supplied with size 2 AWG THW copper feeder conductors from the main switchboard. The panelboard is located three-hundred (300) feet from the main switchboard. What is the MAXIMUM load, in amperes, the conductors can carry without exceeding a three percent voltage drop?

 A. 62 amperes
 B. 54 amperes
 C. 38 amperes
 D. 79 amperes

ANSWER - (A) 62 amperes

 CM = 66,360 (2 AWG)
 VD = 208 x .03 = 6.24 volts
 K = 12.9 ohms (copper)
 D = 300 feet

$$I = \frac{66,360 \times 6.24}{1.732 \times 12.9 \times 300} = \frac{414,086}{6,703} = 61.77 \text{ amperes}$$

☐ Another method of determining the voltage drop of the conductors for **single-phase circuits only** is to apply the Ohm's Law Method, using the following formula:
VD = I x R

FORMULA DEFINITIONS:

VD = Volts dropped from a circuit
I = Intensity of the current, or the load, in amperes, at 100 percent.
R = Total conductor resistance, which can be found in **Chapter 9**, **Table 8** of the NEC®, under the ohm/KFT column. Using this method, you must take into consideration the **total length** of both the conductors to find total resistance.

EXAMPLE - Two (2) size 12 AWG THWN/THHN 120-volt, single-phase, copper branch circuit conductors are to supply a 15 ampere load located one-hundred (100) feet from the panelboard. Determine the approximate voltage drop.

 A. 3 volts
 B. 6 volts
 C. 9 volts
 D. 12 volts

ANSWER - (B) 6 volts

 R = 1.98 ohms per 1,000 feet **(Chapter 9, Table 8)**

 $R = \dfrac{1.98}{1,000}$ = 0.00198 ohms per ft. x 200 ft = .396 ohms total

 I = 15 amperes

 VD = 15 amps x .396 ohms = 5.94 volts

EXAMPLE - A 240-volt, single-phase branch circuit is to supply a 32 ampere load with size 8 AWG THWN copper conductors. The load is one-hundred and fifty (150) feet from the panelboard; determine the voltage drop.

 A. 4 volts
 B. 15 volts
 C. 7.5 volts
 D. 6 volts

ANSWER - (C) 7.5 volts

 R = .778 ohms per 1,000 feet **(Chapter 9, Table 8)**

 $R = \dfrac{.788}{1,000}$ = 0.000788 ohms per ft. = .2334 ohms total

 VD = 32 amps x .2334 ohms = 7.46 volts

UNIT 6
SELF-ASSESSMENT QUIZ

1. Voltage drop can be limited in a circuit by:

 I. increasing the conductor size.
 II. reducing the load.

 A. I only
 B. II only
 C. either I or II
 D. neither I nor II

2. The NEC® recommends the voltage drop on 120-volt branch circuits to be limited to
 _____.

 A. 3.6 volts
 B. 3 volts
 C. 6 volts
 D. 4.5 volts

3. The cross-sectional area of a conductor is expressed in _____.

 A. mils
 B. square inches
 C. cubic inches
 D. circular mils

4. The resistance of a conductor is determined by the _____.

 A. conductors cross-sectional area
 B. material type
 C. length of the conductor
 D. all of these

5. A size 6 AWG copper conductor has a cross-sectional area of _____.

 A. 24,640 CM
 B. 26,240 CM
 C. 16,510 CM
 D. 41,740 CM

6. A common formula that can be used to determine the voltage drop on the conductors of a

single-phase circuit is:

A. VD = $\dfrac{1.732 \times K \times I \times D}{CM}$

B. VD = $\dfrac{2 \times K \times I \times CM}{D}$

C. VD = $\dfrac{CM \times D}{2 \times K \times I}$

D. VD = $\dfrac{2 \times K \times I \times D}{CM}$

7. A 240-volt, single-phase branch circuit, using size 8 AWG copper conductors, is to supply a 32 ampere load located eighty (80) feet from the panelboard. Determine the approximate voltage drop. (K=12.9)

 A. 2 volts
 B. 4 volts
 C. 6 volts
 D. 8 volts

8. Determine the voltage drop on the conductors of a control circuit given the following:

 • current = 5 amperes
 • total conductor length = 300 feet
 • conductor resistance = 4 ohms per 1,000 feet

 A. 0.02 volts
 B. 0.12 volts
 C. 6.00 volts
 D. 1.20 volts

9. A 10,800 VA, 240-volt, single-phase load is located two-hundred (200) feet from the panelboard and is supplied with size 6 AWG THWN copper conductors. Determine the approximate voltage drop on the circuit. (K=12.9)

 A. 9 volts
 B. 5 volts
 C. 12 volts
 D. 18 volts

10. A size 1 AWG aluminum USE feeder cable is to supply a 100 ampere, 120/240 volt, single-phase load located one hundred and forty (140) feet from the panelboard. Determine the

approximate voltage drop on this feeder circuit. (K=21.2)

 A. 14 volts
 B. 7 volts
 C. 4 volts
 D. 9 volts

11. A 208Y/120-volt, three-phase feeder, using size 300 kcmil copper conductors is to supply a 275 ampere demand load located one hundred and twenty-five (125) feet from the switchboard. Determine the approximate voltage drop on this feeder circuit. (K=12.9)

 A. 2.50 volts
 B. 5.00 volts
 C. 6.75 volts
 D. 4.50 volts

12. A 240-volt, single-phase 114 ampere load is located one hundred and sixty (160) feet from the panelboard. What MINIMUM size copper branch circuit conductors should be used to supply this load when voltage drop is to be limited to 3 percent? (K=12.9)

 A. 1/0 AWG
 B. 1 AWG
 C. 3 AWG
 D. 2 AWG

13. A three-phase, 208Y/120-volt forty (40) ampere continuous load is to be located three hundred (300) feet from the panelboard. Determine the MINIMUM size copper branch circuit conductors required to serve the load. Assume the voltage drop is to be limited to not more than 3 percent. (K=12.9)

 A. 4 AWG
 B. 3 AWG
 C. 2 AWG
 D. 1 AWG

14. A three-phase 208Y/120-volt feeder, consisting of aluminum conductors, is to supply a panelboard with a 36 kVA continuous load. If the voltage drop is to be limited to six (6) volts, and the panelboard is located two hundred (200) feet from the voltage source, what MINIMUM size conductors are required? (K=21.2)

 A. 2/0 AWG
 B. 3/0 AWG
 C. 4/0 AWG

D. 250 kcmil

15. Determine the approximate MAXIMUM distance a 240-volt, single-phase 32 ampere load, supplied with a size 8 AWG copper branch circuit conductors can be located from the panelboard, when the voltage drop is to be limited to 3 percent. (K=12.9)

 A. 140 feet
 B. 170 feet
 C. 70 feet
 D. 60 feet

NOTES

PRACTICAL CALCULATIONS FOR ELECTRICIANS
UNIT 6
SELF-ASSESSMENT QUIZ
ANSWER KEY

ANSWER		REFERENCE	NEC PG. #
1.	C	Trade Knowledge	
2.	A	210.19(A)(1) Info note#4	pg. 61

120 volts x 0.03 = 3.6 volts

3.	D	Chapter 9, Table 8	pg. 689
4.	D	Trade Knowledge	
5.	B	Chapter 9, Table 8	pg. 689
6.	D	Trade Knowledge	
7.	B	Single-phase Voltage Drop Formula	
		Chapter 9, Table 8	pg. 689

$$VD = \frac{2 \times K \times I \times D}{CM} = \frac{2 \times 12.9 \times 32 \times 80}{16,510} = \frac{66,048}{16,510} = 4 \text{ volts}$$

8.	C	Ohms Law	

$$\text{Resistance} = \frac{4 \text{ ohms}}{1,000} = 0.004 \text{ ohms per ft.}$$

0.004 ohms x 300 ft. = 1.2 ohms total resistance
VD = I x R VD = 5 amperes x 1.2 ohms = 6 volts dropped

9. A

Single-phase current formula
Chapter 9, Table 8 pg. 689
1 Ø Voltage Drop Formula

First, determine the current.

$$I = \frac{10,800 \text{ VA}}{240 \text{ volts}} = 45 \text{ amperes}$$

$$VD = \frac{2 \times K \times I \times D}{CM}$$

$$VD = \frac{2 \times 12.9 \times 45 \times 200}{26,240} = \frac{232,200}{26,240} = 8.84 \text{ volts}$$

10. B

Chapter 9, Table 8 pg. 689
1 Ø Voltage Drop Formula

$$VD = \frac{2 \times K \times I \times D}{CM}$$

$$VD = \frac{2 \times 21.2 \times 100 \times 140}{83,690} = \frac{551,200}{83,690} = 7.09 \text{ volts}$$

11. A

Chapter 9, Table 8 pg. 689
3 Ø Voltage Drop Formula

$$VD = \frac{1.732 \times K \times I \times D}{CM}$$

$$VD = \frac{1.732 \times 12.9 \times 275 \times 125}{300,000} = \frac{768,034}{300,000} = 2.5 \text{ volts}$$

12. D

Chapter 9, Table 8 pg. 689
1 Ø Wire Size Formula

First find allowable voltage drop:

$$VD = 240 \times .03 = 7.2 \text{ volts}$$

$$CM = \frac{2 \times K \times I \times D}{VD}$$

$$CM = \frac{2 \times 12.9 \times 114 \times 160}{7.2} = \frac{470,592}{7.2} = 65,360 \text{ CM}$$

***NOTE** – Size 2 AWG copper conductors with a CMA of 66,360 CM are required.

13. C 210.19(A)(1)(a) pg. 62
 3 Ø Wire Size Formula
 Chapter 9, Table 8 pg. 689

Allowable voltage drop (VD) – 208 volts x 3% = 6.24 volts
Load (I) – 40 amperes x 125% (continuous load) = 50 amperes

$$CM = \frac{1.732 \times K \times I \times D}{VD}$$

$$CM = \frac{1.732 \times 12.9 \times 50 \times 300}{6.24} = \frac{335,142}{6.24} = 53,709 \; CM$$

NOTE – Size 2 AWG copper conductors with a CMA of 66,360 CM are required.

14. B 3 Ø current formula
 215.2(A)(1)(a) pg. 67
 3 Ø Wire Size Formula
 Chapter 9, Table 8 pg. 689

First find current:

$$I = \frac{kVA \times 1,000}{E \times 1.732} = \frac{36 \times 1,000}{208 \times 1.732} = \frac{36,000}{360.25} = 100 \; amperes$$

100 amperes x 125% (continuous load) = 125 amperes

$$CM = \frac{1.732 \times K \times I \times D}{VD}$$

$$CM = \frac{1.732 \times 21.2 \times 125 \times 200}{6} = \frac{917,960}{6} = 152,993 \; CM$$

NOTE – Size 3/0 AWG aluminum conductors with a CMA of 167,800 CM are required.

15. A 1 Ø Distance Formula
 Chapter 9, Table 8 pg. 689

First find permitted VD:

240 volts x .03 = 7.2 volts

$$D = \frac{CM \times VD}{2 \times K \times I}$$

$$D = \frac{16,510 \times 7.2}{2 \times 12.9 \times 32} = \frac{118,872}{826} = 144 \; feet$$

UNIT 7

AC MOTOR CALCULATIONS

Upon successfully completing this unit of study the student will be familiar with the concept of properly sizing conductors, overcurrent protection, overload protection, and disconnects for single-phase and three-phase ac electric motors.

UNIT 7

AC MOTOR CALCULATIONS

RELATED INFORMATION:

☐ In general, when sizing the conductors, disconnecting means and overcurrent protection for **continuous-duty** ac motors, the full-load current values of the motor(s) given in **Tables 430.247** through **430.250** shall be used, instead of the actual current rating marked on the motor nameplate. **[430.6(A)(1)]** Note this rule does not apply for motors built for low speeds (less than 1,200 RPM) or high torque which may have higher full-load currents and multispeed motors which will have full-load current varying with the speed. For these motors the current values given on the motor(s) nameplate shall be used instead of the NEC® tables.

☐ **All** motors shall be considered to be for **continuous-duty** unless the nature of the apparatus it drives is such that the motor cannot operate continuously with load under any condition of use. **[430.33]** Examples of motors **not** considered as continuous duty are motors operating elevators, cranes and assembly line machines.

☐ In general, in order to properly size branch circuit conductors supplying a single continuous duty motor you are to comply with **430.22** which requires the conductors to have an ampacity of at least **125 percent** of the motor's full-load current (FLC) rating as determined in the related tables in the NEC®. The actual conductor sizes are to be selected from **Tables 310.15(B)(16)** or from **Table 400.5(A)**. The conductors are to be sized according to the temperature ratings (60°C or 75°C) of the equipment terminations.

EXAMPLE - Determine the MINIMUM size THHN copper conductors required to supply a 3 hp, 240-volt, single-phase continuous-duty motor when all terminations have a rating of 75°C.

 A. 14 AWG
 B. 12 AWG
 C. 10 AWG
 D. 8 AWG

ANSWER - (B) 12 AWG

 motor FLC = 17 amperes **[Table 430.248]**
 17 amperes x 125% **[430.22]** = 21.25 amperes
 Size 12 AWG THHN is rated at 25 amperes at 75°C
 [Table 310.15(B)(16)]

 ☐ Conductors that supply a motor used in a short-time, intermittent, or varying duty application are permitted to have an ampacity of not less than the percentage values shown on **Table 430.22(E)**, based the full-load current rating indicated on the **motor's nameplate**.

EXAMPLE - Conductors supplying a 40 hp, 480-volt, three-phase, 5 minute rated elevator motor with an ampere rating of 50 amperes marked on the nameplate, shall have an ampacity of at least _____.

 A. 42.5 amperes
 B. 45.9 amperes
 C. 62.5 amperes
 D. 67.5 amperes

ANSWER - (A) 42.5 amperes

 motor FLA = 50 amperes x 85% **[Table 430.22(E)]** = 42.5 amps

 ☐ In general, conductors that supply more than one continuous-duty motor on a single circuit and/or motor(s) and other load(s), are required to have an ampacity of not less than **125 percent** of the full-load current rating of the **highest** rated motor in the group plus **100 percent** of the full-load current ratings of all the **remaining motors** in the group, also the ampacity required for the other load(s).**[430.24]**

EXAMPLE - Determine the MINIMUM size THWN/THHN copper feeder conductors required to supply two (2) induction type, 208-volt, three-phase, continuous-duty motors; one (1) 10 hp and one (1) 15 hp. Consider all terminations are rated 75°C.

 A. 6 AWG
 B. 4 AWG
 C. 3 AWG
 D. 2 AWG

ANSWER - (C) 3 AWG

 10 hp FLC = 30.8 amps **[Tbl. 430.250]** x 100% = 30.80 amperes
 15 HP FLC = 46.2 amps **[Tbl. 430.250]** x 125% = <u>57.75 amperes</u>
 88.55 amperes

 Size 3 AWG THWN is rated at 100 amperes. **[Table 310.15(B)(16)]**

☐ Each motor and its accessories is required to have branch circuit, short-circuit and ground fault protection by the use of overcurrent protective devices such as fuses or circuit breakers. The overcurrent protective devices are to be sized no larger than the percentage values given in **Table 430.52**. **[430.52(C)(1)]** Where the values for overcurrent protection determined from **Table 430.52** does not correspond with the standard sizes or ratings as listed per **240.6(A)** the next higher standard overcurrent protection device is permitted to be used. **[430.52(C)(1), Ex 1]** This is known as **initial sizing**.

EXAMPLE - Determine the MAXIMUM initial rating of nontime delay fuses to be used for branch-circuit, short-circuit and ground-fault protection for a 5 hp, 230-volt, three-phase, squirrel cage, continuous-duty motor.

 A. 40 amperes
 B. 45 amperes
 C. 50 amperes
 D. 60 amperes

ANSWER - (C) 50 amperes

 5 hp FLC = 15.2 amperes **[Table 430.250]**
 15.2 amperes x 300% = 45.6 amperes **[Table 430.52]**

 Since 45.6 amperes is not a standard rating for nontime delay fuses, as per **430.52(C)(1) Ex. 1**, you are permitted to go up to the next standard size fuse which is rated at 50 amperes.

☐ When sizing overcurrent protection for motors, the selected rating or setting, if adjustable, should be as low as possible for MAXIMUM protection. However, if the motor is under severe starting conditions, the rating or setting designated in **Table 450.52** or as permitted by **430.52(C)(1) Ex. 1** is not large enough for the starting current of the motor, you are permitted to go up to a higher value as allowed by **430.52(C)(1) Ex. 2**. This is known as **MAXIMUM** or **absolute MAXIMUM** sizing.

EXAMPLE - Determine the absolute MAXIMUM standard size time-delay fuses permitted for short-circuit, branch-circuit and ground-fault protection for a 40 hp, 480-volt, three-phase, induction type, continuous-duty motor.

 A. 100 amperes
 B. 110 amperes
 C. 115 amperes
 D. 125 amperes

ANSWER - (B) 110 amperes

40 hp FLC = 52 amperes **[Table 430.250]**
52 amperes x 225% = 117 amperes **[430.52(C)(1)Ex.2(b)]**

Since you are NOT permitted to exceed 225% of the FLC of the motor, you must go down to the next smaller standard size fuse as listed in **240.6(A).**

☐ In general, to properly size the overcurrent protection device for **feeder** conductors supplying two or more motors, the rules as specified in **430.62(A)** are to be applied which states, the protective device is to be sized by:

(1) not greater than the largest overcurrent protection device provided for any motor in the group,

(2) plus the sum of the full-load currents of the other motors of the group.

When sizing **feeder** overcurrent protection for motors, when the value you select does not correspond with a standard rating as listed per **240.6(A)** you are NOT permitted to go up to the next standard size, you must go **down**.

EXAMPLE - What standard size time-delay fuses are required for the feeder overcurrent protection of a feeder supplying four (4), 15 hp, 480-volt, three-phase, continuous-duty induction-type motors, each protected with 40 ampere rated time-delay fuses?

A. 100 amperes
B. 110 amperes
C. 125 amperes
D. 150 amperes

ANSWER - (A) 100 amperes

15 hp FLC = 21 amperes **[Table 430.250]**

40 A (largest OCP in group) + 21 A + 21 A + 21 A = 103 amps

You are required to go down to 100 ampere rated fuses.
[240.6(A)]

☐ In addition to overcurrent protection, most continuous-duty electric motors rated more than 1 hp and motors automatically started having a rating of 1 hp or less, are required to be protected from harmful **overloads**. **[430.32(A)]** To properly size the overload protective devices, they shall be selected to trip at no more than the

percentage values of the motors nameplate rating given in **430.32(A)(1)**, **(MINIMUM)** or **430.32(C)**, **(MAXIMUM)** instead of the full-load current values from Tables 430.248, 430.249 and 430.250. Today, many manufacturers have adjustable overloads installed in motor controllers or starters for protecting the motor against overloads, which are harmful to it.

The ampere trip setting value of the separate overloads is based upon **service factor** and **temperature rise** of the motor, as indicated on the motor **nameplate**. The running overload protection may range from **115%** to **125% (MINIMUM)** **[430.32(A)(1)]** to no more than **140% (MAXIMUM) [430.32(C)]** of the motor's ampere **nameplate** rating. The service factor indicated on the nameplate usually ranges from **1.00** to **1.30**. For example, if a motor has a service factor rating of 1.15 this means that the motor can operate up to **115%** of its rating without undue harm where the ambient temperature is not more than 104°F or 40°C. The temperature rise indicated on the motors nameplate relates to the heating effect of the motor when it is running properly in relation to the ambient temperature. The higher the temperature rise indicated on the nameplate the hotter the motor runs. For example, a motor with a 40°C temperature rise means, under normal operating conditions the motor should not get warmer than 40°C or 104°F. If too great a load is put on the motor or the ambient temperature is elevated, the motor will become excessively hot, causing probable injury to the insulation of the windings.

EXAMPLE - What is the MINIMUM (initial) size running overload protection, in amperes, required for a 2 hp, 208-volt, single-phase, squirrel cage motor with a temperature rise of 42°C and a FLA of 12 amperes indicated on the nameplate?

 A. 13.20 amperes
 B. 15.18 amperes
 C. 15.00 amperes
 D. 13.80 amperes

ANSWER - (D) 13.80 amperes

 2 hp FLA (nameplate) = 12 amperes

 12 amps x 115% (all other motors) = 13.8 amps **[430.32(A)(1)]**

EXAMPLE - Refer to the previous example. Assume the ampere rating you have selected is not sufficient to start the motor and trips. Determine the MAXIMUM size overload protection permitted.

 A. 15.00 amperes
 B. 15.60 amperes
 C. 16.80 amperes

D. 17.16 amperes

ANSWER - (B) 15.60 amperes

2 hp FLA (nameplate) = 12 amperes

12 amps x 130% (all other motors) = 15.60 amps **[430.32(C)]**

☐ Some motors are provided with a **thermal protector integral** with the motor, located inside the motor housing, for overload protection. **[430.32(A)(2)]** Under this condition, the ultimate trip setting, in amperes, shall not exceed the percentage values as expressed in **430.32(A)(2)**, multiplied by the motor's full-load current as given in **Table 430.248**, **Table 430.249** or **Table 430.250**.

EXAMPLE - Determine the MAXIMUM current setting permitted for overload protection for a motor that has a thermal protector integral with the motor, given the following:

- 1 hp – squirrel cage
- single-phase, 120-volts

A. 24.96 amperes
B. 20.80 amperes
C. 22.40 amperes
D. 27.20 amperes

ANSWER - (A) 24.96 amperes

1 hp FLC = 16 amperes **[Table 430.248]**

16 amperes x 156% **[430.32(A)(2)]** = 24.96 amperes

☐ In general, each motor must be provided with some form of approved manual **disconnecting means**. The disconnecting means is required to have an ampere rating of not less than **115 percent** of the full-load current rating of the motor as determined in **Table 430.248** through **430.250**.**[430.110(A)]** For motors rated 2 hp through 100 hp the disconnecting means may be a general-use switch, rated in horsepower, a circuit breaker, or a manual motor controller when marked **"Suitable as Motor Disconnect"**. **[430.109(A)(6)]**

EXAMPLE - When an inverse time circuit breaker is used as a disconnecting means only for a 7½ hp, single-phase, 240-volt, ac motor, the circuit breaker must have a standard ampacity rating of at LEAST _____.

 A. 40 amperes
 B. 50 amperes
 C. 100 amperes
 D. 46 amperes

ANSWER - (B) 50 amperes

 7½ hp FLA = 40 amperes **[Table 430.248]**

 40 amperes x 115% = 46 amperes **[430.110A]**

 As per **240.6(A),** the next standard size circuit breaker has a rating of 50 amperes.

☐ For stationary ac motors of 2 hp or less and 300 volts or less the disconnecting means is permitted to be an ac general-use snap switch where the motor full-load current rating is not more than **80 percent** of the ampere rating of the switch. **[430.109(C)(2)]**

EXAMPLE - A 20 ampere rated ac general-use snap switch is permitted for use as a disconnecting means for a 120-volt, single-phase, ac motor when the motor has a rating of 2 hp or less and a full-load current rating of _____ or less.

 A. 20 amperes
 B. 16 amperes
 C. 12 amperes
 D. 25 amperes

ANSWER - (B) 16 amperes
 20 amperes (switch rating) x 80% = 16 amperes
 [430.109(C)(2)]

UNIT 7
SELF-ASSESSMENT QUIZ

1. In general, when sizing the conductors, disconnecting means or overcurrent protection for a continuous-duty ac motor, they are to be sized based on the _____.

 A. starting current of the motor
 B. locked rotor current of the motor
 C. motors stopping current
 D. running current of the motor at usual speed

2. For continuous-duty motors, the motor nameplate ampere rating is used to determine the size of the _____ for motors.

 A. disconnecting means
 B. branch-circuit conductors
 C. short-circuit protection
 D. overload protection

3. Branch-circuit conductors that supply a single, continuous-duty ac motor shall have an ampacity of not less than _____ of the full-load current of the motor.

 A. 80 percent
 B. 100 percent
 C. 125 percent
 D. 150 percent

4. When determining the required ampacity of the branch-circuit conductors to supply a three-phase, continuous-duty motor, the full-load current values of the motor given on _____ shall be used.

 A. Table 430.250 of the NEC®
 B. Table 430.52 of the NEC®
 C. Table 430.248 of the NEC®
 D. the motor's nameplate

5. When determining the initial standard size, time-delay fuses required for branch-circuit, short-circuit and ground-fault protection of a single-phase, 240 volt, ac motor, the fuses

shall have a rating of _____ of the full-load current of the motor. When the value determined does not correspond to a standard ampere rating, the next higher standard rating shall be permitted.

 A. 175 percent
 B. 150 percent
 C. 225 percent
 D. 300 percent

6. Motors with a service factor of not less than 1.15 indicated on the nameplate, shall have the overload protection sized at _____ of the full-load ampere rating of the motor when modifications of the value selected in not necessary.

 A. 115 percent
 B. 125 percent
 C. 130 percent
 D. 140 percent

7. The full-load running current of a 3 hp, 208-volt, single-phase, continuous-duty, ac motor is _____.

 A. 10.6 amperes
 B. 13.2 amperes
 C. 18.7 amperes
 D. 19.6 amperes

8. Branch-circuit conductors supplying a three-phase, 208-volt, 10 hp continuous duty, induction-type, Design B motor, are required to have an ampacity of at LEAST _____.

 A. 30.80 amperes
 B. 35.42 amperes
 C. 38.50 amperes
 D. 46.20 amperes

9. Determine the MINIMUM (initial) ampere rating for an adjustable trip overload protective device responsive to motor current, used to protect a 20 hp, 230 volt, three-phase, induction type, ac motor with temperature rise of 48°C and a full-load ampere rating of 54 amperes indicated on the nameplate.

 A. 54.0 amperes
 B. 62.1 amperes
 C. 70.2 amperes
 D. 75.6 amperes

10. Refer to the previous question. If the trip setting you selected was not adequate to start the motor and trips, determine the absolute MAXIMUM ampere setting of the adjustable overload protective device as permitted by the NEC®.

A. 62.1 amperes
B. 67.5 amperes
C. 70.2 amperes
D. 75.6 amperes

11. Determine the MINIMUM size Type SO cord, from a motor controller, permitted to supply a 40 hp, 460 volt, three-phase, continuous-duty, wound rotor ac motor installed in an area with an ambient temperature of 86°F.

 A. 2 AWG
 B. 4 AWG
 C. 3 AWG
 D. 6 AWG

12. The branch-circuit conductors supplying a 7½ hp, 240-volt, single-phase, continuous-duty ac motor must be at least size _____ copper conductors, when the conductors and all terminations are rated for 75°C and ambient temperature is not a consideration.

 A. 4 AWG
 B. 10 AWG
 C. 3 AWG
 D. 8 AWG

13. Where an ac motor has a thermal protector integral with the motor, determine the MAXIMUM current setting permitted for overload protection for a 2 hp, 120-volt, single-phase motor having a FLA of 22.5 amperes indicated on the nameplate.

 A. 35.1 amperes
 B. 31.5 amperes
 C. 37.4 amperes
 D. 33.6 amperes

14. Determine the MINIMUM size THWN/THHN copper conductors required to supply three (3) induction-type, 480-volt, three-phase, continuous-duty motors; one (1) 10 hp, one (1) 15 hp and one (1) 20 hp. Consider all terminations are rated for 75°C.

 A. 6 AWG
 B. 4 AWG
 C. 3 AWG
 D. 2 AWG

15. The MAXIMUM standard initial rating of time-delay fuses provided for the branch circuit, short-circuit and ground-fault protection required for a 7½ hp 240-volt, single-phase

continuous-duty motor have a rating of _____.

A. 50 amperes
B. 60 amperes
C. 70 amperes
D. 80 amperes

16. Assume the motor in the previous question is under heavy load when starting and the fuses blow. Determine the absolute MAXIMUM standard rating permitted for overcurrent protection for the motor.

A. 100 amperes
B. 90 amperes
C. 80 amperes
D. 70 amperes

17. If the motor in question 15 is provided with an inverse time circuit breaker as overcurrent protection, the initial standard rating of the circuit breaker would be _____.

A. 70 amperes
B. 80 amperes
C. 90 amperes
D. 100 amperes

18. In general, a general-use fused switch used as a disconnecting means for a 25 hp, 480-volt, three-phase motor with a FLA of 32 amperes indicated on the nameplate, must have an ampere rating of at LEAST _____.

A. 39 amperes
B. 50 amperes
C. 56 amperes
D. 79 amperes

19. What MAXIMUM standard size time-delay fuses are required for the feeder overcurrent protection of a feeder supplying two (2) 20 hp, 480-volt, three-phase continuous-duty induction-type motors, each protected with 50 ampere rated time-delay fuses, and two (2) 30 hp, 480-volt, three-phase continuous duty induction-type motors, each protected with 70 ampere rated time-delay fuses?

A. 200 amperes
B. 125 amperes
C. 150 amperes
D. 175 amperes

20. What MINIMUM size THWN/THHN copper branch-circuit conductors are required to supply a continuous-duty, induction-type, 15 hp, 208-volt, three-phase motor, when installed in an area with an ambient temperature of 120°F? Consider all terminations are rated 75°C.

A. 6 AWG
B. 4 AWG
C. 8 AWG
D. 3 AWG

NOTES

PRACTICAL CALCULATIONS FOR ELECTRICIANS
UNIT 7
SELF-ASSESSMENT QUIZ
ANSWER KEY

ANSWER		REFERENCE	NEC PG. #
1.	D	430.6(A)(1)	pg. 297
2.	D	430.6(A)(2)	pg. 298
3.	C	430.22	pg. 302
4.	A	430.6(A)(1)	pg. 297
5.	A	Table 430.52	pg. 308
		430.52(C)(1), Exception 1	pg. 307
6.	B	430.32(A)(1)	pg. 305
7.	C	Table 430.248	pg. 321
8.	C	430.6(A)(1)	pg. 297
		Table 430.250	pg. 322
		430.22	pg. 302

10 hp FLC = 30.8 amperes x 125% = 38.5 amperes

9.	B	430.32(A)(1)	pg. 305

motor FLA = 54 amperes x 115% = 62.1 amperes

10.	C	430.32(C)	pg. 305

motor FLA = 54 amperes x 130% = 67.5 amperes

11. C 430.6 & 430.6(A)(1) pg. 297
 Table 430.250 pg. 322
 430.22 pg. 302
 Table 400.5(A)(1), Column A pg. 248

40 hp FLC = 52 amperes x 125% = 65 amperes

Table 400.5(A)(1) indicates a size 3 AWG SO cord having an ampacity of 70 amperes is required.

12. D 430.6(A)(1) pg. 297
 Table 430.248 pg. 321
 430.22 pg. 302
 Table 310.15(B)(16) pg. 150

7½ hp FLC = 40 amperes x 125% = 50 amperes

Table 310.15(B)(16) indicates size 8 AWG 75°C copper conductors should be selected.

13. D 430.32(A)(2) pg. 305
 Table 430.248 pg. 321

2 hp FLC = 24 amperes x 140% = 33.6 amperes

14. B 430.24(1)&(2) pg. 303
 Table 430.250 pg. 322
 Table 310.15(B)(16) pg. 150

10 hp FLC = 14 amperes x 100% = 14.00
15 hp FLC = 21 amperes x 100% = 21.00
20 hp FLC = 27 amperes x 125% = 33.75
 TOTAL = 68.75 amperes

Table 310.15(B)(16) indicates size 4 AWG 75°C conductors with an ampacity of 85 amperes should be selected.

15. C 430.6(A)(1) pg. 297
 Table 430.248 pg. 321
 Table 430.52 pg. 308

7½ hp FLC = 40 amperes x 175% = 70 amperes

16. B 430.52(C)(1), Exception 2(b) pg. 307

7½ hp FLC = 40 amperes x 225% = 90 amperes

17. D Table 430.52 pg. 308

 7½ hp FLC = 40 amperes x 250% = 100 amperes

18. A 430.6(A)(1) pg. 297
 Table 430.250 pg. 322
 430.110(A) pg. 315

 25 hp FLC = 34 amperes x 115% = 39.1 amperes

19. C 430.62(A) pg. 310
 Table 430.250 pg. 322
 Table 240.6(A) pg. 95

 Largest OCP in group = 70 amperes
 30 hp FLC = 40 amperes
 20 hp FLC = 27 amperes
 20 hp FLC = <u>27 amperes</u>
 TOTAL = 164 amperes

 *NOTE – You are required to go down to 150 ampere rated fuses.

20. B Table 430.250 pg. 322
 430.22 pg. 302
 Table 310.15(B)(2)(a) pg. 147
 Table 310.15(B)(16) pg. 150

 15 hp FLC = 46.2 amperes

 46.2 amperes x 125% = 57.75 amperes

$$\frac{57.75 \text{ amps}}{.75 \text{ (temp. cor.)}} = 77 \text{ amperes}$$

 Size 4 AWG copper conductors rated for 75°C with an ampacity of 85 amperes should be selected.

UNIT 8

SINGLE-FAMILY DWELLING SERVICE CALCULATIONS

After completing this unit of study, the successful student will be familiar with the concept of properly sizing services for one-family dwellings.

UNIT 8

SINGLE-FAMILY DWELLING SERVICE CALCULATIONS

RELATED INFORMATION:

☐ A single-family dwelling is considered a building consisting solely of one dwelling unit with living and sleeping quarters and having permanent provisions for cooking, cleaning, and laundering.

☐ In order to properly size services for dwelling units you are to comply with the requirements as set forth in **Article 220** of the NEC® and additional Articles such as **210**, **230** and **240** that may also apply. As indicated in **Section 310.15(B)(7)**, for sizing residential **120/240-volt, 3-wire, single phase** ungrounded (line) service conductors rated **100 through 400 amperes,** they are permitted to have an ampacity not less than **83 percent** of the service rating. For example, if the dwelling unit has a service rating of 150 amperes, the service-entrance conductors are permitted to have a rating of 125 amperes. 150 amperes x .83 = 124.5 amperes

☐ The NEC® recognizes two (2) methods when calculating dwelling services, the **general method**, also known as the **standard method** and the **optional method**. The standard method starts at **220.12** and the optional method starts at **220.80.** Generally, the optional method is easier to use because you simply add the nameplate values of the utilization equipment together and apply only one demand factor. With the general method, there are several demand factors applied. With either method the most common service provided for a one-family dwelling unit is 120/240-volts, single-phase.

☐ When using either calculation method, the **MINIMUM** size service for a one-family dwelling is required to be rated **100 amperes** because the ampacity for the ungrounded conductors shall not be less than the rating of the service disconnecting means **[230.42(B)]** and the service disconnecting means shall have a rating of not less than **100 amperes**. **[230.79(C)]**

☐ **Annex D** of the NEC® shows examples of both calculation methods and the steps and procedures to be used. We will follow these examples and steps to learn how to properly size services for one-family dwellings. First, we will look at the general (standard) method of calculation. You will find a completed example of this form using the standard method of calculation on page 123 of this text.

General Calculation Method

Step 1 - Determine the total connected load, in VA, of the general lighting and general-purpose receptacles by applying **Table 220.12**. Use the outside dimension of the house but, do not include garages, open porches and enclosed areas not adaptable for future use. **[220.12]**

EXAMPLE - What is the total connected load, in VA, for the general lighting and general-use receptacles of a one-family dwelling having 30 feet by 60 feet of livable space?

 A. 2,100 VA
 B. 3,600 VA
 C. 5,400 VA
 D. 6,300 VA

ANSWER - (C) 5,400 VA

 First, find the area, in square feet, of the livable space, then multiply by the value given in **Table 220.12**.

 30 ft. x 60 ft. = 1,800 sq. ft. x 3 VA **[Table 220.12]** = 5,400 VA

Step 2 - Find the total connected load of the small appliance and laundry branch circuits. A MINIMUM of **two (2)** small appliance branch circuits are required **[210.11(C)(1)]** and they shall be calculated at **1,500 VA** per circuit. **[220.52(A)]** A MINIMUM of **one (1)** branch circuit is required to supply the laundry **[210.11(C)(2)]** and shall be calculated at **1,500 VA** per circuit. **[220.52(B)]**

EXAMPLE - What is the MINIMUM total connected load, in VA, for the small appliance and laundry loads in a single-family dwelling?

 A. 4,500 VA
 B. 3,000 VA
 C. 6,000 VA
 D. 1,500 VA

ANSWER - (A) 4,500 VA

 2 small appl. circuits @ 1,500 VA each = 3,000 VA
 1 laundry circuit @ 1,500 VA = 1,500 VA
 TOTAL = 4,500 VA

Step 3 - Apply the demand factors specified in **Table 220.42** for the general-purpose lighting and receptacle loads, plus the loads required for the small appliance and laundry branch circuits. **[220.42]**

EXAMPLE - What is the demand load, in VA, for a dwelling unit having a 5,400 VA total connected lighting load and a 4,500 VA connected load for small appliance and laundry branch-circuits?

 A. 9,900 VA
 B. 5,415 VA
 C. 6,780 VA
 D. 3,465 VA

ANSWER - (B) 5,415 VA

 5,400 VA (ltg.) + 4,500 VA (laundry & sm. appl.) = 9,900 VA total

 1st 3,000 VA @ 100% **[Table 220.42]** = 3,000 VA
 9,900 VA – 3,000 VA = 6,900 VA (remainder) x 35% = 2,415 VA
 DEMAND LOAD = 5,415 VA

Step 4 - Apply a demand factor of **75 percent** of the nameplate rating of **four (4)** or more fastened in place appliances.

 *NOTE – This rule does **not apply** for electric ranges, clothes dryers, space heating or air-conditioning equipment. **[220.53]**

EXAMPLE - A one-family dwelling is to have the following fastened in place appliances:

 garbage disposal – 864 VA
 dishwasher – 1,100 VA
 trash compactor – 1,188 VA
 water heater – 4,500 VA
 attic fan – 750 VA
 swimming pool pump – 1,250 VA
Where using the standard method of calculation for dwelling units, determine the demand load.

 A. 7,652 VA
 B. 9,652 VA
 C. 6,757 VA
 D. 7,239 VA

ANSWER - (D) 7,239 VA

 garbage disposal - 864 VA
 dishwasher - 1,100 VA
 trash compactor – 1,188 VA
 water heater – 4,500 VA
 attic fan - 750 VA
 pump - 1,250 VA
 TOTAL = 9,652 VA (connected load)
 x 75%
 7,239 VA (demand load)

Step 5 - Determine the electric clothes dryer demand load, using **5,000 watts (volt –
amperes)** as a MINIMUM or the nameplate rating, **whichever is larger**, for each
dryer served. **[220.54]** You are permitted to use the demand factors shown in
Table 220.54. A demand of **70 percent** of this value may be applied to the **neutral**
(grounded) conductor. **[220.61(B)(1)]**

EXAMPLE - When a one-family dwelling is to have only one (1) 4,500 VA electric clothes dryer
installed, the demand load will be _____ on the ungrounded service-entrance
conductors and _____ on the grounded (neutral) conductor.

 A. 4,500 VA – 3,500 VA
 B. 3,500 VA – 4,500 VA
 C. 4,500 VA – 5,000 VA
 D. 5,000 VA – 3,500 VA

ANSWER - (D) 5,000 VA – 3,500 VA

 5,000 VA MINIMUM ungrounded conductors **[220.54]**
 5,000 VA x 70% = 3,500 VA neutral conductor **[220.61(B)(1)]**

Step 6 - Determine the demand load for the cooking appliances in accordance with **Table
220.55. [220.55]** This is explained in **Unit 3** of this book. A further demand of **70
percent** of the demand load on the ungrounded conductors may be applied to the
neutral (grounded) conductor. **[220.61(B)(1)]**

EXAMPLE - A 12 kW electric range installed in a one-family dwelling will have a demand load of
_____ on the ungrounded service-entrance conductors and a demand load of _____
on the grounded neutral conductor.

 A. 8,000 VA – 5,600 VA
 B. 12,000 VA – 8,400 VA
 C. 12,000 VA – 8,000 VA
 D. 8,000 VA – 3,920 VA

ANSWER - (A) 8,000 VA – 5,600 VA

ungrounded conductors demand – 8 kW = 8,000 VA
[Table 220.55, Col. C]
grounded conductor – 8,000 VA x 70% = 5,600 VA
[220.61(B)(1)]

Step 7 - Determine the demand load for the fixed electric space heating or air-conditioning load; you are permitted to **omit the smaller** of the two because these loads are considered noncoincident loads, meaning, they are unlikely to be in use simultaneously. **[220.60]**

EXAMPLE - A one-family dwelling unit to be constructed will have a 10 kW (kVA), 240-volt, single-phase, fixed electric space heating unit and a 32 ampere, 240-volt, single-phase air-conditioning unit. When calculating the total load on the dwelling unit, what is the demand that should be applied to the service-entrance conductors?

A. 10,000 VA
B. 10,800 VA
C. 9,600 VA
D. 19,600 VA

ANSWER - (A) 10,000 VA

First, compare the two loads.

A/C unit - P = I x E P = 32 amperes x 240 volts = 7,680 VA
Heating unit - 10 kW = 10 kW x 1,000 = 10,000 VA

*NOTE – The heating unit is the larger of the loads, this value should be applied.

Step 8 - Add an additional **25 percent** of the full-load current of the **largest motor** in the dwelling. **[220.50]** Generally, the largest motor in the house is the air-conditioning unit.

EXAMPLE - A one-family dwelling will have the following motor loads installed:

garbage disposal – 864 VA
trash compactor – 1,188 VA
attic fan – 750 VA
pump motor – 1,250 VA

When applying the largest motor rule for residential service calculations, how many

VA should be added?

> A. 1,013 VA
> B. 1,563 VA
> C. 1,266 VA
> D. 313 VA

ANSWER - (D) 313 VA

> Largest motor (pump) 1,250 VA x 25% = 313 VA

Step 9 - Add together the values determined from steps 3-8 to find the required volt-amperes. Next, apply the current formula **(I=P/E)** to determine the demand load. Then, multiply the current value by **83%** and size the service-entrance conductors using **Table 310.15(B)(16)**. Use **Table 250.66** for sizing the grounding electrode conductor.

EXAMPLE - After all demand factors have been taken into consideration for a one-family dwelling unit, a demand load of 35,967 VA is determined. What MINIMUM size THWN aluminum ungrounded service-entrance conductors are required when the house is to have a 120/240-volt, single-phase, electrical system?

> A. 1 AWG
> B. 1/0 AWG
> C. 2/0 AWG
> D. 3/0 AWG

ANSWER - (C) 2/0 AWG

> First, find the load in amperes and multiply by 83%.

> $I = \dfrac{P}{E} = \dfrac{35,967}{240 \text{ volts}}$ = 150 amperes x 83% = 124.5 amperes

> **Table 310.15(B)(16)** indicates size 2/0 AWG aluminum conductors having an ampacity of 135 amperes should be selected.

STANDARD CALCULATION: ONE-FAMILY DWELLING

<table>
<tr><td colspan="3">

1. GENERAL LIGHTING & RECEPTACLES: *Table 220.12*
_____ sq. ft. x 3 VA = _____ VA
</td></tr>
</table>

1. GENERAL LIGHTING & RECEPTACLES: *Table 220.12*
 _____ sq. ft. x 3 VA = _____ VA

2. SMALL APPLIANCES 220.52(A) & LAUNDRY 220.52(B)
 1,500 VA x _____ circuits = _____ VA

3. APPLY DEMAND FACTORS: *Table 220.42*
 Total of gen. ltg. & small appl. _____ VA
 First 3000 VA x 100% = 3,000 VA
 Next _____ VA x 35% = _____ VA **LINE** **NEUTRAL**
 Remaining _____ VA x 25% = _____ VA
 Total _____ VA _____ VA _____VA

4. FIXED APPLIANCES: 220.53
 Water Heater = _____ VA
 Disposal = _____ VA
 Compactor = _____ VA
 Dishwasher = _____ VA
 _____ = _____ VA
 _____ = _____ VA
 _____ = _____ VA
 Total _____ VA (x 75% if 4 or more)= _____ VA _____ VA

5. DRYER: 220.54; *Table 220.54*
 _____ VA = _____ VA x 70%=_____ VA

6. COOKING EQUIPMENT: *Table 220.55 & Notes*
 Col A _____ VA x _____% = _____ VA
 Col B _____ VA x _____% = _____ VA
 Col C _____ VA = _____ VA
 Total _____ VA _____ VA x 70%=_____ VA

7. HEATING or A/C (largest): 220.60
 Heating unit = _____ VA x 100% =_____ VA
 A/C unit = _____ VA x 100% =_____ VA
 Heat pump = _____ VA x 100% =_____ VA
 Largest Load _____ VA

8. LARGEST MOTOR: 220.14(C)
 _____ VA x 25% = _____ VA _____ VA

9. TOTAL _____ VA _____ VA
 Line I = _____ VA = _____ amperes
 240 volts
 Neutral I = _____ VA = _____ amperes
 240 volts

Conductors are permitted to be sized @ 83% of the demand load if 120/240-volts, single-phase and not greater than 400 amperes.

STANDARD CALCULATION: ONE-FAMILY DWELLING

1. GENERAL LIGHTING & RECEPTACLES: *Table 220.12*
1,800 sq. ft. x 3 VA = 5,400 VA

2. SMALL APPLIANCES *220.52(A)* & LAUNDRY *220.52(B)*
1,500 VA x ___3___ circuits = 4,500 VA

3. APPLY DEMAND FACTORS: *Table 220.42*

		LINE	NEUTRAL
Total of gen. ltg. & small appl. 9,900 VA			
First 3000 VA x 100% =	3,000 VA		
Next 6,900 VA x 35% =	2,415 VA		
Remaining -0- VA x 25% =	-0- VA		
Total	5,415 VA	5,415 VA	5,415 VA

4. FIXED APPLIANCES: *220.53*

Water Heater =	4,500 VA	
Disposal =	864 VA	
Compactor =	1,188 VA	
Dishwasher =	1,110 VA	
Attic fan =	750 VA	
Pump =	1,250 VA	
-0- =	-0- VA	

		LINE	NEUTRAL
Total	9,652 VA (x 75% if 4 or more)=	7,239 VA	7,239 VA

5. DRYER: *220.54*; *Table 220.54*
5,000 VA = 5,000 VA x 70%= 3,500 VA

6. COOKING EQUIPMENT: *Table 220.55 & Notes*

		LINE	NEUTRAL
Col A -0- VA x -0- % =	-0- VA		
Col B -0- VA x -0- % =	-0- VA		
Col C 8,000 VA =	8,000 VA		
Total	8,000 VA	8,000 VA x 70%= 5,600 VA	

7. HEATING or A/C (largest): *220.60*

Heating unit = 10,000 VA x 100%	=10,000 VA		
A/C unit = 7,680 VA x 100%	=7,680 VA		
Heat pump = -0- VA x 100%	= -0- VA		
Largest Load		10,000 VA	

8. LARGEST MOTOR: *220.14(C)*

	LINE	NEUTRAL
1,250 VA x 25% =	313 VA	313 VA

9. TOTAL

	LINE	NEUTRAL
	35,967 VA	22,067 VA

Line I = 35,967 VA = 150 amperes
 240 volts

Neutral I = 22,067 VA = 92 amperes
 240 volts

Conductors are permitted to be sized @ 83% of the demand load if 120/240-volts, single-phase and not greater than 400 amperes.

Optional Calculation Method

☐ In general, the **optional calculation method** for dwelling units provides an easier and less complex method than the standard (general) method for computing the total demand load for service-entrance conductors. The optional calculation method is reserved for dwelling units served by a single service with a connected load of **100 amperes or greater. [220.82(A)]** Therefore, since most one-family homes currently being constructed have a connected load of 100 amperes or more, this calculation method is frequently used. You will find a completed example of this form of calculation method on page 130 of this text.

☐ When using the **optional calculation method**, the calculated load shall not be less than **100 percent** of the **first 10 kW**, plus **40 percent** of the remainder of the **"general loads"**, including, general lighting and receptacles, laundry and small appliance branch circuits and nameplate VA rating of all fastened in place motors and appliances, plus the larger of the air-conditioner or heating load. **[220.82(A)]** The following steps may be applied when using the optional calculation method for dwellings.

Step 1 - Compare the heating and air-conditioning loads. As per **220.82(C)**, include the **largest** of the following:

1. 100 percent of the nameplate rating(s) of the air-conditioning equipment.
2. 100 percent of the nameplate rating(s) of the heat pump(s) only.
3. 100 percent of the nameplate ratings of electric thermal storage and other heating systems where the usual load is expected to be continuous.

4. 100 percent of the nameplate rating(s) of the heat pump compressor and 65 percent of the supplemental electric heating for central electric space heating systems. If the heat pumps compressor is interlocked with the supplementary heat in a manner that both cannot be operated at the same time, the heat pump does not need to be added.

5. 65 percent of the nameplate rating(s) of electric space heating, if there are less than four (4) units having separate controls.

6. 40 percent of the nameplate rating(s) of electric space heating, if there are four (4) or more units with separate controls.

EXAMPLE - A one-family dwelling is to have the following heating and air-conditioning
equipment:

 two (2) 10 kW (kVA) electric space heating systems
 two (2) 240-volt, single-phase, 50 ampere rated air-conditioners

 When using the optional method of calculation for one-family dwellings, what demand, in VA, should be applied to the ungrounded service-entrance conductors for the heating or air-conditioning loads?

 A. 20,000 VA

 B. 24,000 VA
 C. 15,600 VA
 D. 13,000 VA

ANSWER -　(B)　24,000 VA

 Space heaters **[220.82(C)(5)]**
 10 kVA + 10 kVA = 20 kVA x 1,000 = 20,000 VA
 20,000 VA x 65% = 13,000 VA

 A/C Equipment **[220.82(C)(1)]**
 50 amps + 50 amps = 100 amperes x 240 volts = 24,000 VA

 The A/C equipment with a computed load of 24,000 VA is to be
used for this calculation.

Step 2 -　Determine the connected load, in VA, of the general lighting and general-use receptacles; calculated from the outside dimensions of the 　　　 dwelling using 3 VA per square foot. Do not include open porches, 　 garages or unused or unfinished spaces not adapted for future use. 　 **[220.82(B)(1)]**

EXAMPLE -　Before demand factors are taken into consideration, determine the connected load, in VA, for the general lighting and general-use receptacles for a one-family dwelling having 5,000 square feet of livable space, a 600 square foot garage and a 350 square foot open porch.

 A. 15,000 VA
 B. 17,500 VA
 C. 17,850 VA
 D. 5,000 VA

ANSWER -　(A)　15,000 VA

 5,000 sq. ft. x 3 VA **[220.82(B)(1)]** = 15,000 VA

Step 3 -　Find the total connected load of the small appliance and laundry branch circuits; each circuit is to be calculated at **1,500 VA each**. **[220.82(B)(2)]** A MINIMUM of two (2) small-appliance branch circuits are required **[210.11(C)(1)]** and a MINIMUM of one (1) laundry branch circuit is required. **[210.11(C)(2)]**

EXAMPLE -　A one-family dwelling is to have three (3) small-appliance branch circuits and one (1) laundry branch circuit installed. Before demand factors are taken into consideration, what is the total connected load of these circuits?

 A. 1,500 VA
 B. 3,000 VA
 C. 4,500 VA

D. 6,000 VA

ANSWER - (D) 6,000 VA

> Small appliance circuits 3 x 1,500 VA = 4,500 VA **[220.52(A)]**
> Laundry circuit 1 x 1,500 VA = <u>1,500 VA</u> **[220.52(B)]**
> TOTAL Connected Load = 6,000 VA

Step 4 - Find the total connected load of all fastened in place appliances, such as electric ranges, cooktops, ovens, clothes dryers and water heaters. This total is to be based on the nameplate rating of the appliances. **[220.82(B)(3)]** Also include the nameplate ratings of all motors, such as attic fans, sump pumps and water well and swimming pool pumps. **[220.82(B)(4)]**

EXAMPLE - A single family dwelling is to have the following fastened in place appliances and motors:

> one – 12 kVA electric range
> one – 6 kVA electric clothes dryer
> one – 1,250 VA dishwasher
> one – 1,176 VA trash compactor
> one – 1,656 VA garbage disposer
> one – 6,000 VA water heater
> one – 1,176 VA attic fan
> one – 1,250 VA microwave oven

What is the total connected load of this utilization equipment?

> A. 26,508 VA
> B. 30,508 VA
> C. 25,508 VA
> D. 26,805 VA

ANSWER - (B) 30,508 VA

> range - 12 kVA x 1,000 = 12,000 VA
> clothes dryer - 6 kVA x 1,000 = 6,000 VA
> dishwasher = 1,250 VA
> trash compactor = 1,176 VA
> garbage disposer = 1,656 VA
> water heater = 6,000 VA
> attic fan = 1,176 VA
> microwave oven = <u> 1,250 VA</u>
> TOTAL Connected Load = 30,508 VA

Step 5 - Total the **"general load"** as determined in steps 2, 3 and 4, then apply the demand factors as per **220.82(B)**, **100 percent** of the **first 10 kVA (10,000 VA)**, plus **40 percent** of the remainder.

EXAMPLE - Using the optional calculation method for one-family dwellings, determine the demand load on the ungrounded service-entrance conductors for a dwelling that has the following total connected general loads:

General lighting and receptacles - 15,000 VA
Small appliance and laundry circuits - 6,000 VA
Fastened in place appliances and motors - 30,500 VA

 A. 51,500 VA
 B. 25,000 VA
 C. 26,600 VA
 D. 25,600 VA

ANSWER - (C) 26,600 VA

 General lighting and receptacles - 15,000 VA
 Small appliance and laundry circuits - 6,000 VA
 Fastened in place appliances and motors - 30,500 VA
 TOTAL General Load = 51,500 VA

 1st 10,000 VA @ 100% - 10,000 VA
 Remainder (total – 10,000) = 41,500 VA @ 40% - 16,600 VA
 DEMAND LOAD = 26,600 VA

Step 6 - Add together the values determined from steps 1 and 5 to find the required volt-amperes. Next, apply the current formula **(I=P/E)** to determine the demand load. Then, multiply the current value by **83%** and size the service-entrance conductors using **Table 310.15(B)(16)**. Use **Table 250.66** for sizing the grounding electrode conductor.

EXAMPLE - When applying the optional method of calculation for a one-family dwelling, after all demand factors have been considered, a demand load of 50,600 VA is determined. Using standard overcurrent protective devices, determine the MAXIMUM ampere rating of the service overcurrent protective device and the MINIMUM size of 75ºC aluminum ungrounded service-entrance conductors required. The electrical system is 120/240-volts, single-phase.

 A. 200 amperes OCP – 4/0 AWG aluminum conductors
 B. 250 amperes OCP – 4/0 AWG aluminum conductors
 C. 250 amperes OCP – 250 kcmil aluminum conductors
 D. 225 amperes OCP – 4/0 AWG aluminum conductors

ANSWER - (D) 225 amperes – 4/0 AWG aluminum conductors

First, find the load in amperes.

$$I = \frac{P}{E} = \frac{50,600 \text{ VA}}{240 \text{ volts}} = 210.8 \text{ amperes (demand load)}$$

This value does not correspond with the standard ampere rating of an overcurrent protective device. Therefore, as per **240.4(B)**, the next higher standard overcurrent device is permitted to be used. **Table 240.6(A)** indicates a **225 ampere** rating is the next higher standard OCP rating.

To find the required ampacity of the conductors:

210.8 amperes **x 83% = 175 amperes**

Size 4/0 AWG 75ºC aluminum conductors with an ampacity of 180 amperes should be selected from **[Table 310.15(B)(16)]**.

OPTIONAL CALCULATION: ONE-FAMILY DWELLING

1. HEATING or A/C: 220.82(C)(1-6)

Heating units (3 or less) = _____ VA x 65% = _____ VA
Heating units (4 or more) = _____ VA x 40% = _____ VA
A/C unit = _____ VA x 100% = _____ VA
Heat pump = _____ VA x 100% = _____ VA **LINE**
Largest Load = _____ VA
Total = _____ VA _____ VA

2. GENERAL LIGHTING: 220.82(B)(1) **NEUTRAL**

_____ sq. ft. x 3 VA per sq. ft. = _____ VA _____ VA

3. SMALL APPLIANCE & LAUNDRY LOADS: 220.82(B)(2)

1,500 VA x _____ circuits _____ VA _____VA

4. FIXED APPLIANCES & MOTORS: 220.82(B)(3)&(4)

Dishwasher =		_____ VA		_____ VA
Disposal =		_____ VA		_____ VA
Compactor =		_____ VA		_____ VA
Water heater =		_____ VA		_____ VA
Range =		_____ VA	@ 70%	_____ VA
Cooktop =		_____ VA	@ 70%	_____ VA
Oven =		_____ VA	@ 70%	_____ VA
Dryer =		_____ VA	@ 70%	_____ VA
_____ =		_____ VA		_____ VA
_____ =		_____ VA		_____ VA
_____ =		_____ VA		_____ VA
	Total =	_____ VA		_____ VA

5. APPLY DEMAND FACTORS: 220.82(B)

First 10,000 VA x 100% = 10,000 VA
Remaining _____ VA x 40% = _____ VA
Total _____ VA _____ VA _____ VA

6. TOTAL _____ VA _____ VA

LINE I = __VA__ = _____amperes
240 volts

NEUTRAL I = __VA__ = _____amperes
240 volts

Conductors are permitted to be sized @ 83% of the demand load if 120/240-volts, single-phase, or 100% if 208Y/120-volts, three-phase, or the load is greater than 400 amperes.

OPTIONAL CALCULATION: ONE-FAMILY DWELLING

1. HEATING or A/C: *220.82(C)(1-6)*

Heating units (3 or less) = <u>20,000</u> VA x 65%	= <u>13,000</u> VA		
Heating units (4 or more) = _____ VA x 40%	= _____ VA		
A/C unit = <u>24,000</u> VA x 100%	= <u>24,000</u> VA		
Heat pump = _____ VA x 100%	= _____ VA	**LINE**	
Largest Load	= <u>24,000</u> VA		
Total	= <u>24,000</u> VA	<u>24,000</u> VA	

2. GENERAL LIGHTING: *220.82(B)(1)*

NEUTRAL

<u>5,000</u> sq. ft. x 3 VA per sq. ft. = <u>15,000</u> VA <u>15,000</u> VA

3. SMALL APPLIANCE & LAUNDRY LOADS: *220.82(B)(2)*

1,500 VA x __4__ circuits = <u>6,000</u> VA <u>6,000</u> VA

4. FIXED APPLIANCES & MOTORS: *220.82(B)(3)&(4)*

Dishwasher	=	<u>1,250</u> VA		<u>1,250</u> VA
Disposal	=	<u>1,656</u> VA		<u>1,656</u> VA
Compactor	=	<u>1,176</u> VA		<u>1,176</u> VA
Water heater	=	<u>6,000</u> VA		<u>6,000</u> VA
Range	=	<u>12,000</u> VA	@ 70%	<u>8,400</u> VA
Cooktop	=	<u>-0-</u> VA	@ 70%	<u>-0-</u> VA
Oven	=	<u>-0-</u> VA	@ 70%	<u>-0-</u> VA
Dryer	=	<u>6,000</u> VA	@ 70%	<u>4,200</u> VA
Attic fan	=	<u>1,176</u> VA		<u>1,176</u> VA
Microwave	=	<u>1,250</u> VA		<u>1,250</u> VA
_____	=	_____ VA		_____ VA
	Total =	<u>51,508</u> VA		_____ VA

5. APPLY DEMAND FACTORS: *220.82(B)*

First 10,000 VA x 100% =	10,000 VA		
Remaining <u>41,508</u> VA x 40% =	<u>16,603</u> VA		
Total =	<u>26,603</u> VA	<u>26,603</u> VA	<u>46,108</u> VA

6. TOTAL

50,603 VA 46,108 VA

LINE I = <u>50,603 VA</u> = __211__ amperes
 240 volts

NEUTRAL I = <u>46,108 VA</u> = __192__ amperes
 240 volts

Conductors are to be sized per Table 310.15(B)(7) if 120/240 volts, single-phase, or Table 310.15(B)(16) if 208Y/120 volts, three-phase, or the load is greater than 400 amperes.

UNIT 8
SELF-ASSESSMENT QUIZ

1. The ungrounded service-entrance conductors for a one-family dwelling are required to have an ampacity of at LEAST _____.

 A. 60 amperes
 B. 100 amperes
 C. 75 amperes
 D. 150 amperes

2. When calculating the general lighting and general-use receptacle load for a dwelling unit, the _____ dimension of the dwelling is to be used.

 I. outside
 II. inside

 A. I only
 B. II only
 C. either I or II
 D. neither I or II

3. When sizing service-entrance conductors for a dwelling, a unit load of _____ shall be used for calculating the general lighting and general-use receptacle load.

 A. 3 VA per cubic foot
 B. 3.5 VA per square foot
 C. 3 VA per square foot
 D. 4 VA per square foot

4. What is the MINIMUM size copper SE cable with type THHW insulation that may be used as ungrounded service-entrance conductors for a 150-ampere rated 120/240-volt, 3-wire, single-phase residential service?

 A. 1/0 AWG
 B. 1 AWG
 C. 2 AWG
 D. 3 AWG

5. When calculating the total load for a one-family dwelling, what is the MINIMUM load, in VA, that must be added for the two (2), required small appliance branch circuits?

A. 1,200 VA
B. 2,400 VA
C. 1,500 VA
D. 3,000 VA

6. It shall be permissible to apply a demand factor of _____ to the nameplate rating load of four (4) or more fastened-in-place appliances when using the general method of calculation for dwellings.

 A. 75 percent
 B. 60 percent
 C. 50 percent
 D. 25 percent

7. When calculating the service for a dwelling, electric clothes dryers are to be calculated at a MINIMUM of _____ watts (VA) or the nameplate rating, which ever is larger.

 A. 3,000
 B. 4,500
 C. 5,000
 D. 6,000

8. A demand factor of _____ may be applied to the neutral loads of 240-volt, single-phase, electric clothes dryers and cooking equipment when doing residential service calculations.

 A. 75 percent
 B. 70 percent
 C. 60 percent
 D. 50 percent

9. Using the standard method of calculation for a single-family dwelling, determine the demand load, in VA, on the ungrounded service-entrance conductors when the residence has the following fixed appliances installed:

 Water heater - 4.5 kW – 240 volts
 Dishwasher - 1,250 VA – 120 volts
 Garbage disposer - 3/4 HP – 120 volts
 Trash compactor - 1/2 HP – 120 volts

Attic fan - 1/3 HP – 120 volts

 A. 7,085 VA
 B. 7,460 VA
 C. 9,446 VA
 D. 6,612 VA

10. When using the standard method of calculation for a one-family dwelling unit, determine the neutral demand load, in VA, for a 9 kW, 240-volt, single-phase electric range.

 A. 6,300 VA
 B. 6,750 VA
 C. 8,400 VA
 D. 5,600 VA

11. Determine the demand, in VA, on the ungrounded (line) service-entrance conductors for a 30 ampere, 240-volt, single-phase electric clothes dryer when using the standard method of calculation for a one-family dwelling.

 A. 5,000 VA
 B. 5,040 VA
 C. 7,200 VA
 D. 3,500 VA

12. What is the total connected load, in VA, for the general lighting and general-use receptacles, of a one-family residence having 35 feet by 75 feet of livable space?

 A. 2,625 VA
 B. 5,250 VA
 C. 9,188 VA
 D. 7,875 VA

13. When applying the standard calculation method for dwelling units, a demand load of _____ is to be applied to the first 3,000 VA of the general lighting and receptacle loads.

 A. 100 percent
 B. 80 percent
 C. 70 percent
 D. 35 percent

14. A single-family dwelling to be built will have 2,500 square feet of livable space, a 500 square foot garage, a 200 square foot open porch, a 1,250 square foot unfinished basement (adaptable for future use), three (3) small-appliance branch circuits and one (1) branch circuit for the laundry room. Determine the demand load, in VA, on the ungrounded (line) service-entrance conductors for the general lighting and receptacle loads using the standard method of calculation for a one-family dwelling.

 A. 12,000 VA
 B. 6,150 VA
 C. 17,250 VA
 D. 7,988 VA

15. When applying the optional method of calculation for a one-family dwelling, the air conditioning load, if used, is assessed at _____ of the nameplate rating(s) of the unit(s).

 A. 100 percent
 B. 125 percent
 C. 80 percent
 D. 70 percent

16. When applying the optional method of calculation for a one-family dwelling, when the electric space equipment load is used, and if there are less than four (4) separately controlled units, the load is assessed at _____ of the nameplate rating(s) of the unit(s).

 A. 100 percent
 B. 80 percent
 C. 70 percent
 D. 65 percent

17. What is the demand load, in VA, on the ungrounded (line) service-entrance conductors for one (1) 10 kW electric range when using the optional method of calculation for a one-family residence?

 A. 8,000 VA
 B. 9,000 VA
 C. 10,000 VA
 D. 12,000 VA

18. Refer to the previous question. Determine the demand load, in VA, on the neutral (ungrounded) service-entrance conductor for the range.

 A. 10,000 VA

B. 7,000 VA
C. 8,000 VA
D. 5,000 VA

19. When using the optional method of calculation for a one-family dwelling, the first _____ of the "general loads" shall be calculated at not less than 100 percent plus 40 percent of the remainder.

 A. 3,000 VA
 B. 1,000 VA
 C. 8 kVA
 D. 10 kVA

20. A one-family dwelling unit to be constructed will have the following total connected general loads:

 - General lighting and receptacles = 17,500 VA
 - Small appliance and laundry circuits = 7,500 VA
 - Fastened in place appliances and motors = 40,500 VA

 What is the demand load, in VA, on the ungrounded service-entrance conductors for the above referenced loads? (Use the optional method of calculation.)

 A. 65,500 VA
 B. 32,200 VA
 C. 26,200 VA
 D. 62,500 VA

NOTES

PRACTICAL CALCULATIONS FOR ELECTRICIANS
UNIT 8
SELF-ASSESSMENT QUIZ
ANSWER KEY

ANSWER		REFERENCE	NEC PG. #
1.	B	230.42(B)	pg. 87
		230.79(C)	pg. 90
2.	A	220.12	pg. 70
3.	C	Table 220.12	pg. 71
4.	B	310.15(B)(7)(1)	pg. 149
		Table 310.15(B)(16)	pg. 150

150 amperes x 83% = 124.5 amperes
Size 1 AWG THHW copper conductors rated 75ºC with an ampacity of 130 amperes should be selected from Table 310.15(B)(16).

5.	D	220.52(A)	pg. 73
		210.11(C)(1)	pg. 60

1,500 VA x 2 circuits = 3,000 VA

6.	A	220.53	pg. 73
7.	C	220.54	pg. 73
8.	B	220.61(B)(1)	pg. 75
9.	A	220.53	pg. 73
		Table 430.248	pg. 321

water heater	- 4.5 kW x 1,000	= 4,500 VA
dishwasher	- 1,250 VA	= 1,250 VA
garbage disposal	- 3/4 HP – 13.8 amps x 120 volts	= 1,656 VA
trash compactor	- 1/2 HP – 9.8 amps x 120 volts	= 1,176 VA
attic fan	- 1/3 HP – 7.2 amps x 120 volts	= 864 VA
	Connected Load	= 9,446 VA
	(Demand)	x 75%
	Demand Load	= 7,085 VA

10. D Table 220.55 pg. 74
 220.61(B)(1) pg. 75

 8kW (Table 220.55) x 70% = 5,600 VA

11. C 1 Ø Power Formula
 220.54 pg. 73

 P = I x E = 30 amperes x 240 volts = 7,200 VA

12. D Table 220.12 pg. 71

 35 feet x 75 feet = 2,625 square feet
 2,625 square feet x 3 VA = 7,875 VA

13. A Table 220.42 pg. 72

14. D 220.12 pg. 70
 Table 220.12 pg. 71
 220.52(A)&(B) pg. 73
 Table 220.42 pg. 72

 2,500 sq. ft. + 1,250 sq. ft. = 3,750 sq. ft.

 3,750 sq. ft. x 3 VA = 11,250 VA
 3 small appl. circuits x 1,500 VA = 4,500 VA
 1 laundry circuit x 1,500 VA = <u>1,500 VA</u>
 TOTAL CONNECTED LOAD = 17,250 VA

 First, 3,000 VA at 100% = 3,000 VA
 remainder (17,250 – 3,000) 14,250 VA at 35% = <u>4,988 VA</u>
 7,988 VA

15. A 220.82(C)(1) pg. 75

16. D 220.82(C)(4) pg. 75

17. C 220.82(B)(3)b. pg. 75

 10 kW x 1,000 = 10,000 VA

18. B 220.82(A) pg. 75
 220.61(B)(1) pg. 75

 10,000 VA x 70% = 7,000 VA

19. D 220.82(B) pg. 75

20. B 220.82(B) pg. 75

- General lighting and receptacles = 17,500 VA
- Small appliance and laundry circuits = 7,500 VA
- Fastened in place appliances and motors = 40,500 VA
- TOTAL GENERAL LOAD = 65,500 VA

1st 10,000 VA @ 100% = 10,000 VA
Remainder (total – 10,000) = 55,500 VA @ 40% = 22,200 VA
DEMAND LOAD = 32,200 VA

UNIT 9

MULTI-FAMILY DWELLING SERVICE CALCULATIONS

After successfully completing this unit of study, the student will have the ability to properly size services for multiple-family dwelling units.

UNIT 9

MULTI-FAMILY DWELLING SERVICE CALCULATIONS

RELATED INFORMATION:

☐ A multi-family dwelling unit is considered a building containing three or more dwelling units; examples are apartments, condominiums, and town houses.

☐ Many similarities exist between multi-family dwelling service calculations and one-family dwelling service calculations. Both can be calculated using the **standard (general) method** as well as the **optional method**. I suggest you become familiar with one-family dwelling calculations before attempting multi-family dwelling calculations.

☐ For multi-family dwellings the service-entrance conductor sizes are to be selected from **Table 310.15(B)(16).** The neutral load is permitted to be determined per **Section 220.61**. The rule in **Section 310.15(B)(7)(a)** that permits a reduction in the ampacity of service conductors, is reserved for one-family dwellings and individual units in a two-family or multifamily dwelling.

☐ **Annex D** of the NEC® shows examples of both calculation methods and the steps and procedures to be used. We will follow these examples and steps to learn to properly size services for multi-family dwellings. First, we will look at the general (standard) method of calculation. You will find a completed example of the general (standard) method of calculation on page 145 of this text.

General Calculation Method

Step 1 - Determine the total connected load, in VA, of the general lighting and general-use receptacles. Simply multiply the number of units by the square footage of one unit, when they are all the same size, and multiply by **3 VA** per Table **220.12**. Do not include open porches, garages, and enclosed areas not adaptable for future use. **[220.12]**

EXAMPLE - What is the total connected load, in VA, for the general lighting and general-use receptacles for a six (6) unit multi-family dwelling, when each apartment is 750 square feet?

 A. 2,250 VA
 B. 4,500 VA

C. 13,500 VA
D. 15,300 VA

ANSWER – (C) 13,500 VA

First, find the area, in square feet, of the habitable spaces.

6 units X 750 sq.ft. = 4,500 sq.ft.

Next, multiply by 3 VA **[Table 220.12]**

4,500 sq. ft. X 3 VA = 13,500 VA

Step 2 - Find the total connected load of the small appliance and laundry branch circuits. A minimum of **two (2)** small appliance branch circuits are required per unit **[210.11(C)(1)]** and they shall be calculated at **1,500 VA** per circuit. **[220.52(A)]**. A minimum of **one (1)** branch circuit calculated at **1,500 VA** is required to supply the laundry of each unit having a laundry. **[210.11(C)(2)] & [220.52(B)]**. When the multi-family dwelling unit has a common laundry facility provided on the premises and available to all building occupants, this is considered a "house load" and the laundry load can be omitted in this step.

EXAMPLE - What is the minimum total connected load, in VA, for the small appliance and laundry loads for a six (6) unit multi-family dwelling, having laundry facilities in each unit?

A. 27,000 VA
B. 18,000 VA
C. 12,000 VA
D. 9,000 VA

ANSWER - (A) 27,000 VA

2 small appl. circuits @ 1,500 VA X 6 units = 18,000 VA
1 laundry circuit @ 1,500 VA X 6 units = 9,000 VA
 Total = 27,000 VA

Step 3 - Apply the demand factors specified in **Table 220.42** for the general purpose lighting and receptacle loads, plus the loads required for the small appliance and laundry branch circuits. **[220.42]**

EXAMPLE - What is the demand load, in VA, for a multi-family dwelling unit having a total connected general-purpose receptacle and lighting load of 13,500 VA and a total connected small appliance and laundry branch

circuit load of 27,000 VA? (Use general method of calculation.)

> A. 13,125 VA
> B. 16,125 VA
> C. 37,500 VA
> D. 40,500 VA

ANSWER - (B) 16,125 VA

> General purpose lighting & receptacles = 13,500 VA
> Laundry & small appliances = 27,000 VA
> Total Connected Load = 40,500 VA
>
> 1st 3,000 VA @ 100% **[Table 220.42]** = 3,000 VA
> 40,500 VA – 3,000 VA = 37,500 VA
> 37,500 VA (Remainder) X 35% = 13,125 VA
> Demand Load = 16,125 VA

Step 4 - Apply a demand factor of **75%** of the nameplate rating of **four (4)** or more fastened in place appliances. Examples include, water heater, dishwasher, trash compactor, garbage disposal, etc. **[220.53]** Note that this rule **does not apply** for electric ranges, clothes dryers, space heating or air conditioning equipment.

EXAMPLE - Using the standard (general) method of calculation for dwellings, determine the demand load, in VA, of a six (6) unit multi-family dwelling unit having the following fixed appliances installed in each unit:

> dishwasher - 1,100 VA
> water heater - 3,500 VA
> garbage disposal - 850 VA

> A. 32,700 VA
> B. 23,700 VA
> C. 22,890 VA
> D. 24,525 VA

ANSWER - (D) 24,525 VA

> Dishwasher - 1,100 VA X 6 = 6,600 VA
> Water Heater - 3,500 VA X 6 = 21,000 VA
> Garbage Disposal - 850 VA X 6 = 5,100 VA
> Total Connected Load = 32,700 VA
> X 75% (demand)
> Demand Load = 24,525 VA

Step 5 - Determine the electric clothes dryer demand load, using **5,000 watts** (volt amperes) as the minimum or the nameplate rating, **whichever is larger**, for each dryer served. **[220.54]** Apply the demand factors listed in **Table 220.54**. A further demand of **70 percent** of this value may be applied to the **neutral** (grounded) conductor. **[220.61(B)(1)]**

EXAMPLE - When the standard (general) method of calculation for dwellings is applied, where a six (6) unit multifamily apartment building having a 3.5 kW electric clothes dryer in each unit, the demand load, in VA, on the ungrounded (line) service-entrance conductors is _____.

 A. 15,750 VA
 B. 21,000 VA
 C. 22,500 VA
 D. 30,000 VA

ANSWER - (C) 22,500 VA

 5,000 VA (minimum) x 6 = 30,000 VA
 Demand **[Table 220.54]** x 75 %
 22,500 VA

STEP 6 - Determine the demand load for the cooking appliances in accordance with **Table 220.55 [220.55]**. This is explained in **Unit 3** of this book. A further demand of **70 percent** of the demand load on the ungrounded conductors may be applied to the **neutral** (grounded) conductor. **[220.61(B)(1)]**

EXAMPLE - An 8 kW electric range installed in each unit of a six (6) unit multifamily apartment building will have a demand load of _____ on the ungrounded (line) service-entrance conductors and demand load of _____ on the grounded (neutral) conductor, when the standard method of calculation for dwellings is applied.

 A. 43,000 VA – 30,100 VA
 B. 20,640 VA – 14,448 VA
 C. 48,000 VA – 33,600 VA
 D. 43,000 VA – 32,250 VA

ANSWER - (B) 20,640 VA – 14,448 VA

 ungrounded conductor – **[Table 220.55, Column B.]**

8 kW x 6 units x 43% = 20.64 kW
20.64 kW x 1,000 = 20,640 VA

grounded conductor – **[220.61(B)(1)]**

20,640 VA x 70% = 14,448 VA

STEP 7 - Determine the demand load for the fixed electric space heating or air
 conditioning load; the smaller of the two is permitted to be omitted,
 because these loads are considered noncoincident loads, meaning they are
unlikely to be used at the same time. **[220.60]**

EXAMPLE - A six (6) unit multifamily apartment building to be constructed will
 have a 3 kW (kVA), 240-volt, single-phase, fixed electric space
 heating unit and a 17 ampere, single-phase, 240-volt, air conditioning
 unit, installed in each dwelling unit. When using the standard
 (general) method of calculation for dwellings, what is the demand, in
 VA, that should be applied to the ungrounded (line) service-entrance
 conductors?

 A. 24,480 VA
 B. 18,000 VA
 C. 7,080 VA
 D. 42,840 VA

ANSWER - (A) 24,480 VA

 First compare the two loads.
 A/C unit – P = I x E P= 17 amps x 240 volts = 4,080 VA
 Heating unit – 3 kW x 1,000 = 3,000 VA

 4,080 VA (larger) x 6 units = 24,480 VA

STEP 8 - Add the values determined from steps 3 – 7 together to find the
 required volt ampere rating of the service. Next, apply the current
 formula **(I = P ÷ E)**, and size the ungrounded service-entrance
 conductors using **Table 310.15(B)(16)**.

EXAMPLE - After all demand factors have been taken into consideration for a
 multifamily dwelling unit, a demand load of 108,270 VA is determined
 for the ungrounded service-entrance conductors. What minimum size
 THWN copper ungrounded conductors are required for the dwelling
 service? (120/240-volt, 3-wire, single-phase electrical system.)

 A. 400 kcmil
 B. 500 kcmil

C. 600 kcmil
D. 700 kcmil

ANSWER - (D) 700 kcmil

First, find the load in amperes.

$I = P \div E$

$I = \dfrac{108,270 \text{ VA}}{240 \text{ volts}} = 451.125$

Table 310.15(B)(16) is to be used for sizing the conductors. Size 700 kcmil conductors with an ampacity of 460 amperes should be selected.

STANDARD CALCULATION: MULTI-FAMILY DWELLING

1. GENERAL LIGHTING & RECEPTACLES: *Table 220.12*
_____ sq. ft. x 3 VA = _____ VA

2. SMALL APPLIANCES *220.52(A)* & LAUNDRY *220.52(B)*
1,500 VA x _____ circuits = _____ VA

3. APPLY DEMAND FACTORS: *Table 220.42*
Total of gen. ltg. & small appl. _____ VA
First 3000 VA x 100% = 3,000 VA
Next _____ VA x 35% = _____ VA **LINE** **NEUTRAL**
Remaining _____ VA x 25% = _____ VA
Total = _____ VA _____ VA _____VA

4. FIXED APPLIANCES: *220.53*
Water Heater _____ VA x _____ units = _____ VA
Disposal _____ VA x _____ units = _____ VA
Compactor _____ VA x _____ units = _____ VA
Dishwasher _____ VA x _____ units = _____ VA
_____ _____ VA x _____ units = _____ VA
_____ _____ VA x _____ units = _____ VA
_____ _____ VA x _____ units = _____ VA

Total = (x 75% if 4 or more) _____ VA = _____ VA _____ VA

5. CLOTHES DRYERS: *220.54*; *Table 220.54*
_____ VA x _____ units = _____VA x _____% _____ VA x 70%= _____ VA

6. COOKING EQUIPMENT: *Table 220.54 & Notes*
Col A _____ VA x _____units x _____ % = _____ VA
Col B _____ VA x _____units x _____ % = _____ VA
Col C _____ VA x _____units = _____ VA
Total = _____ VA _____ VA x 70%= _____ VA

7. HEATING or A/C at 100% (largest): *220.60*
Heating unit = _____ VA x _____ units = _____ VA
A/C unit = _____ VA x _____ units = _____ VA
Heat pump = _____ VA x _____ units = _____ VA
Largest Load = _____ VA

8. TOTAL _____ VA _____ VA
Line I = _____ VA = _____ amperes
 240 volts
Neutral I = _____ VA = _____ amperes
 240 volts

Conductors are to be sized per Table 310.15(B)(16).

STANDARD CALCULATION: MULTI-FAMILY DWELLING

1. GENERAL LIGHTING & RECEPTACLES: *Table 220.12*

 <u>4,500</u> sq. ft. x 3 VA = <u>13,500</u> VA

2. SMALL APPLIANCES *220.52(A)* **& LAUNDRY** *220.52(B)*

 1,500 VA x <u>18</u> circuits = <u>27,000</u> VA

3. APPLY DEMAND FACTORS: *Table 220.42*

				LINE	NEUTRAL
Total of gen. ltg. & small appl.	<u>40,500</u> VA				
First 3000 VA x 100%	=	3,000 VA			
Next <u>37,500</u> VA x 35%	=	<u>13,125</u> VA			
Remaining _____ VA x 25% =		_____ VA			
Total		<u>16,125</u> VA		<u>16,125</u> VA	<u>16,125</u> VA

4. FIXED APPLIANCES: *220.53*

 Water Heater <u>3,500</u> VA x <u>6</u> units = <u>21,000</u> VA
 Disposal <u>850</u> VA x <u>6</u> units = <u>5,100</u> VA
 Compactor _____ VA x _____ units = _____ VA
 Dishwasher <u>1,100</u> VA x <u>6</u> units = <u>6,600</u> VA
 _____ _____ VA x _____ units = _____ VA
 _____ _____ VA x _____ units = _____ VA
 _____ _____ VA x _____ units = _____ VA

 Total (x 75% if 4 or more) <u>32,700</u> VA = <u>24,525</u> VA <u>24,525</u> VA

5. CLOTHES DRYERS: *220.54*; *Table 220.54*

 <u>5,000</u> VA x <u>6</u> units =<u>30,000</u>VA x <u>75</u> % <u>22,500</u> VA x 70% =<u>15,750</u> VA

6. COOKING EQUIPMENT: *Table 220.54* & Notes

 Col A _____ VA x _____units x _____% =_____ VA
 Col B <u>8,000</u> VA x <u>6</u> units x <u>43</u> % = <u>20,640</u> VA
 Col C _____VA x _____units = _____ VA
 Total = <u>20,640</u> VA <u>20,640</u> VA x 70% =<u>14,448</u> VA

7. HEATING or A/C at 100% (largest): *220.60*

 Heating unit = <u>3,000</u> VA x _____units =_____ VA
 A/C unit = <u>4,080</u> VA x <u>6</u> units = <u>24,480</u> VA
 Heat pump = _____ VA x _____ units =_____ VA
 Largest Load = <u>24,480</u> VA

8. TOTAL <u>108,270</u> VA <u>70,848</u> VA

$$\text{Line} \quad I = \frac{108{,}270 \text{ VA}}{240 \text{ volts}} = 451 \text{ amperes}$$

220.61(B)(2)

$$\text{Neutral} \quad I = \frac{70{,}848 \text{ VA}}{240 \text{ volts}} = 295 \text{ amperes}$$

 – First 200 amps @ 100% = 200 amperes
 Next 95 amps @70% <u>= 67 amperes</u>
 TOTAL NEUTRAL = 267 amperes

Conductors are to be sized per Table 310.15(B)(16).

OPTIONAL CALCULATION METHOD

☐ When calculating the service size for multi-family dwellings, the **optional**

calculation method is commonly applied, because it is an easier and less complex calculation method than the general (standard) method; less steps are used and it results in a smaller service size. The optional method is specifically designed for dwelling units having an electrical load of greater than 100 amperes. **[220.82(A)]** You will find a completed example of this calculation method on page 152 of this text.

☐ In general, the optional calculation method for multifamily dwellings may be applied when all of the following conditions are met: **[220.84(A)]**

1. No dwelling unit is supplied by more than one feeder.

2. Each dwelling unit is equipped with electric cooking equipment.

3. Each dwelling unit is equipped with either electric space heating or air conditioning, or both.

☐ The following steps may be applied when using the optional calculation method for multifamily dwellings. Notice the first two steps are the same for both calculation methods.

STEP 1 - Determine the total connected load, in VA, of the general lighting and general-use receptacle. Simply multiply the number of units by the square footage of all units of the same size and multiply by 3 VA per square foot. **[220.84(C)(1)]** Do not include open porches, balconies, and garages.

EXAMPLE - What is the connected load, in VA, for the general lighting and general-use receptacles for an eight (8) unit multifamily dwelling, when each apartment has 840 square feet of livable space?

A. 20,160 VA
B. 10,080 VA
C. 16,020 VA
D. 6,720 VA

ANSWER - (A) 20,160 VA

First, find the total area in square feet.

8 units x 840 sq. ft. = 6,720 sq. ft.

Next, multiply by 3 VA **[220.84(C)(1)]**

6,720 sq. ft. x 3 VA = 20,160 VA

STEP 2 - Find the connected load of the small appliances and laundry branch
circuits. **[220.84(C)(2)]** Each unit is required to have at least
two (2) small appliance branch circuits, **[210.11(C)(1)]** and
one (1) laundry branch circuit, **[210.11(C)(2)]** and they shall be
calculated at **1,500** VA per circuit. **[220.52(A)&(B)]**

EXAMPLE - Determine the minimum connected load, in VA, for the small appliance
and laundry loads for an eight (8) unit multifamily apartment building
having a laundry facility in each unit.

 A. 24,000 VA
 B. 36,000 VA
 C. 42,000 VA
 D. 12,000 VA

ANSWER- (B) 36,000 VA

 2 small appl. circuits @ 1,500 VA x 8 units = 24,000 VA
 1 laundry circuit @ 1,500 va x 8 units = 12,000 VA
 TOTAL 36,000 VA

STEP 3 - Calculate the connected load, at the nameplate rating, of all fastened
in place appliances, such as electric ranges, cooktops, ovens, clothes,
dryers, dishwashers, garbage disposers, and water heaters.
[220.84(C)(3)]

EXAMPLE - An eight (8) unit multifamily apartment building is to have the
following fastened in place appliances installed in each unit.

water heater	– 3.6 kW	– 240 volts
electric range	– 8 kW	– 240 volts
dishwasher	– 1.1 kW	– 120 volts
garbage disposal	– 850 VA	– 120 volts
clothes dryer	– 3.5 kW	– 240 volts

Determine the total connected load, in VA, for the appliances.

A. 17,050 VA
B. 102,300 VA
C. 136,400 VA
D. 51,150 VA

ANSWER - (C) 136,400 VA

water heater	- 3,600 VA x 8 units = 28,800 VA
electric range	- 8,000 VA x 8 units = 64,000 VA
dishwasher	- 1,100 VA x 8 units = 8,800 VA
garbage disposal	- 850 VA x 8 units = 6,800 VA
clothes dryer	- 3,500 VA x 8 units = 28,000 VA
	TOTAL 136,400 VA

STEP 4 - Calculate the connected load of the larger of the air-conditioning or space heating equipment. Omit the smaller. **[220.84(C)(5)]**

EXAMPLE - An eight (8) unit multifamily apartment building to be constructed will have a 3.5 kW (kVA), 240 volt, single-phase, fixed electric space heating unit and a 17 ampere, single-phase, 240-volt air-conditioning unit installed in each dwelling unit. When applying the optional method of calculations for multifamily dwellings for services and feeders, what MINIMUM value, in VA, is permitted to be used?

A. 60,640 VA
B. 28,000 VA
C. 24,480 VA
D. 32,640 VA

ANSWER - (D) 32,640 VA

First, compare the two loads.
A/C unit – P = I x E P= 17 amps x 240 volts = 4,080 VA
Heating unit – 3.5 kW x 1,000 = 3,500 VA

4,080 (larger) x 8 units = 32,640 VA

STEP 5 - Add steps 1 through 4 to determine the total connected VA load of the dwelling units and apply the demand factors as per **Table 220.84**.

EXAMPLE - An eight (8) unit multifamily apartment building has the following total connected loads:

general lighting & receptacles	– 20,160 VA
small appliances & laundry circuits	– 36,000 VA
Fixed appliances	- 136,400 VA
A/C- heating equipment	– 32,640 VA

Use the optional method of calculation for multifamily dwellings, and determine the demand load, in VA, on the ungrounded service-entrance conductors.

A. 96,836 VA
B. 222,500 VA
C. 225,500 VA
D. 99,088 VA

ANSWER - (A) 93,836 VA

20,160 VA	
36,000 VA	
136,400 VA	
32,640 VA	
225,200 VA	(connected load)
x 43%	**Table 220.84**
96,836 VA	(demand load)

STEP 6 - Add the "house loads" at the nameplate rating of the equipment. When the multifamily dwelling has a common laundry facility provided on the premises and available to all building occupants, this is considered a commercial occupancy and dwelling demand factors are **not** to be applied. If there are no "house loads," this step is omitted.

STEP 7 - Add the values determined from steps 5 and 6 (if any) together to find the required volt ampere rating of the service. Next, apply the current formula **(I = P ÷ E)** and size the service-entrance conductors using **Table 310.15(B)(16)**. The neutral load is determined per **220.61**.

EXAMPLE - After all demand factors have been taken into consideration for a multifamily dwelling, a demand load of 96,836 VA is determined for the ungrounded service-entrance conductors. What minimum size THWN/THHN copper ungrounded conductors are required for the service? (120/240-volts, single-phase electrical system)

A. 500 kcmil

B. 600 kcmil
C. 700 kcmil
D. 750 kcmil

ANSWER - (B) 600 kcmil

First, find the load in amperes.

$I = P \div E$

$I = \dfrac{96,836 \text{ VA}}{240 \text{ volts}} = 403$ amperes

Select 75°C rated conductors from **Table 310.15(B)(16).**
Size 600 kcmil conductors with an ampacity of 420 amperes should be selected.

OPTIONAL CALCULATION: MULTI-FAMILY DWELLING

		Line	Neutral
1. GENERAL LIGHTING & RECEPTACLES: *220.84(C)(1)*			
_____ sq. ft. x 3 VA =		(___) VA	(_____) VA

2. SMALL APPLIANCES & LAUNDRY 220.84(C)(2)

	Line	Neutral
Small Appl. 1,500 VA x _____ circuits x _____ units=	_____ VA	_____ VA
Laundry 1,500 VA x _____ circuits x _____ units=	_____ VA	_____ VA
Total =	(_____) VA	(_____) VA

3. FIXED APPLIANCES: *220.84(C)(3)*

		Line	Neutral
Water Heater _____ VA x _____ units =		_____ VA	_____ VA
Disposal _____ VA x _____ units =		_____ VA	_____ VA
Compactor _____ VA x _____ units =		_____ VA	_____ VA
Dishwasher _____ VA x _____ units =		_____ VA	_____ VA
Range _____ VA x _____ units =	_____ VA x 70%	_____ VA	
Cooktop _____ VA x _____ units =	_____ VA x 70%	_____ VA	
Oven _____ VA x _____ units =	_____ VA x 70%	_____ VA	
Dryer _____ VA x _____ units =	_____ VA x 70%	_____ VA	
_____ _____ VA x _____ units =		_____ VA	_____ VA
_____ _____ VA x _____ units =		_____ VA	_____ VA
Total =		(_____) VA	(_____) VA

4. HEATING or A/C at 100% (largest): *220.84(C)(5)*

Heating unit = _____ VA x _____ units =_____ VA		
A/C unit = _____ VA x _____ units =_____ VA		
Heat pump = _____ VA x _____ units =_____ VA		
Largest Load = _____ VA x _____ units =_____ VA	(_____) VA	(_____) VA

5. APPLY DEMAND FACTORS: *Table 220.84 Total of steps 1 -4*

	Line	Neutral
LINE _____ VA x _____ % =	[_____] VA	
NEUTRAL _____ VA x _____ % =		[_____] VA

6. HOUSE LOADS: *220.84(B)*

		Line	Neutral
Lighting _____ VA		_____ VA	_____ VA
Receptacles _____ VA		_____ VA	_____ VA
Motors _____ VA		_____ VA	_____ VA
_____ _____ VA		_____ VA	_____ VA
_____ _____ VA		_____ VA	_____ VA
Total =		[____] VA	[____] VA

7. TOTAL of STEPS 5 & 6

	Line	Neutral
	_____ VA	_____ VA

Line I = _____ VA = _____ amperes
 240 volts

Neutral I = _____ VA = _____ amperes
 240 volts

Conductors are to be sized per Table 310.15(B)(16).

OPTIONAL CALCULATION: MULTI-FAMILY DWELLING

	Line	Neutral
1. GENERAL LIGHTING & RECEPTACLES: *220.84(C)(1)*		
6,720 sq. ft. x 3 VA =	(20,160) VA	(20,160) VA

2. SMALL APPLIANCES & LAUNDRY *220.84(C)(2)*

	Line	Neutral
Small Appl. 1,500 VA x __2__ circuits x __8__ units=	24,000 VA	24,000 VA
Laundry 1,500 VA x __1__ circuits x __8__ units=	12,000 VA	12,000 VA
Total =	(36,000) VA	(36,000) VA

3. FIXED APPLIANCES: *220.84(C)(3)*

		Line	Neutral
Water Heater	**3,600** VA x __8__ units =	28,800 VA	28,800 VA
Disposal	**850** VA x __8__ units =	6,800 VA	6,800 VA
Compactor	_____ VA x _____ units =	_____ VA	_____ VA
Dishwasher	**1,100** VA x __8__ units =	8,800 VA	8,800 VA
Range	**8,000** VA x __8__ units =	64,000 VA x 70%	44,800 VA
Cooktop	_____ VA x _____ units =	_____ VA x 70%	_____ VA
Oven	_____ VA x _____ units =	_____ VA x 70%	_____ VA
Dryer	**3,500** VA x __8__ units =	28,000 VA x 70%	19,600 VA
_____	_____ VA x _____ units =	_____ VA	_____ VA
_____	_____ VA x _____ units =	_____ VA	_____ VA
Total =		(136,400) VA	(108,800) VA

4. HEATING or A/C at 100% (largest): *220.84(C)(5)*

			Line	Neutral
Heating unit	= **3,500** VA x _____ units	= _____ VA		
A/C unit	= **4,080** VA x __8__ units	= 32,640 VA		
Heat pump	= _____ VA x _____ units	= _____ VA		
Largest Load	= **4,080** VA x __8__ units	= 32,640 VA	(32,640) VA	(0) VA

5. APPLY DEMAND FACTORS: *Table 220.84 Total of steps 1 -4*

		Line	Neutral
LINE	225,200 VA x **43** % =	[96,836] VA	
NEUTRAL	164,960 VA x **43** % =		[70,933] VA

6. HOUSE LOADS: *220.84(B)*

		Line	Neutral
Lighting	_____ VA	_____ VA	_____ VA
Receptacles	_____ VA	_____ VA	_____ VA
Motors	_____ VA	_____ VA	_____ VA
_____	_____ VA	_____ VA	_____ VA
_____	_____ VA	_____ VA	_____ VA
Total =		[_____] VA	[_____] VA

7. TOTAL of STEPS 5 & 6

96,836 VA	70,933 VA

Line I = **96,836** VA = **403** amperes
 240 volts **220.61(B)(2)**

Neutral I = **70,933** VA = **296** amperes – First 200 amps @100% = 200 amperes
 240 volts Next 96 amps @ 70% = 67 amperes
 TOTAL NEUTRAL = 267 amperes

Conductors are to be sized per Table 310.15(B)(16).

UNIT 9
SELF-ASSESSMENT QUIZ

1. When calculating the service-entrance conductors supplying multifamily dwellings, the actual conductor sizes are to be selected from Table _____ of the NEC®.

 A. 310.15(B)(7)
 B. 310.15(B)(16)
 C. 220.61
 D. 310.15(B)(2)(a)

2. Each unit of a multifamily dwelling is required to have at LEAST _____ small appliance branch circuit(s) rated at _____ each.

 A. one -1,500 VA
 B. one – 2,400 VA
 C. three – 1,500 VA
 D. two – 1,500 VA

3. When applying the general method of calculation for multifamily dwellings, a demand factor of _____ may be applied to the nameplate rating of four (4) or more fastened in place appliances.

 A. 75 percent
 B. 60 percent
 C. 80 percent
 D. 50 percent

4. When sizing feeder and service-entrance conductors for a multifamily dwelling and the general method of calculation is used, before demand factors are applied electric clothes dryers are to be calculated at a MINIMUM of _____.

 A. the nameplate rating of the dryer
 B. 5,000 watts each
 C. 4,000 watts each
 D. 3,500 watts each

5. Feeder or service-entrance conductors supplying household cooking equipment and electric clothes dryers shall be permitted to have an additional demand factor of _____ applied to the neutral (grounded) conductor after the initial demand factors have been applied to

the grounded conductors.

 A. 50 percent
 B. 60 percent
 C. 75 percent
 D. 70 percent

6. When sizing feeders and services for multifamily dwellings, that portion of the neutral (grounded) load that is in excess of 200 amperes an additional demand factor _____ of may be applied.

 A. 50 percent
 B. 60 percent
 C. 70 percent
 D. 75 percent

7. For sizing feeders and services, the optional calculation method is specifically designed for dwelling units having an electrical load of at LEAST greater than _____.

 A. 100 amperes
 B. 200 amperes
 C. 300 amperes
 D. 400 amperes

8. In general, when sizing feeders and services for multifamily dwellings, the optional calculation method may be applied when _____.

 I. no dwelling is supplied by more than one feeder.
 II. each dwelling is equipped with either electric space heating or air conditioning, or both.

 A. I only
 B. II only
 C. either I or II
 D. both I and II

9. When calculating services and/or feeders supplying multifamily dwellings, when determining the load to be used for the heating and air-conditioning equipment the _____ is required to be applied.

 A. air-conditioning load only
 B. heating load only
 C. sum of the two loads
 D. larger of the two

10. Determine the total area, in square feet of a multifamily apartment building having four (4) units of 900 sq. ft. each and six (6) units of 1,100 sq. ft. each.

 A. 9,800 sq. ft.
 B. 10,200 sq. ft.
 C. 10,000 sq. ft.
 D. 12,200 sq. ft.

11. Use the general method of calculation for multifamily dwellings and determine the general lighting, small appliance and laundry minimum demand load for an apartment building consisting of twenty (20) units, each having a living area of 840 sq. ft., when the laundry facilities are provided on the premises and available to all tenants.

 A. 50,400 VA
 B. 40,950 VA
 C. 110,400 VA
 D. 49,800 VA

12. In a 16 unit multifamily dwelling, each unit is provided with a garbage disposal (864 VA), a dishwasher (1,250 VA) and a water heater (3,600 VA). Apply the general (standard) method of calculation for dwellings, and determine the service demand load, in VA, for the fixed appliances.

 A. 91,424 VA
 B. 63,997 VA
 C. 68,568 VA
 D. 73,139 VA

13. Each unit in a 10 unit multifamily apartment building contains a 4 kW rated electric clothes dryer. Apply the general (standard) method of calculation and determine the demand load, in VA, on the ungrounded (line) service-entrance conductors.

 A. 37,500 VA
 B. 27,500 VA
 C. 25,000 VA
 D. 20,000 VA

14. In a 12 unit multifamily apartment building, six (6) units are provided with a 8 kW electric range in each unit and six (6) units are provided with a 9 kW Electric range in each unit. Apply the general (standard) method of calculations for dwellings and determine the demand load, in VA, on the ungrounded (line) service-entrance conductors.

 A. 27,000 VA
 B. 41,640 VA
 C. 32,640 VA
 D. 102,000 VA

15. If an apartment building, with cooking facilities provided in each dwelling unit, has a general lighting and general use receptacle, laundry and small appliance connected load of 200.2 kW, what is the demand load, in VA, on the ungrounded service-entrance conductors? (Apply the general (standard) method of calculation.)

 A. 64,000 VA
 B. 64,750 VA
 C. 65,300 VA
 D. 70,080 VA

16. Each unit of a 14 unit multifamily dwelling has a habitable area of 1,250 sq. ft. Using the optional method of calculation for multi-family dwellings, what is the demand load, in VA, that must be applied to the service-entrance conductors for the general lighting and general-use receptacles, laundry and small appliance circuits?

 A. 46,200 VA
 B. 37,800 VA
 C. 54,000 VA
 D. 115,500 VA

17. Using the optional calculation method for multifamily dwellings, determine the demand load, in VA, that must be applied to the ungrounded service- entrance conductors for a 14 unit apartment building having a 4 kW electric clothes dryer in each unit.

 A. 22,400 VA
 B. 28,000 VA
 C. 32,500 VA
 D. 56,000 VA

18. Using the optional calculation method for multifamily dwellings, determine the demand load, in VA, that must be applied to the neutral (grounded) service-entrance conductors for a 14 unit apartment building provided with a 8 kW, 240-volt, single-phase electric range in each unit.

 A. 112,000 VA
 B. 44,800 VA
 C. 35,840 VA
 D. 31,360 VA

19. A 16 unit multifamily apartment building has the following 240-volt, single-phase heating and air-conditioning equipment installed in each apartment.

 * A/C unit – 3 hp
 * Heating unit – 5 kW
 * Circulating Motor – ½ hp (common for both htg. & A/C.)

Use the optional calculation method for multi-family dwellings and determine the demand load, in VA, on the ungrounded service-entrance conductors for the above listed equipment.

A. 31,200 VA
B. 38,538 VA
C. 35,383 VA
D. 32,797 VA

20. What MINIMUM size THWN/THHN copper ungrounded service-entrance conductors are required for a multifamily dwelling unit provided with a 120/240-volt, single-phase service, when the building has a demand load of 90 kW on the service?

A. 400 kcmil
B. 500 kcmil
C. 600 kcmil
D. 700 kcmil

NOTES

PRACTICAL CALCULATIONS FOR ELECTRICIANS
UNIT 9
SELF-ASSESSMENT QUIZ
ANSWER KEY

ANSWER	REFERENCE	NEC® PG. #
1. B	310.15(B)(7)	pg. 149
	Table 310.15(B)(16)	pg. 150
2. D	210.11(C)(1)	pg. 60
	220.52(A)	pg. 73
3. A	220.53	pg. 73
4. B	220.54	pg. 73
5. D	220.61(B)(1)	pg. 75
6. C	220.61(B)(2)	pg. 75
7. A	220.82(A)	pg. 75
8. D	220.84(A)(1)&(3)	pg. 76
9. D	220.60	pg. 73
10. B	General Knowledge	

900 sq. ft. x 4 units = 3,600 sq. ft.
1,100 sq. ft. x 6 units = 6,600 sq. ft.
 Total = 10,200 sq. ft.

11. B	Table 220.12	pg. 71
	210.11(C)(1)	pg. 60
	220.52(A)	pg. 73

General Lighting – 840 sq. ft. x 20 units x 3 VA = 50,400 VA
Small appl. circuits – 15,000 VA x 2 x 20 units = 60,000 VA
Laundry Circuit = -0-
 Total Connected Load = 110,400 VA

Apply demand factors – Table 220.42
First 3,000 VA @ 100% = 3,000 VA
Remainder (110,400 – 3,000) 107,400 @ 35% = 37,590 VA
 Demand Load = 40,590 VA

12. C 220.53 pg. 73

Disposal – 846 VA x 16 units = 13,824 VA
Dishwasher – 1,250 VA x 16 units = 20,000 VA
Water Heater – 3,600 VA x 16 units = 57,600 VA
 91,424 VA
 (Demand Factor) x 75%
 68,568 VA

13. C 220.54 pg. 73
 Table 220.54 pg. 73

5,000 VA (MINIMUM) x 10 units = 50,000 VA
 (demand) x 50%
 25,000 VA

14. A Table 220.55 pg. 74

Col. B – 8,000 VA x 6 units = 48,000 VA x 43% = 20,640 VA
Col. C – 9,000 VA – demand for 6 ranges = 21,000 VA
 41,640 VA

*NOTE: Column C of Table 220.55 indicates a demand of 27 kW for twelve
ranges. The smaller value is permitted to be used instead of the higher value.

15. A Table 220.42 pg. 72

Connected Load = 200.2 kW x 1,000 = 200,200 VA

First 3,00 VA @ 100% = 3,000 VA
Next 117,000 VA @ 35% = 40,950 VA
Remainder (200.2 kW -120 kW) = 80,200 VA @ 25% = 20,050 VA
 Demand = 64,000 VA

16. A 220.84(A)(1)&(2) pg. 76
 210.11(C)(1)&(2) pg. 60
 220.84(C)(2) pg. 76
 Table 220.84 pg. 76

General lighting 1,250 sq. ft. x 3 VA x 14 units = 52,500 VA
Small appl. circuits 1,500 VA x 2 x 14 units = 42,000 VA
Laundry Circuits 1,500 VA x 1 x 14 units = 21,000 VA
 115,500 VA
 (demand) x 40%
 demand load = 46,200 VA

17. A 220.84(C)(3)c. pg. 76
 Table 220.84 pg. 76

 4,000 VA x 14 units = 56,000 VA
 (demand) x 40%
 22,400 VA

18. D 220.84(C)(3)b. pg. 76
 220.84(A)(3) pg. 76
 220.61(B)(1) pg. 75

 8,000 VA x 14 units = 112,000 VA (Connected load)
 x 40% [Table 220.84]
 44,800
 x 70% [220.61(B)(1)]
 31,360 VA (demand)

19. B 220.84(C)(5) pg. 76
 Table 430.248 pg. 321

 First, compare the two loads.

 A/C = 17 amperes x 240 volts = 4,080 VA
 Heat = 5,000 VA

 Circulating motor – 4.9 amperes x 240 volts = 1,176 VA

 Under this condition the heating load is the larger load, omit the smaller A/C load.

 Heating = 5,000 + 1,176 VA (cir. motor) = 6,176 VA
 x 16 units
 98,816 VA
 x 39%
 (demand load) 38,538 VA

20. B Single-phase current formula
 Table 310.15(B)(16) pg. 150

 I = P ÷ E I = 90 kW x 1,000 = 90,000 = 375 amperes
 240 volts 240

 *NOTE: Table 310.15(B)(16) indicates 75ºC rated size 500 kcmil conductors
 with an ampacity of 380 amperes should be selected.

UNIT 10

COMMERCIAL LOAD CALCULATIONS

Upon successfully completing this unit of study, the student will be familiar with the concept of properly sizing overcurrent protection, branch circuit, feeder, and service conductors for commercial occupancies.

UNIT 10

COMMERCIAL LOAD CALCULATIONS

RELATED INFORMATION:

☐ Examples of commercial occupancies are office buildings, banks, retail stores, restaurants, warehouses, laundries, mobile home and recreational vehicle (RV) parks, automobile dealerships, sporting facilities, motels, etc.

☐ The loads in commercial locations are diversified and are to be calculated based upon the type of occupancy, how the loads are to be used in the electrical system, and the requirements of the equipment to be supplied. A good example of a commercial occupancy with diverse loads would be a motel or hotel. The sleeping rooms are calculated much like residential occupancies but the lobby, hallways, meeting rooms, restaurant, and area lighting are considered commercial locations. Let's look at some of the requirements that apply to commercial occupancies.

☐ Most of the lighting for commercial locations is to be considered a **continuous load**. Examples of exceptions to this statement would be the sleeping rooms of hotels and motels, which will be addressed later in this unit, and temporary commercial storage facilities and warehouses. The definition of a **continuous load** is a load where the maximum current is expected to continue for **3 hours** or more. **[Article 100]**

☐ In general, branch circuit conductors shall have an allowable ampacity (current carrying capacity) of NOT less than **125%** of the **continuous load**, plus **100%** of the **non-continuous** load to be served. **[210.19(A)(1)(a)]**

EXAMPLE - A branch circuit conductor supplying a continuous load of 24 amperes, must have an ampacity of at least _____.

 A. 24 amperes
 B. 30 amperes
 C. 19 amperes
 D. 36 amperes

ANSWER - (B) 30 amperes

24 amperes x 125% = 30 amperes

☐ In general, overcurrent devices (fuses and circuit breakers) protecting branch circuits, shall have a rating of not less that **125%** of the **continuous load** to be served plus **100%** of the **non-continuous** load to be served. **[210.20(A)]** Another way to look at it is, fuses and circuit breakers protecting branch circuits are not permitted to be loaded more than **80%** of their rated value when protecting **continuous loads**.

EXAMPLE - When a 30 ampere rated circuit breaker is used to protect a branch circuit supplying a continuous load, the load shall not exceed_____.

 A. 30 amperes
 B. 38 amperes
 C. 24 amperes
 D. 36 amperes

ANSWER - (C) 24 amperes

30 amperes x 80% = 24 amperes

☐ If the overcurrent device is listed for **continuous operation**, it shall be permitted to have a rating of **100%** of the **continuous load(s)** to be supplied. **[210.20(A)EX.]** But, circuit breakers are **NOT** listed for continuous operation, unless they have a rating of at least **400 amperes** or more. The NEC® does not address this issue.

☐ This continuous load requirement also applies to feeders **[215.2(A)(1)]** & **[215.3]** and services. **[230.42(A)(1)&(2)]**

Lighting Loads

☐ In general, 15- or 20-ampere rated branch circuits are used to supply lighting loads. **[210.23(A)]**

☐ General lighting loads for specific occupancies shall be based on the unit load per square feet depending on the type of occupancy as shown on Table **220.12**, and calculated from the outside dimensions of the building. **[220.12]** This is a **MINIMUM** requirement.

☐ Most commercial occupancies now contain fluorescent and/or HID lighting systems. When the occupancies contain lighting systems of this category, the **larger** of either the area load of the VA per square foot of the facility, or the total

connected load of the ampere ratings of the ballast or transformers of the luminaries (lighting fixtures) shall be used to size branch circuit, feeder, and service-entrance conductors. **[220.18(B)]**

EXAMPLE - A retail department store having dimensions of 100 feet by 150 feet is to be constructed. The store will have three-hundred (300) fluorescent luminaires (lighting fixtures) installed for general lighting. Each luminaire will contain two (2), 120-volt ballasts that draw 0.75 amperes each. Determine the demand load, in VA, that must be applied to the service-entrance conductors for the general lighting.

A. 45,000 VA
B. 54,000 VA
C. 56,250 VA
D. 67,500 VA

ANSWER - (D) 67,500 VA

Compare the two methods and use the larger value.

Table 220.12
150 ft. x 100 ft. = 15,000 sq. ft.

15,000 sq. ft. x 3 VA = 45,000 VA
 (continuous load) x 125%
 56,250 VA

220.18(B)
300 (fixt.) x 2 (ballast) x 120 volts x .75 amps = 54,000 VA
 (continuous load) x 125%
 67,500 VA

☐ Show window lighting for retail stores is commonly calculated at 200 volt-amperes per linear foot of show window. **[220.43(A)]** Such lighting is usually considered a **continuous load** because it is normally operated continuously for three (3) hours or more. Multiply **200 VA** per linear foot times **125%** to determine the load in VA.

EXAMPLE - A retail store is to have 125 feet of show window lighting, which will be operated continuously during the business day. Determine the demand load in VA.

A. 31,250 VA
B. 25,000 VA
C. 28,125 VA
D. 12,500 VA

ANSWER - (A) 31,250 VA

200 VA x 125 ft. x 125% = 31,250 VA

☐ When calculating the number of branch circuits required for lighting systems or receptacles, you can use the following formula:

$$\text{Number of circuits} = \frac{\text{Load VA}}{\text{circuit VA}}$$

EXAMPLE - The total demand load for the show window lighting of a retail store is determined to be 31,250 VA. Determine the MINIMUM number of 120 volt, 20 ampere branch circuits required to supply the show window lighting.

 A. ten
 B. twelve
 C. thirteen
 D. none of these

ANSWER - (C) thirteen

$$\text{\# of circuits} = \frac{31,250 \text{ VA}}{120 \text{ volts x 20 amps}} = \frac{31,250 \text{ VA}}{2,400 \text{ VA}} = 13 \text{ circuits}$$

☐ In addition to the general lighting, many commercial occupancies, particularly retail stores, have track lighting mounted for display or accent lighting. Again, commercial lighting systems are usually considered as continuous use. For track lighting in non-dwelling occupancies a load of **150 volt-amperes** shall be included for every **two (2) feet** of track. **[220.43(B)]** Multiply **150 VA** per linear foot times **125%** and divide by **two (2)** to determine the load in VA.

EXAMPLE - A retail store is to have eighty (80) feet of accent track lighting installed and will be in use continuously during business hours. For the purpose of sizing branch-circuits, feeders and service-entrance conductors, determine the load in VA.

 A. 15,000 VA
 B. 10,000 VA
 C. 12,500 VA
 D. 7,500 VA

ANSWER - (D) 7,500 VA

150 VA x 80 ft. x 125% = 15,000 = 7,500 VA

2 2

☐ The general lighting and general-use receptacles for the guest rooms and suites of hotels and motels are permitted to be calculated by applying a demand load of **2 VA** per square foot **[Table 220.12]** and is permitted to be reduced by applying the demand factors as shown in **Table 220.42**. Even though this is a commercial occupancy, loads of this category are not considered as continuous use.

EXAMPLE - Determine the general lighting and general-use receptacle demand load, in VA, for the guest rooms of a twenty-four (24) unit motel. Each guest room has 600 square feet of living area.

 A. 14,400 VA
 B. 13,520 VA
 C. 21,600 VA
 D. 28,800 VA

ANSWER - (B) 13,520 VA

24 units x 600 x 2 VA **[Table 220.12]** = 28,800 VA

First 20,000 VA at 50% = 10,000 VA **[Table 220.42]**
8,800 VA at 40% = 3,520 VA
 Demand Load = 13,520 VA

Electric Sign Loads

☐ The NEC® requires each commercial occupancy with grade level access to pedestrians to be provided with at least one (1) outlet for an exterior electric sign or outline lighting system. The outlet(s) is/are to be supplied by a branch-circuit rated at least 20 amperes. **[600.5(A)]**

☐ The branch-circuits that supply electric signs with incandescent and fluorescent lighting are not to exceed 20 amperes. **[600.5(B)(1)]**

☐ When calculating feeder and service-entrance conductors, each electric sign branch-circuit is to be calculated at a MINIMUM of **1,200 VA. [220.14(F)]** This VA rating is to be multiplied by **125%**; for the purpose of calculations electric signs are to be considered continuous loads. **[600.5(B)]**

EXAMPLE - A motel to be constructed will have two (2) 20 ampere, 120-volt branch-circuits provided for the exterior electric signs. Determine the

minimum demand load, in VA, on the feeder and service-entrance conductors.

> A. 2,400 VA
> B. 3,000 VA
> C. 4,800 VA
> D. 6,000 VA

ANSWER - (B) 3,000 VA

1,200 VA x 2 (signs) x 125% = 3,000 VA

Receptacle Loads

☐ For non-dwelling occupancies each general-use receptacle outlet is to be calculated at **180 VA** for each single or duplex receptacle on one yoke or strap **[220.14(I)]**; receptacle loads are permitted to be made subject to the demand factors given in **Table 220.44** when calculating the demand loads on feeders and services. **[220.44]** General-use receptacle loads are generally not considered to be a continuous load.

Table 220.44 Demand Factors for Non-dwelling Receptacle Loads

Portion of Receptacle Load to Which Demand Factor Applies (Volt-Ampere)	Demand Factor (Percent)
First 10 kVA or less	100
Remainder over 10 kVA at	50

EXAMPLE – What is the service demand load, in VA, for one-hundred and fifty (150), 20 ampere, 120-volt general-use duplex receptacles installed in an office building?

> A. 27,000 VA
> B. 23,125 VA
> C. 24,250 VA
> D. 18,500 VA

ANSWER - (D) 18,500 VA

150 receptacles x 180 VA = 27,000 VA (connected load)

First 10 kVA at 100% = 10,000 VA

remainder (17,000 VA) at 50% = <u>8,500 VA</u>
Total = 18,500 VA

☐ When the exact number of general-use receptacle outlets to be installed in a bank or an office building has not yet been determined, **one (1) VA** per square foot of interior space is to be applied when calculating feeders or services. **[Table 220.12, Note B]** and **[220.14(K)]** When this condition occurs, the receptacle loads are **not** permitted to be made subject to the demand factors given in **Table 220.44. [220.44]**

EXAMPLE - A 20,000 square foot bank building is to be constructed and the exact number of general-use receptacles to be installed in unknown.
Determine the demand load, in VA, on the service-entrance conductors for the unknown receptacles.

 A. 20,000 VA
 B. 18,000 VA
 C. 36,000 VA
 D. 60,000 VA

ANSWER - (A) 20,000 VA

20,000 sq. ft. x 1 VA = 20,000 VA

☐ When calculating the service and/or feeder demand load for multioutlet assemblies installed in commercial, industrial and educational facilities, the calculation is to be based on the use of the supplied cord-connected equipment that is expected to be used at the same time. **[220.14(H)]** (1) Where the cord-connected equipment are **unlikely** to be used simultaneously, each **five (5) feet** or fraction thereof shall be considered as one (1) outlet of not less than **180 VA**. (2) Where the cord-connected equipment are **likely** to be used simultaneously each **one (1) foot** or fraction thereof shall be considered as one outlet of not less than **180 VA**.

☐ The demand factors shown on **Table 220.44** may also be applied to fixed multioutlet assemblies when located in non-dwelling occupancies. Multioutlet assembly receptacles are generally not to be considered a continuous load; if they are **continuous, multiply by 125%.**

EXAMPLE - What is the service demand load, in VA, for one-hundred (100), 20 ampere, 120-volt, general-use receptacles and one-hundred (100) feet of multioutlet assembly, installed in an office building, where the cord connected appliances are unlikely to be used simultaneously?

 A. 21,600 VA
 B. 15,800 VA
 C. 10,800 VA
 D. 8,100 VA

ANSWER - (B) 15,800 VA

 Receptacles – 180 VA x 100 = 18,000 VA
 Multioutlet assembly – 100 ft. / 5 = 20 x 180 VA = 3,600 VA
 connected load = 21,600 VA

 Apply demand factors **[Table 220.44]**

 First 10 kVA at 100% = 10,000 VA
 Remainder (11,600 VA) at 50% = 5,800 VA
 demand load = 15,800 VA

EXAMPLE - Refer to the previous example and consider the cord-connected
 appliances are to be used simultaneously and determine the demand
 load.

 A. 15,800 VA
 B. 36,000 VA
 C. 23,000 VA
 D. 18,000 VA

ANSWER - (C) 23,000 VA

 Receptacles – 180 VA x 100 = 18,000 VA
 Multioutlet assembly – 100 ft. x 180 VA = 18,000 VA
 Connected load = 36,000 VA

 First 10 kVA at 100% = 10,000 VA
 Remainder (26,000 VA) at 50% = 13,000 VA
 Demand Load = 23,000 VA

Air Conditioning Loads

 ☐ When sizing overcurrent protection, branch-circuit, feeder and service conductors
 for air-conditioning equipment, you will find many air-conditioning condensing
 units are sized according to **TONS** and not horsepower. The NEC® does not
 address this issue. A useful and practical method to convert **tons** to **VA** is to
 consider **one (1) ton** of air-conditioning condensing load equals **2,400 VA**. To
 find the load, in amperes, simply apply the current formula I = P ÷ E. Multiply
 2,400 VA times the tonage of the A/C unit and divide by the voltage. For the
 purpose of calculating loads in this text this is the method that will be used.

EXAMPLE - A 240-volt, single-phase, 3½ ton A/C condensing unit will draw_____
 of current.

 A. 30 amperes

B. 35 amperes
C. 40 amperes
D. 45 amperes

ANSWER - (B) 35 amperes

$$I = \frac{3.5 \times 2{,}400 \text{ VA}}{240 \text{ volts}} = \frac{8{,}400}{240} = 35 \text{ amperes}$$

☐ Branch-circuit conductors supplying a single air-conditioning condensing unit are required to have a current-carrying capacity (ampacity) of not less than **125 percent** of the rated-current of the air-conditioning unit supplied. **[440.32]**

EXAMPLE - Branch-circuit conductors supplying an air-conditioning condensing unit having a rated-current of 35 amperes, are required to have an ampacity of at LEAST _____.

A. 28 amperes
B. 35 amperes
C. 44 amperes
D. 53 amperes

ANSWER - (C) 44 amperes

35 amperes x 125% = 43.75 amperes

☐ A value of not less than **100%** of the rated-current of the air-conditioning equipment is to be applied to feeder and service equipment and conductors.

☐ Fuses and circuit breakers provided for the protection of air-conditioning equipment shall be capable of carrying the starting current of the motor. **[440.22(A)]** The overcurrent protection device is mandated to be sized between **175 percent** and no more than **225 percent** of the rated-current of the air-conditioning equipment.

EXAMPLE - A circuit breaker provided to protect an air-conditioning condensing unit with a rated current of 35 amperes is required to have a MAXIMUM ampere rating of no more than _____.

A. 60 amperes
B. 80 amperes
C. 75 amperes
D. 70 amperes

ANSWER - (D) 70 amperes

35 amperes x 225% = 78.75 amperes

*NOTE: Under this condition, you must go down to the next standard size circuit breaker, because you may not exceed **225%** of the rated-current of the A/C unit.

Electric Space-Heating Loads

◻ All fixed space heating equipment, including blower motors, shall be considered as **continuous load(s)**, when sizing branch-circuit conductors and overcurrent protection for the heating units. **[424.3(B)]** The branch-circuit conductors supplying electric space-heating equipment are required to have an ampacity of not less than **125 percent** of the current rating of the heating unit(s) to be served.**[210.19(A)(1)]** This rule does not apply when sizing feeders and/or services. The feeder and/or service demand load is calculated at **100 percent** of the total heating load. **[220.51]**

EXAMPLE - The branch-circuit conductors supplying a 240-volt, single-phase, 15 kW rated fixed electric space heater provided with a 10 ampere blower motor are required to have an ampacity of at LEAST _____.

 A. 63 amperes
 B. 78 amperes
 C. 91 amperes
 D. 109 amperes

ANSWER - (C) 91 amperes

First find the current rating of the heater.

$$I = P \div E \quad I = \frac{15 \text{ kW x 1,000}}{240 \text{ volts}} = 62.5 \text{ amperes}$$

 62.5 amperes (heater)
+10.0 amperes (blower)
 72.5 amperes x 125% = 91 amperes

EXAMPLE - The overcurrent protection device for the above referenced heating unit is required to have a standard rating of not less than _____.

 A. 75 amperes
 B. 80 amperes
 C. 90 amperes
 D. 100 amperes

ANSWER - (D) 100 amperes

The next standard size overcurrent device has a rating of 100 amperes. **[240.6(A)]**

EXAMPLE - Determine the service demand load, in VA, for an office building

that has three (3), 208-volt, three-phase, 10 kW fixed electric space heaters, provided with a 1,945 VA blower motor in each heating unit.

A. 35,835 VA
B. 44,794 VA
C. 53,585 VA
D. 55,583 VA

ANSWER - (A) 35,835 VA

10,000 VA + 1,945 VA = 11,945 x 3 units = 35,835 VA

☐ When determining the demand load on the service-entrance conductors for the fixed electric space heating or air-conditioning load, the smaller of the two loads is permitted to be omitted; because both loads are unlikely to be used at the same time. **[220.60]** Apply only the largest load(s) that will be used at one time for calculating the total load on feeder or service conductors.

EXAMPLE - A retail store is to have a ten (10) ton A/C unit and a thirty-five (35) kW electric heating unit installed. Both units are 240-volts, single-phase. Determine the demand load, in amperes on the service-entrance conductors for the A/C and heating equipment.

A. 100 amperes
B. 125 amperes
C. 146 amperes
D. 183 amperes

ANSWER - (C) 146 amperes

First compare the two loads.

A/C Unit
10 tons x 2,400 VA = 24,000 VA
$I = \dfrac{24,000 \text{ VA}}{240 \text{ volts}} = 100$ amperes

Heating Unit
$I = \dfrac{35 \text{ kW x } 1,000}{240 \text{ volts}} = \dfrac{35,000}{240} = 146$ amperes

*NOTE: The heating unit is the larger load therefore, the A/C unit is permitted to be omitted.

☐ Today, many buildings are provided with roof-mounted heating and cooling systems that are in one complete unit in order to save space. The cooling capacity usually range from 5 tons up to 200 tons. Examples of good applications for roof-mounted heating and cooling systems are schools, office buildings, retail stores, super markets and manufacturing facilities.

Kitchen Equipment

☐ For electric kitchen equipment in commercial occupancies the branch circuits and overcurrent protection are sized according to the nameplate rating on the appliance. When sizing feeder and service conductors the demand factors shown on **Table 220.56** may be applied. However, the feeder or service demand load is **not** permitted to be **less** than the sum of the **two (2) largest** kitchen equipment loads. **[220.56]**

EXAMPLE - A catering service is to have the following cooking related equipment
in the kitchen:

- water heater – 5.5 kW
- booster heater – 7.0 kW
- dishwasher – 2.0 kW
- sterilizer - 2.5 kW
- oven - 6.0 kW
- grill - 5.0 kW
- mixer - 3.0 kW
- freezer - 3.5 kW
- refrigerator - 2.5 kW

What is the demand load, in kW, on the service-entrance conductors
for the appliances?

A. 37.00 kW
B. 25.90 kW
C. 13.00 kW
D. 24.05 kW

ANSWER - (D) 24.05 kW

water heater	- 5.5 kW
booster heater	- 7.0 kW
dishwasher	- 2.0 kW
sterilizer	- 2.5 kW
oven	- 6.0 kW
grill	- 5.0 kW
mixer	- 3.0 kW
freezer	- 3.5 kW
refrigerator	- 2.5 kW
(connected load)	37 kW
(demand)	x 65 % **[Table 220.56]**
Demand Load	= 24.05 kW

Laundry Equipment

☐ The branch-circuit conductors and overcurrent protection for laundry equipment in
commercial occupancies are to be sized in accordance to the appliance
nameplate rating. The NEC® does not permit a demand factor to be applied to
service, feeder or branch-circuit conductors for commercial laundry equipment
therefore, the laundry equipment demand load is to be calculated at **100%.**

EXAMPLE - The laundry room of a multi-family dwelling will have the following
laundry equipment installed:

- two – clothes dryers - 7,000 VA each
- three – washing machines - 1,920 VA each
- three – washing machines - 1,500 VA each

What is the demand load, in VA, on the service and feeder conductors for the listed appliances?

A. 24,260 VA
B. 18,500 VA
C. 16,982 VA
D. 14,000 VA

ANSWER - (A) 24,260 VA

clothes dryers	– 2 x 7,000 VA =	14,000 VA
washing machine	– 3 x 1,920 VA =	5,760 VA
washing machine	– 3 x 1,500 VA =	4,500 VA
	TOTAL =	24,260 VA

Mobile Home and Manufactured Home Parks

☐ The distribution system to mobile home lots is required to be 120/240 volts, single-phase. **[550.30]** Because appliances, luminaries, and other equipment are installed in a mobile home when manufactured and are rated 120/240-volts single-phase; three-phase systems and systems of a different voltage would not be compatible to the loads to be supplied.

☐ Each mobile home lot is required to be calculated on the basis of the larger of (1) a minimum of not less than **16,000 VA** for each mobile home lot or (2) the calculated load of the largest typical mobile home the lot will accommodate. **[550.31]** However, for each mobile home to be served the service equipment is to be rated at least 100 amperes, **[550.32(C)]** and the mobile home lot feeder conductors shall have a current carrying capacity (ampacity) of not less than 100 amperes. **[550.33(B)]**

☐ When sizing service-entrance conductors for a mobile home park the demand factors, based on the number of mobile homes in the park, displayed in **Table 550.31** are permitted to be applied.

EXAMPLE - What is the MINIMUM demand load, in amperes, on the service conductors of a mobile home park consisting of fifteen (15) lots?

A. 250 amperes
B. 260 amperes
C. 400 amperes
D. 1,000 amperes

ANSWER - (B) 260 amperes

 15 lots x 16,000 VA (MINIMUM) = 240,000 VA
 demand = x .26 **[Tbl. 550.31]**
 demand load = 62,400 VA

$$I = P \div E$$
$$I = \frac{62,400 \text{ VA}}{240 \text{ volts}} = 260 \text{ amperes}$$

EXAMPLE - A twenty-five (25) lot mobile home park is to be constructed. Each lot in the park is capable of accommodating a mobile home with a rating of 24,000 VA. Determine the demand load, in amperes, on the park service conductors.

 A. 1,000 amperes
 B. 650 amperes
 C. 400 amperes
 D. 600 amperes

ANSWER - (D) 600 amperes

 25 lots x 24,000 VA = 600,000 VA
 x .24 **[Tbl.550.31]**
 Demand load = 144,000 VA

$$I = P \div E$$
$$I = \frac{144,000 \text{ VA}}{240 \text{ volts}} = 600 \text{ amperes}$$

Recreational Vehicle Parks

- For recreational vehicle parks the NEC® requires electrical equipment connected line-to-line shall have a voltage rating of 208-230 volts. **[551.40(A)]** Therefore, recreational vehicle parks are permitted to be provided with 120-volt, 120/240-volt, single-phase or 208Y/120-volt, three-phase electrical systems. Typically, most older recreational vehicle parks have 120/240-volt, single-phase distribution systems.

- When sizing service-entrance or feeder conductors for a recreational vehicle park, the demand factors, reflected in **Table 551.73(A)**, based on the number of sites in the park, are permitted to be applied.

- **Each RV site** supplied with electrical power is required to be provided with at least **one (1) 20 ampere**, 125-volt receptacle outlet. **[551.71(A)]** For the basis of calculation, 20 ampere, 120-volt sites are considered as **2,400 VA per site**. **[551.73(A)]**

- At least **20 percent** of existing and **40 percent** of new RV sites in the park supplied with electrical power are required to be provided with a **50 ampere**, 125/250-volt receptacle outlet. **[551.71(C)]** The 50 ampere sites are considered

as **12,000 VA** per site, for the basis of calculation. **[551.73(A)]** Where the RV site has more than one (1) receptacle outlet, the calculated load shall only be calculated for the highest rated receptacle.

EXAMPLE - When a newly constructed forty (40) site RV park supplies all the
RV sites with electrical power, the NEC® requires at LEAST _____ of
the sites to be provided with a 50 ampere, 125/250-volt receptacle.

 A. eight
 B. ten
 C. twelve
 D. sixteen

ANSWER- (D) sixteen

40 sites x 40% = 16 sites

☐ At least **70 percent** of all RV sites in the park supplied with electrical power are required to be provided with a **30-ampere**, 125-volt receptacle. **[551.71(B)]** For the basis of calculation 30-ampere, 125-volt, RV sites are considered as **3,600 VA** per site. **[551.73(A)]**

EXAMPLE - Refer to the previous example. How many sites in the RV park are
required to be provided with a 30-ampere, 125-volt receptacle outlet?

 A. eight
 B. twelve
 C. twenty-eight
 D. forty

ANSWER - (C) twenty-eight

40 sites x 70% = 28 sites

☐ Dedicated **tent sites** in a RV park that are provided with only 20 ampere, 125-volt receptacles are considered as **600 VA** per site, for the basis of calculation. Because these sites are not intended to accommodate recreational vehicles, the calculated load is permitted to be smaller. **[551.73(A)]**

☐ When determining the total load for a recreational vehicle park, you must take into consideration the loads required for the recreational buildings, swimming pools, stores, service buildings, etc. These amenities are to be considered commercial loads and are to be sized separately and then added to the value calculated for the RV sites, where they are all supplied by one service. **[551.73(B)**

☐ Typically, recreational vehicle parks are provided with one service and the RV sites are supplied from a common feeder through one or more sub-panel(s). The demand factors shown on **Table 551.73(A)** are to be applied when sizing RV site feeders and service-entrance conductors.

EXAMPLE - What is the feeder/service demand load, in amperes, for the RV sites
of a recreational vehicle park that has twenty (20) sites provided with 50
ampere 125/250-volt receptacles, fifteen (15) sites provided with
both 30 ampere and 20 ampere receptacles and five (5) RV sites
provided with 20 ampere, 125-volt receptacles? The electrical system
is 120/240-volts, single-phase.

 A. 392 amperes
 B. 553 amperes
 C. 441 amperes
 D. 535 amperes

ANSWER - (B) 553 amperes

50 ampere sites – 12,000 VA x 20 sites = 240,000 VA
30/20 ampere sites – 3,600 VA x 15 sites = 54,000 VA
20 ampere sites – 2,400 VA x 5 sites = 12,000 VA
 306,000 VA
Table 551.73(A) (demand) x .41
 Demand Load = 125,460 VA

$I = P \div E$
$I = \dfrac{125,460 \text{ VA}}{240 \text{ volts}} = 553 \text{ amperes}$

Electric Welders

☐ The NEC® provides rules governing two general types of electric welding
machines.
 1. <u>Arc welders</u>
 Non-motor generator – a transformer supplies current for an AC arc
welder.
 Motor generator – A generator or rectifier supplies current for DC
arc welder.
 2. <u>Resistance welders</u>, which are commonly referred to as "spot" welders
which derive their power from an AC power source.

☐ The ampacity of the supply conductors to individual arc welders is determined by
selecting the appropriate factor shown in **Table 630.11(A)** based on the type of
welding machine and the duty cycle of the welder. **[630.11(A)]** An arc welder
with a 60% duty cycle means the welding machine will be used approximately for
6 minutes out of every 10 minutes. The selected factor is then multiplied by the
primary current rating displayed on the welder nameplate to determine the
minimum current-carrying capacity (ampacity) of the circuit conductors. The
actual size of the conductors are selected from **Table 310.15(B)(16).**

EXAMPLE - The minimum ampacity of the branch-circuit conductors supplying a
transformer arc welder with a 60 percent duty cycle and a primary
current of 50 amperes indicated on the nameplate is _____.

 A. 40 amperes
 B. 44 amperes
 C. 39 amperes

D. 50 amperes

ANSWER - (C) 39 amperes

50 amperes x .78 (multiplier) = 39 amperes

☐ When a feeder supplies more than one arc welding machine the conductor ampacity rating is based on the sum of the current ratings of the individual arc welders determined by applying **Table 630.11(A)** and multiplying by **100 percent** of the **two** largest welders, plus **85 percent** of the **third** largest welder, plus **70 percent** of the **fourth** largest welder, plus **60 percent** of **all remaining** welders in the group. **[630.11(B)]**

EXAMPLE - A feeder at a school welding shop is to supply the following listed transformer arc welders all with a 50 percent duty cycle.

- two (2) 60 ampere primary current
- two (2) 50 ampere primary current
- two (2) 40 ampere primary current

The feeder is required to have an ampacity of at LEAST _____.

A. 213 amperes
B. 196 amperes
C. 182 amperes
D. 176 amperes

ANSWER - (D) 176 amperes

60 amperes x .71 = 43 x 100% = 43 amperes
60 amperes x .71 = 43 x 100% = 43 amperes
50 amperes x .71 = 36 x 85% = 31 amperes
50 amperes x .71 = 36 x 70% = 25 amperes
40 amperes x .71 = 28 x 60% = 17 amperes
40 amperes x .71 = 28 x 60% = <u>17 amperes</u>
 176 amperes

☐ The ampacity of the supply conductors for a resistance type welder, when the primary current and duty cycle are known, shall not be less than the product of the actual primary current when welding and the multiplication factors shown in **Table 630.31(A)(2).**

EXAMPLE - A resistance type (spot) welder with a duty cycle of 25 percent and with an actual primary current of 30 amperes is to be served. The conductors supplying the welder are required to have an ampacity of at LEAST _____.

A. 15 amperes
B. 20 amperes
C. 25 amperes
D. 30 amperes

ANSWER - (A) 15 amperes

30 amperes x .50 = 15 amperes

☐ When conductors supply two or more resistance type welding machines, the conductors ampacity rating is based on the sum of the primary current of the individual welders determined by applying **Table 630.31(A)(2)** and multiplying by 100% of the largest welder, plus 60 percent of the values obtained for all remaining welders in the group. **[630.31(B)]**

EXAMPLE - Three (3) spot welders, each having a primary current of 30 amperes and a duty cycle of 10 percent are to be supplied by a common branch circuit. The branch-circuit conductors are required to have an ampacity of at LEAST_____.

A. 15 amperes
B. 22 amperes
C. 66 amperes
D. 99 amperes

ANSWER - (B) 22 amperes

30 amperes x .32 = 10 amperes x 100% = 10 amperes
30 amperes x .32 = 10 amperes x 60% = 6 amperes
30 amperes x .32 = 10 amperes x 60% = 6 amperes
 22 amperes

Commercial Service and Feeder Sizing

☐ For the purpose of sizing the service for a commercial building, the following steps may be used to determine the demand load.

Step 1 Determine the lighting load. Include:
(1) the **larger** of the area load of the VA per square foot of the facility **[Table 220.12]** or the connected loads of the lighting fixtures **[220.18(B)]** and apply **Table 220.42 if applicable**,
(2) sign lighting, **[220.14(F)]**
(3) show windows, **[220.43(A)]**
(4) track lighting **[220.43(B)]**

Step 2 Calculate the receptacle load. Include:
(1) 180 VA per receptacle outlet **[220.14(I)]**
(2) fixed multi-outlet assemblies **[220.14(H)]** apply demand factors per **Table 220.44**

Step 3 Compare the air-conditioning loads or the space heating loads. Use the **larger** of the two loads at **100%**.

Step 4 Determine the kitchen equipment load. Apply **Table 220.56** for 3 or more units of kitchen equipment.

Step 5 Calculate the laundry equipment at **100%**

Step 6 Add any other miscellaneous loads not covered in the above steps. Examples: walk-in coolers, water heaters, frozen food display cases, welders, exhaust fans, motors, etc.

Step 7 Add the value determined from the above listed steps together to find the volt ampere rating of the service. Next, apply the current formula $(I = P \div E)$ and size the service-entrance conductors using 75°C conductors selected from **Table 310.15(B)(16)**.

EXAMPLE - A hair salon is 4,000 square feet; the service is 208Y/120-volts, three-phase. Determine the service demand load and the service conductor size for the hair salon which has the following equipment.

- 20 feet of show window lighting
- 150 feet of track lighting
- 120 feet of fixed multi-outlet assembly (appliances will be used simultaneously)
- 50 – 120-volt, 20 ampere duplex receptacles
- one – 12 ton A/C unit, 3-phase (gas heating)
- one – 5 kW cooktop, 208-volt, single-phase
- one – 4 kW oven, 208-volt, single-phase
- one – 1,200 VA, microwave oven
- one – 1,200 VA, refrigerator/freezer
- two – 1,800 VA, washing machines
- one – 5 kW, clothes dryer, 208-volt, single-phase
- one – electric sign circuit

SOLUTION -

LIGHTING

General lighting	– 4,000 sq. ft. x 3 VA x 125%	= 15,000 VA
Show Window	- 20 ft. x 200 VA x 125%	= 5,000 VA
Track Lighting	- 150 ft.÷2 x 150 VA x 125%	= 14,063 VA
Sign Circuits	- 1 x 1,200 VA x 125%	= 1,500 VA

RECEPTACLES

Multi-outlet Assembly	– 120 ft. x 180 VA	= 21,600 VA
Receptacles	- 50 x 180 VA	= 9,000 VA
		30,600 VA

Table 220.44

1st 10 kVA @ 100%	= 10,000 VA	
20,600 VA @50%	= 10,300 VA	
	20,300 VA	= 20, 300 VA

COMPARE A/C VERSUS HEATING

A/C – 12 ton x 2,400 VA per ton	= 28,800 VA	= 28,800 VA
HTG. – N/A	= N/A	

KITCHEN EQUIPMENT

Cooktop	- 5 kW	= 5,000 VA
Oven	- 4 kW	= 4,000 VA
Microwave	- 1,200 VA	= 1,200 VA
Refrigerator	- 1,200 VA	= 1,200 VA
		11,400 VA

Table 220.56 x .8

9,120 VA = 9,120 VA

LAUNDRY EQUIPMENT

Washing Machine	– 2 x 1,800 VA	= 3,600 VA
Clothes Dryer	- 1 x 5,000 VA	= 5,000 VA
		8,600 VA = 8,600 VA

DEMAND LOAD = 102,383 VA

$$I = \frac{102,383 \text{ VA}}{208 \times 1.732} = \frac{102,383 \text{ VA}}{368.25} = 284 \text{ amperes}$$

Size 300 kcmil copper 75ºC rated service-entrance conductors or size 500 kcmil aluminum 75ºC rated service-entrance conductors should be selected from **Table 310.15(B)(16).**

*NOTE – See page 182 of this text for an example of this calculation method using the following completed form.

COMMERCIAL CALCULATION

1. LIGHTING: *Table 220.12 or 220.18(B)*

General Lighting: _____ sq. ft. x _____ VA x 125% = _____ VA

220.18(B): _____ fixtures x _____ VA x 125% = _____ VA

Show Window: _____ ft. x 200 VA x 125% = _____ VA

Track Lighting: _____ ft. / 2 x 150 VA x 125% = _____ VA

Sign Ckts. _____ x 1,200 VA x 125% = _____ VA

Misc. Lighting: _____ VA

Total Lighting = (_____) VA [_____] VA

2. RECEPTACLES: 220.14(I) and/or 220.14(H)

Receptacles: 180 VA x _____ receptacles = _____ VA

Multi-outlet Assembly: 180 VA x _____ ft. = _____ VA

Total = (_____) VA

Table 220.44

First 10,000 VA x 100% = _____ VA

Remainder: _____ VA x 50% = _____ VA

Demand = (_____) VA [_____] VA

3. HEATING or A/C at 100% (largest):

Heating unit = _____ VA x _____ units = _____ VA

A/C unit = _____ VA x _____ units = _____ VA

Heat pump = _____ VA x _____ units = _____ VA

Largest Load = _____ VA x _____ units = _____ VA (_____) VA [_____] VA

4. KITCHEN EQUIPMENT: 220.56

Range _____ VA x _____ units = _____ VA

Cooktop _____ VA x _____ units = _____ VA

Oven _____ VA x _____ units = _____ VA

Dishwasher _____ VA x _____ units = _____ VA

Water Heater _____ VA x _____ units = _____ VA

_____ _____ VA x _____ units = _____ VA

_____ _____ VA x _____ units = _____ VA

Total = (_____) VA

Table 220.56 x_____%

Demand = (_____) VA [_____] VA

5. LAUNDRY EQUIPMENT:

Washing Machine _____ VA x _____ units _____ VA

Clothes Dryer _____ VA x _____ units _____ VA

Water Heater _____ VA x _____ units _____ VA

_____ _____ VA x _____ units _____ VA

Total = (_____) VA [_____] VA

6. MISCELLANEOUS LOADS:

_____ VA

_____ VA

Total = (_____) VA [_____] VA

7. TOTAL

_____ VA

Line I = _____ VA = _____ amperes
 volts

Conductors are to be sized per Table 310.15(B)(16)

COMMERCIAL CALCULATION

1. LIGHTING: *Table 220.12 or 220.18(B)*

General Lighting: **4,000** sq. ft. x ___**3**___ VA x 125% = **15,000** VA

220.18(B): _____ fixtures x _____ VA x 125% = _____ VA

Show Window: **20** ft. x 200 VA x 125% = **5,000** VA

Track Lighting: **150** ft. / 2 x 150 VA x 125% = **14,063** VA

Sign Ckts. **1** x 1,200 VA x 125% = **1,500** VA

Total Lighting = (**35,563**) VA [**35,563**] VA

2. RECEPTACLES: 220.14(I) and/or 220.14(H)

Receptacles: 180 VA x **50** receptacles = **9,000** VA

Multi-outlet Assembly: 180 VA x **120** ft. = **21,600** VA

Total = (**30,600**) VA

Table 220.44

First 10,000 VA x 100% = **10,000** VA

Remainder: **20,600** VA x 50% = **10,300** VA

Demand = (**20,300**) VA [**20,300**] VA

3. HEATING or A/C at 100% (largest):

Heating unit = **20,000** VA x **1** units = **20,000** VA

A/C unit = **28,800** VA x **1** units = **28,800** VA

Heat pump = _____ VA x _____ units = _____ VA

Largest Load = **28,800** VA x **1** units = **28,800** VA (**28,800**) VA [**28,800**] VA

4. KITCHEN EQUIPMENT: 220.56

Range _____ VA x _____ units = _____ VA

Cooktop **5,000** VA x **1** units = **5,000** VA

Oven **4,000** VA x **1** units = **4,000** VA

Dishwasher _____ VA x _____ units = _____ VA

_____ _____ VA x _____ units = _____ VA

Microwave **1,200** VA x **1** units = **1,200** VA

Refrigerator **1,200** VA x **1** units = **1,200** VA

Total = (**11,400**) VA

Table 220.56 x **80** %

Demand = (**9,120**) VA [**9,120**] VA

5. LAUNDRY EQUIPMENT:

Washing Machine **1,800** VA x **2** units **3,600** VA

Clothes Dryer **5,000** VA x **1** units **5,000** VA

Water Heater _____ VA x _____ units _____ VA

_____ _____ VA x _____ units _____ VA

Total = (**8,600**) VA [**8,600**] VA

6. MISCELLANEOUS LOADS:

_____ VA

_____ VA

Total = (_____) VA [_____] VA

7. TOTAL

102,383 VA

Line I = **102,383** VA = **284** amperes

208 x 1.732

Conductors are to be sized per Table 310.15(B)(16).

UNIT 10
SELF-ASSESSMENT QUIZ

1. A retail occupancy is to have seventy-five (75) 120-volt, 15-ampere rated duplex receptacle outlets installed. Determine the MINIMUM demand load, in VA, on the service-entrance conductors for these receptacles.

 A. 13,000 VA
 B. 13,500 VA
 C. 12,225 VA
 D. 11,750 VA

2. What is the general lighting demand load, in VA, on the ungrounded (phase) service-entrance conductors for a 2,750 square foot office?

 A. 8,250 VA
 B. 9,625 VA
 C. 10,313 VA
 D. 12,031 VA

3. Determine the MINIMUM number of 120-volt, 20-ampere lighting branch circuits required for one-hundred and fifty (150) linear feet of show window lighting in a retail store.

 A. 13
 B. 14
 C. 15
 D. 16

4. A 75,000 sq. ft. office building with 277-volt lighting is required to have at least _____ 20-ampere, single-phase general lighting branch-circuits.

 A. 48
 B. 60
 C. 109
 D. 137

5. A department store is to have 36 continuous linear feet of cord-and-plug connected show window lighting. How many receptacle outlets must be provided directly above the show window for the lighting?

- 232 -

A. two
B. three
C. four
D. five

6. A grocery store will have sixty (60) feet of track lighting installed above the meat display case for accent lighting. What demand load, in VA, must be applied to the ungrounded (phase) service-entrance conductors for this track lighting?

A. 11,250 VA
B. 9,600 VA
C. 5,625 VA
D. 4,500 VA

7. A 208-volt, three-phase, 10 ton A/C condensing unit will draw approximately _____ amperes of current.

A. 67 amperes
B. 100 amperes
C. 115 amperes
D. 134 amperes

8. An automobile dealership is to have four (4) 20-ampere, 120-volt branch- circuits provided for the exterior electric signs. What is the MINIMUM demand load, in VA, that must be applied to the service conductors for these signs?

A. 4,000 VA
B. 4,800 VA
C. 6,000 VA
D. 9,600 VA

9. A 6,000 square foot bank building to be constructed is to have one (1) electric sign circuit and the exact number of receptacle outlets to be provided is not yet determined. Determine the MINIMUM number of 20-ampere, 120-volt branch-circuits that must be provided for the general lighting, receptacles and the sign.

A. 14
B. 15
C. 16
D. 12

10. A 20,000 sq. ft. office building is to be provided with a 208Y/120-volt, 3- phase electrical system. The building will have two-hundred (200), 120-volt, general-use receptacles and seventy-five (75) feet of multioutlet assembly where the cord connected appliances are unlikely to be used simultaneously. Determine the MINIMUM demand load, in amperes, on the ungrounded (phase) service conductors for the general lighting and receptacle load.

Copyright© 2017

A. 262 amperes
B. 466 amperes
C. 310 amperes
D. 538 amperes

11. Branch-circuit conductors supplying a 7½ ton, 208-volt, single-phase, A/C condensing unit are required to have an ampacity of at LEAST _____.

A. 86 amperes
B. 117 amperes
C. 94 amperes
D. 108 amperes

12. When a circuit breaker is provided to protect the previous referenced A/C condensing unit, the circuit breaker is required to have an absolute MAXIMUM ampere rating of no more than _____.

A. 125 amperes
B. 150 amperes
C. 175 amperes
D. 200 amperes

13. A commercial occupancy is to have a fifteen (15) ton A/C unit and a thirty (30) kW electric heating unit installed; both units are 208-volts, 3-phase. What is the demand load, in amperes, to be applied on the service for the A/C and heating equipment?

A. 100 amperes
B. 125 amperes
C. 150 amperes
D. 83 amperes

14. A Mexican food restaurant is to have the following cooking related equipment in the kitchen:

- water heater - 9.0 kW
- fryer - 7.5 kW
- grill - 15 kW
- mixer - 2.0 kW
- food warmer - 4.0 kW
- freezer - 3.5 kW
- refrigerator - 2.5 kW

- dishwasher - 2.0 kW
- booster heater - 4.5 kW

What is the demand load, in kW, on the service for the above listed appliances?

 A. 50.00 kW
 B. 42.75 kW
 C. 37.50 kW
 D. 32.50 kW

15. Each lot in a fifteen (15) unit manufactured home park is capable of accommodating a manufactured home with a rating of 36,000 VA. The demand load, in amperes, on the park service conductors is _____.

 A. 540 amperes
 B. 585 amperes
 C. 390 amperes
 D. 687 amperes

16. When a new one-hundred and twenty-five (125) site RV park supplies all the campsites with electrical power, at LEAST _____ of the sites are required to
 be provided with a 50-ampere, 125/250-volt receptacle and at LEAST _____
 of the sites are required to be provided with a 30-ampere, 125-volt receptacle.

 A. 25, 88
 B. 100, 25
 C. 25, 125
 D. 50, 88

17. An RV park has twenty (20) sites with electrical power reserved as dedicated tent sites. Before demand factors are taken into consideration, what is the MINIMUM total calculated load, in VA, of the tent sites?

 A. 48,000 VA
 B. 36,000 VA
 C. 24,000 VA
 D. 12,000 VA

18. A newly constructed recreational vehicle park has a total of one hundred and
 fifty (150) RV sites, all provided with electrical power. Sixty (60) of the sites
 are provided with 50- and 30-ampere, 125/250-volt receptacles and ninety
 (90) of the sites are provided with 30- and 20-ampere rated 125-volt
 receptacles. What is the feeder/service demand load, in amperes, for the
 RV sites where the electrical system is 208Y/120-volts, three-phase?

 A. 1,188 amperes
 B. 956 amperes
 C. 1,435 amperes
 D. 1,120 amperes

19. What MINIMUM size 75°C rated copper branch-circuit conductors are required to supply a 9.0 kW, 208-volt, single-phase storage-type commercial electric water heater?

 A. 10 AWG
 B. 8 AWG
 C. 6 AWG
 D. 4 AWG

20. Refer to the previous question. What MAXIMUM standard size circuit breaker is permitted to be used for overcurrent protection for the water heater?

 A. 50 ampere
 B. 60 ampere
 C. 65 ampere
 D. 70 ampere

NOTES

PRACTICAL CALCULATIONS FOR ELECTRICIANS
UNIT 10
SELF-ASSESSMENT QUIZ
ANSWER KEY

ANSWER	REFERENCE	NEC PG. #

1. D 220.14(I) pg. 71
 Table 220.44 pg. 72

75 receptacles x 180 VA = 13,500 VA (connected load)

1st 10,000 VA at 100% = 10,000 VA
Remainder (3,500 VA) at 50% = 1,750 VA
 11,750 VA (demand load)

2. D Table 220.12 pg. 71
 230.42(A)(1) pg. 87

2,750 sq. ft. x 3.5 VA x 125% = 12,031 VA

3. D 220.43(A) pg. 72
 210.19(A)(1)(a) pg. 62

200 VA x 150 ft. x 125% = 37,500 VA (load)

circuits = $\dfrac{37,500 \text{ VA}}{120 \text{ volts x 20 amps}}$ = $\dfrac{37,500 \text{ VA}}{2,400}$ = 15.6 = 16 circuits

4. B Table 220.12 pg. 71
 210.19(A)(1)(a) pg. 62

75,000 sq. ft. x 3.5 VA x 125% = 328,125 VA (load)

circuits = $\dfrac{328,125 \text{ VA}}{277 \text{ volts x 20 amps}}$ = $\dfrac{328,125}{5,540}$ = 59.2 = 60

5. B 210.62 pg. 66

$$\frac{36 \text{ ft. (length of show window)}}{12 \text{ ft. (length per receptacle)}} = 3 \text{ receptacles}$$

6. C 220.43(B) pg. 72
 230.42(A)(1) pg. 87

$$\frac{150 \text{ VA} \times 60 \text{ ft} \times 125\%}{2} = \frac{11,250}{2} = 5,625 \text{ VA}$$

7. A Trade Knowledge
 3 Ø current formula

*NOTE: 1 ton of A/C load = 2,400 VA

$I = P \div E$
$I = \dfrac{10 \text{ tons} \times 2,400 \text{ VA}}{208 \text{ volts} \times 1.732} = \dfrac{24,000}{360.25} = 66.6 \text{ amperes}$

8. C 220.14(F) pg. 71
 600.5(B) pg. 488
 230.42(A)(1) pg. 87

1,200 VA x 4 circuits x 125% = 6,000 VA

9. B Table 220.12 pg. 71
 210.19(A)(1)(a) pg. 62
 220.14(K)(2) pg. 72
 600.5(A) pg. 488

(lighting) 6,000 sq. ft. x 3.5 VA x 125% = 26,250 VA
(receptacles) 6,000 sq. ft. x 1 VA = 6,000 VA
 32,250 VA

$$\frac{32,250 \text{ VA}}{120 \text{ volts} \times 20 \text{ amps}} = \frac{32,250}{2,400} = 13.4 = 14 \text{ ltg. \& recpt. circuits}$$
 + 1 sign circuit
 TOTAL = 15 circuits

10. C Table 220.12 pg. 71
 230.42(A)(1) pg. 87
 220.14(H)&(I) pg. 71
 Table 220.44 pg. 72
 3 Ø current formula

 Lighting 20,000 sq. ft. x 3.5 VA x 125% =[87,500 VA]

 Receptacles 180 VA x 200 = 36,000 VA
 Multioutlet Assembly 75 ft ÷ 5 = 15 x 180 VA = 2,700 VA
 38,700 VA

 Apply demand factors (Table 220.44)
 First 10 kVA at 100% = 10,000 VA
 28,700 VA (remainder) at 50% = 14,350 VA
 24,350 VA =[24,350 VA]

 TOTAL =111,850 VA

 I = P ÷ E x 1.732
 I = 111,850 VA = 111,850 = 310.4 amperes
 208 volts x 1.732 360.25

11. D Single-phase current formula
 440.32 pg. 327

 *NOTE: 1 ton of A/C = 2,400 VA

 I = P ÷ E
 I = 7.5 tons x 2,400 VA = 18,000 = 86 amperes
 208 volts 208

 86 amperes x 1.25 = 107.5 amperes

12. C 440.22(A) pg. 327
 Table 240.6(A) pg. 95

 86 amperes x 225% = 193.5 amperes

 *NOTE: Under this condition, you must go down to the next standard
 size circuit breaker which has a rating of 175 amperes.

13. A 220.60 pg. 73
 3 Ø current formula

A/C Unit
15 tons x 2,400 VA = 36,000 VA

$$I = \frac{36,000 \text{ VA}}{208 \text{ volts} \times 1.732} = \frac{36,000}{360.25} = 100 \text{ amperes}$$

Heating Unit
$$I = \frac{30 \text{ kW} \times 1,000}{208 \times 1.732} = \frac{30,000}{360.25} = 83 \text{ amperes}$$

*NOTE: The A/C unit is the larger load therefore the heating unit is permitted to be omitted.

14. D Table 220.56 pg. 75

Water heater	- 9.0 kW
fryer	- 7.5 kW
grill	- 15 kW
mixer	- 2.0 kW
food warmer	- 4.0 kW
freezer	- 3.5 kW
refrigerator	- 2.5 kW
dishwasher	- 2.0 kW
booster heater	- 4.5 kW

 50 kW (connected load)
 x 65% [Table 220.56]
 32.5 kW (demand load)

15. B 550.30 pg. 461
 Table 550.31 pg. 461
 Single-phase current formula

15 lots x 36,000 VA = 540,000 VA
 x .26 [Table 550.31]
 140,400 VA (demand)

$$I = P \div E$$
$$I = \frac{140,400 \text{ VA}}{240 \text{ volts}} = 585 \text{ amperes}$$

16. D 551.71(B)&(C) pgs. 470 & 471

50 ampere – 125 sites x 40% = 50 sites w/50 A receptacle outlets
30 ampere – 125 sites x 70% = 88 sites w/30 A receptacle outlets

17. D 551.73(A) pg. 471

20 sites x 600 VA = 12,000 VA

18. A 551.73(A) pg. 471
 Table 551.73(A) pg. 471
 3 Ø current formula

50/30 ampere sites – 12,000 VA x 60 sites = 720,000 VA
30/20 ampere sites – 3,600 VA x 90 sites = 324,000 VA
 1,044,000 VA
 x .41 [Table 51.73(A)]
 428,040 VA (demand load)

$$I = P \div E \times 1.732$$

$$I = \frac{428{,}040 \text{ VA}}{208 \text{ volts} \times 1.732} = \frac{428{,}040}{360.25} = 1{,}188 \text{ amperes}$$

19. C Single-phase current formula
 422.13 pg. 277
 422.10(A) pg. 276
 Table 310.15(B)(16) pg. 150

$$I = P \div E$$
$$I = \frac{9 \text{ kW} \times 1{,}000 \times 125\%}{208 \text{ volts}} = \frac{11{,}250}{208} = 54 \text{ amperes}$$

*NOTE: Table 310.15(B)(16) indicates size 6 AWG conductors should be selected.

20. D Single-phase current formula

422.11(E)(3) pg. 277
Table 240.6(A) pg. 95

$$I = P \div E$$

$$I = \frac{9 \text{ kW} \times 1{,}000 \times 150\%}{208 \text{ volts}} = \frac{13{,}500}{208} = 65 \text{ amperes}$$

*NOTE: A circuit breaker with a 70 ampere rating is permitted
 because you are allowed to go up to the next standard size
 circuit breaker.

JOURNEYMAN ELECTRICIAN'S EXAM PREP GUIDE
EXAM #1

The following questions are based on the 2017 edition of the National Electrical Code® and are typical of questions encountered on most Journeyman Electricians' Licensing Exams. On each question select the best answer from the choices given and review your answers with the answer key included in this book. Typically, the only material permitted for use on this type of exam is a calculator, scratch paper and a current edition of the NEC® book. Each question on this test has a value of 4 points: a passing score is 70%. In order to pass, you therefore need to get 18 of the 25 questions correct.

ALLOTTED TIME: 75 minutes

1. Where multiple driven ground rods are installed, they shall NOT be spaced less than _____ apart.

A. 2 feet
B. 4 feet
C. 6 feet
D. 8 feet

2. Where a one-family dwelling has a 200 ampere, 120/240-volt, single-phase main service panel and is being supplied with size 2/0 AWG THW copper ungrounded service-entrance conductors in rigid metal conduit (RMC), the MINIMUM allowable size of the bonding jumper for this service-entrance conduit is _____ copper.

A. 6 AWG
B. 4 AWG
C. 2 AWG
D. 1/0 AWG

3. A disconnect switch enclosure installed in a Class II, Division 2 location shall be _____.

A. dusttight
B. heavy-duty type
C. raintight
D. general-duty type

4. The interior of enclosures or raceways installed underground shall be considered to be a _____ location.

A. dry
B. damp
C. hazardous
D. wet

5. Determine the MAXIMUM allowable current-carrying capacity of four (4) size 1/0 AWG THW copper current-carrying conductors installed in a common raceway with an ambient temperature of 86 degrees F.

A. 150 amperes
B. 105 amperes
C. 112 amperes
D. 120 amperes

6. The NEC® defines a continuous load to be a load where the maximum current on the circuit is expected to continue for at LEAST_____ hours or more.

A. three
B. four
C. six
D. eight

7. Determine the MINIMUM size THW copper branch-circuit conductors the NEC® requires to supply a 3-phase, continuous-duty, ac motor that draws 70 amperes per phase. Consider all terminations are rated for 75 deg. C.

A. 1 AWG
B. 2 AWG
C. 3 AWG
D. 4 AWG

8. Given: You have determined a conductor has a computed allowable ampacity of 75 amperes. What is the MAXIMUM standard ampere rating of the overcurrent protection device the NEC® permits to protect this circuit where this is not a motor circuit or part of a multioutlet branch circuit supplying more than one receptacle?

A. 70 amperes
B. 75 amperes
C. 80 amperes
D. 85 amperes

9. A 208-volt, 3-phase, 50 hp, squirrel-cage, continuous-duty, ac motor has a full-load running current rating of _____.

A. 130 amperes
B. 143 amperes
C. 162 amperes
D. 195 amperes

10. What is the MAXIMUM distance that a disconnect switch is permitted to be located from the operator's station for a portable carnival ride?

A. 6 feet
B. 10 feet
C. 25 feet
D. 50 feet

11. Determine the MINIMUM trade size electrical metallic tubing (EMT) required to enclose eight (8) size 6 AWG copper conductors with THHW insulation, when installed in a 50 foot conduit run.

A. 1 in.
B. 1¼ in.
C. 1½ in.
D. 2 in.

12. Where exceptions are not applicable, when a feeder supplies a continuous load of 240 amperes, the overcurrent protection device protecting this circuit shall have a rating of at LEAST _____.

A. 240 amperes
B. 300 amperes
C. 250 amperes
D. 275 amperes

13. Liquidtight flexible metal conduit (LFMC) shall be securely fastened WITHIN _____ of each box or other conduit termination.

A. 4½ feet
B. 3 feet
C. 12 inches
D. 18 inches

14. When a pull box contains conductors of size 4 AWG and larger and a straight pull of the conductors is to be made, the length of the box shall NOT be less than _____times the trade diameter of the largest conduit entering the box.

A. six
B. four
C. eight
D. twelve

15. Conduit nipples not over 24 inches long may be filled to a MAXIMUM of _____ of their cross-sectional area.

A. 30 percent
B. 40 percent
C. 54 percent
D. 60 percent

16. Determine the MAXIMUM number of size 14 AWG THHN conductors permitted to be installed in a trade size 3/8 in. flexible metal conduit (FMC) that contains a bare size 14 AWG grounding conductor, when the FMC has external fittings.

A. two
B. three
C. four
D. five

17. Which of the following listed conduits does the NEC® permit to enclose conductors supplying wet-niche underwater pool luminaires?

A. electrical metallic tubing (EMT)
B. electrical nonmetallic tubing (ENT)
C. galvanized rigid metal conduit (RMC)
D. Schedule 40 rigid polyvinyl chloride conduit (PVC)

18. Underground wiring is not permitted under a permanently installed swimming pool or within _____ of the pool, unless the wiring is supplying the associated pool equipment.

A. 10 feet
B. 6 feet
C. 5 feet
D. 8 feet

19. Which of the following listed types of batteries is NOT permitted for use as a source of power for emergency systems?

A. automotive
B. lead acid type
C. alkali type
D. all of these

20. In new installations, the MINIMUM working space the NEC® requires between a 480Y/277-volt, switchboard and a 480-volt motor control center when facing each other is _____.

A. 3 feet
B. 3½ feet
C. 4 feet
D. 6 feet

21. In guest rooms of hotels, motels, and sleeping rooms of dorms a MINIMUM of _____ general purpose receptacles installed in the room is/are required to be readily accessible.

A. one
B. two
C. three
D. all

22. When branch circuit conductors are installed inside a ballast enclosure of a luminaire and are within three (3) inches of the ballast, the conductors shall have a temperature rating NOT lower than _____.

A. 105 deg. C
B. 90 deg. C
C. 75 deg. C
D. 60 deg. C

23. When a size 4 AWG or larger conductor enters a panelboard, which of the following must be provided?

A. A bonding jumper.
B. A grounding clip.
C. An insulated bushing.
D. An insulated grounding conductor.

24. Class _____ locations are those that are hazardous because of the presence of easily ignitible fibers or where materials producing combustible flyings are handled, but in which such fibers/flyings are not likely to be in suspension in the air in quantities sufficient to produce ignitible mixtures.

A. I
B. II
C. III
D. IV

25. A single-phase, 240-volt, 15 kVA standby generator may be loaded to a MAXIMUM of _____ per line.

A. 62.50 amperes
B. 31.25 amperes
C. 41.66 amperes
D. 52.50 amperes

END OF EXAM #1

JOURNEYMAN ELECTRICIAN'S EXAM PREP GUIDE
PRACTICE EXAM #1
ANSWER KEY

ANSWER	REFERENCE	NEC PG. #
1. C	250.53(B)	pg. 113
2. B	250.102(C)(1)	pg. 118
	Table 250.102(C)(1)	pg. 119
3. A	502.10(B)(4)	pg. 365
4. D	300.5(B)	pg. 136
5. D	Table 310.15(B)(16)	pg. 150
	Table 310.15(B)(3)(a)	pg. 148

Size 1/0 AWG THW ampacity = 150 amperes before derating
150 amperes x 80% (adjustment factor) = 120 amperes

6. A	Article 100	pg. 35
7. C	430.22	pg. 302
	Table 310.15(B)(16)	pg. 150

FLC of motor = 70 amperes x 125% = 87.5 amperes
Size 3 AWG THW with an ampacity of 100 amperes should be selected.

8. C	240.4(B)(1),(2)&(3)	pg. 94
	Table 240.6(A)	pg. 95
9. B	Table 430.250	pg. 322
10. A	525.21(A)	pg. 446
11. B	Annex C, Table C.1	pg. 713
12. B	215.3	pg. 68

240 amperes x 125% = 300 amperes

13. C	350.30(A)	pg. 201

14. C	314.28(A)(1)	pg. 180
15. D	Chapter 9, Note 4 to Tables	pg. 679
16. C	Table 348.22	pg. 200
17. D	680.23(B)(2)	pg. 547
18. C	680.10	pg. 544
19. A	700.12(A)	pg. 584
20. C	Table 110.26(A)(1)	pg. 47
21. B	210.60(B)	pg. 66
22. B	410.68	pg. 271
23. C	300.4(G)	pg. 136
24. C	500.5(D)	pg. 351

25. A Single-Phase Current Formula
$$I = P \div E$$

$$\frac{15 \text{ kVA} \times 1,000}{240 \text{ volts}} = \frac{15,000}{240} = 62.50 \text{ amperes}$$

##

JOURNEYMAN ELECTRICIAN'S EXAM PREP GUIDE
EXAM #2

The following questions are based on the 2017 edition of the National Electrical Code® and are typical of questions encountered on most Journeyman Electricians' Licensing Exams. On each question select the best answer from the choices given and review your answers with the answer key included in this book. Typically, the only material permitted for use on this type of exam is a calculator, scratch paper and a current edition of the NEC® book. Each question on this test has a value of 4 points: a passing score is 70%. In order to pass, you therefore need to get 18 of the 25 questions correct.

ALLOTTED TIME: 75 minutes

1. In general, for other than dwelling units, all 15- and 20-ampere, 125-volt, single-phase receptacles installed on rooftops must be provided with _____.

 I. GFCI protection
 II. AFCI protection

A. I only
B. II only
C. Both I and II
D. Neither I nor II

2. Where the motor controller also serves as a disconnecting means, it shall open all _____ conductors to the motor.

A. grounded
B. neutral
C. grounding
D. ungrounded

3. Before demand factors are taken into consideration for commercial buildings, general-purpose receptacle loads are to be computed at NOT less than _____ per outlet.

A. 100 VA
B. 120 VA
C. 150 VA
D. 180 VA

4. Conductors with _____ insulation have a greater ampacity when used in a dry location compared to when used in a wet location.

A. THW
B. RHW
C. THWN
D. THHW

5. Where a submersible pump is used in a metal well casing, the well casing shall be _____ the pump circuit equipment grounding conductor.

A. isolated from
B. connected to
C. exothermic welded to
D. none of these

6. In a health care facility, low voltage electrical equipment that is likely to become energized that is frequently in contact with the bodies of patients, shall operate on a voltage of _____ or less if the equipment is not approved as intrinsically safe, double insulated or moisture resistant.

A. 10 volts
B. 24 volts
C. 100 volts
D. 120 volts

7. When ambient temperature is not a factor, a size 8 AWG single copper conductor with type FEPB insulation, installed in free air, will have a MAXIMUM allowable ampacity of _____.

A. 80 amperes
B. 55 amperes
C. 45 amperes
D. 83 amperes

8. For the purpose of determining conductor fill in a device box, a three-way switch is counted as equal to _____ conductor(s), based on the largest conductor connected to the switch.

A. zero
B. one
C. two
D. three

9. When determining the required ampacity of the branch circuit conductors to supply a 3-phase, continuous duty ac motor, current values given on _____ shall be used.

A. the motors nameplate
B. Table 430.248 of the NEC®
C. Table 430.52 of the NEC®
D. Table 430.250 of the NEC®

10. When calculating the total load for a building or structure, what is the MINIMUM computed branch circuit load, in volt-amps, permitted by the NEC® for a branch circuit serving an exterior electric sign?

A. 1,200 volt amps
B. 1,800 volt amps
C. 1,500 volt amps
D. 2,000 volt amps

11. Determine the MAXIMUM number of size 1 AWG XHHW compact conductors permitted in a trade size 3 in., rigid Schedule 40 PVC conduit more than 24 inches long.

A. 21
B. 19
C. 14
D. 18

12. Infrared commercial and industrial heating appliances shall have overcurrent protection NOT exceeding _____.

A. 20 amperes
B. 40 amperes
C. 50 amperes
D. 60 amperes

13. Class _____ hazardous locations are those in which flammable liquid-produced vapors, or combustible liquid-produced vapors are or may be present in the air in quantities sufficient to produce explosive or ignitible mixtures.

A. I
B. II
C. III
D. IV

14. In indoor areas where walls are frequently washed, such as laundries or car washes, metallic conduit and metallic panelboards shall be mounted with a _____ space between the wall and conduit or panelboard when the equipment is installed exposed.

A. 3/4 in.
B. 1/2 in.
C. 1/8 in.
D. 1/4 in.

15. A branch circuit served by size 12 AWG conductors is a _____ rated branch circuit when protected by a 15-ampere circuit breaker.

A. 20 ampere
B. 25 ampere
C. 15 ampere
D. 10 ampere

16. What is the MAXIMUM overcurrent protection allowed for the protection of resistance-type electric space heating equipment?

A. 30 amperes
B. 40 amperes
C. 48 amperes
D. 60 amperes

17. Information technology equipment shall be permitted to be connected to a branch circuit by a listed power-supply cord having a length NOT to exceed _____.

A. 10 feet
B. 15 feet
C. 12 feet
D. 20 feet

18. Type MI cable shall be supported at intervals NOT exceeding _____ .

A. 2 feet
B. 4 feet
C. 6 feet
D. 10 feet

19. General use snap switches supplying inductive loads shall be loaded to NO more than _____ of the ampere rating of the switch at the applied voltage.

A. 50 percent
B. 60 percent
C. 75 percent
D. 80 percent

20. Direct-buried conductors emerging from grade shall be protected by raceways or covers up to at LEAST _____ above finished grade.

A. 8 feet
B. 10 feet
C. 12 feet
D. 15 feet

21. What is the MINIMUM size equipment grounding conductor for a 50 ampere branch circuit where the conductors are installed in PVC conduit?

A. 12 AWG
B. 10 AWG
C. 8 AWG
D. 6 AWG

22. Disregarding exceptions, all 3-phase, 4-wire, 480Y/277-volt, electrical services, require ground-fault protection for each service disconnecting means, when rated for at LEAST _____ or more.

A. 400 amperes
B. 600 amperes
C. 1,000 amperes
D. 1,500 amperes

23. Determine the conductor ampacity given the following related information:

* conductors are size 500 kcmil copper
* conductor insulation is THWN
* eight (8) current-carrying conductors are in the raceway
* ambient temperature is 125 deg. F
* conduit length is 50 feet
* installation is a wet location

A. 178.2 amperes
B. 199.5 amperes
C. 294.6 amperes
D. 380.0 amperes

24. When connecting to luminaires, trade size 3/8 in. flexible metal conduit (FMC) is permitted to enclose tap conductors, provided the length of the FMC does NOT exceed _____.

A. 3 feet
B. 4 feet
C. 6 feet
D. 8 feet

25. Where a trade size 1/2 in. rigid metal conduit (RMC) is installed in a Class I location and a 1/2 in. conduit seal is required, the MINIMUM thickness of the sealing compound shall NOT be less than _____.

A. 3/8 in.
B. 1/2 in.
C. 5/8 in.
D. 3/4 in.

END OF EXAM #2

JOURNEYMAN ELECTRICIAN'S EXAM PREP GUIDE
PRACTICE EXAM #2
ANSWER KEY

ANSWER	REFERENCE	NEC. PG. #
1. A	210.8(B)(3)	pg. 59
2. D	430.84, Exception	pg. 312
3. D	220.14(I)	pg. 71
4. D	Table 310.104(A)	pg. 167
	Table 310.15(B)(16)	pg. 150
5. B	250.112(M)	pg. 121
6. A	517.64(A)(1),(2)&(3)	pg. 432
7. A	Table 310.15(B)(17)	pg. 151
8. C	314.16(B)(4)	pg. 176
9. D	430.6(A)(1)	pg. 297
10. C	220.14(F)	pg. 71
	600.5(B)	pg. 488
	210.19(A)(1)(a)	pg. 62

$$1{,}200 \text{ VA} \times 125\% = 1{,}500 \text{ VA}$$

ANSWER	REFERENCE	NEC. PG. #
11. A	Annex C, Table C.11(A)	pg. 777
12. C	422.11(C)	pg. 276
13. A	500.5(B)	pg. 350
14. D	300.6(D)	pg. 138
15. C	210.18	pg. 61
16. D	424.22(B)	pg. 282
17. B	645.5(B)(1)	pg. 526
18. C	332.30	pg. 190
19. A	404.14(B)(2)	pg. 257

20. A	300.5(D)(1)	pg. 136
21. B	Table 250.122	pg. 125
22. C	230.95	pg. 91
23. A	Table 310.15(B)(16)	pg. 150
	Table 310.15(B)(2)(a)	pg. 147
	Table 310.15(B)(3)(a)	pg. 148

Size 500 KCMIL THWN copper ampacity before derating = 380 amperes
380 amperes x .67 (temp. correction) x .7 (adjustment factor) = 178.22 amperes

24. C	348.20(A)(2)c.	pg. 199
	410.117(C)	pg. 272
25. C	501.15(C)(3)	pg. 358

##

JOURNEYMAN ELECTRICIAN'S EXAM PREP GUIDE
EXAM #3

The following questions are based on the 2017 edition of the National Electrical Code® and are typical of questions encountered on most Journeyman Electricians' Licensing Exams. On each question select the best answer from the choices given and review your answers with the answer key included in this book. Typically, the only material permitted for use on this type of exam is a calculator, scratch paper and a current edition of the NEC® book. Each question on this test has a value of 4 points: a passing score is 70%. In order to pass, you therefore need to get 18 of the 25 questions correct.

ALLOTTED TIME: 75 minutes

1. As a general rule in a dwelling, branch circuits provided to supply receptacle outlets in an attached garage shall have no other outlets. An exception to this rule is _____.

A. receptacle outlets in an adjacent laundry room
B. readily accessible outdoor receptacle outlets
C. receptacle outlets in the foyer
D. rooftop receptacle outlets

2. A 30 hp, 480-volt, 3-phase wound-rotor, ac motor has a full-load running current rating of _____ .

A. 27 amperes
B. 32 amperes
C. 40 amperes
D. 50 amperes

3. The MAXIMUM ampacity of an individual branch circuit in a flat conductor cable assembly shall be _____.

A. 10 amperes
B. 15 amperes
C. 20 amperes
D. 30 amperes

4. In dwelling units, GFCI protection is required for all 15-and 20-ampere, 125-volt receptacles located within at LEAST _____ of the outside edge of a bathtub or shower stall.

A. 4 feet
B. 6 feet
C. 8 feet
D. 10 feet

5. What MAXIMUM percent of a metal wireway cross-section may be occupied by splices, taps and conductors at any point?

A. 20 percent
B. 30 percent
C. 40 percent
D. 75 percent

6. In an underground rigid polyvinyl chloride conduit (PVC) system that consist of 50 feet length between pulling points, what is the MAXIMUM number of bends this run may have?

A. four (4) - 90 degree
B. six (6) - 90 degree
C. four (4) - 120 degree
D. two (2) - 90 degree

7. Grounding electrodes made of pipe or conduit shall NOT be smaller than _____ electrical trade size.

A. 1/2 in.
B. 3/4 in.
C. 1 in.
D. 1½ in.

8. Liquidtight flexible metallic conduit (LFMC) shall NOT be used:

A. in lengths in excess of 6 feet.
B. in concealed work.
C. in hazardous locations.
D. where subject to physical damage.

9. Determine the allowable ampacity of a size 3 AWG THHN copper conductor where given the following related information.

 * Two (2) current-carrying conductors are in the raceway.
 * The ambient temperature is 35 deg. C.
 * The terminations are rated at 60 deg. C.

A. 105.6 amperes
B. 85 amperes
C. 81.6 amperes
D. 110 amperes

10. As per a general NEC® rule, communications wires and cables shall have a vertical clearance of NOT less than _____ from all points above roofs which they pass.

A. 3 feet
B. 4 feet
C. 6 feet
D. 8 feet

11. Standard trade size 2 in. rigid Schedule 40 polyvinyl chloride conduit (PVC), shall be supported at LEAST every _____.

A. 3 feet
B. 5 feet
C. 6 feet
D. 8 feet

12. For an ac system operating at less than 1000 volts, a main bonding jumper shall connect the grounded conductor(s) to _____.

A. each service disconnecting means enclosure
B. each meter base only
C. the grounding electrode
D. all sub-panels

13. In industrial establishments, where sizes 1/0 AWG through 4/0 AWG single conductor cables are installed in ladder type cable tray, the MAXIMUM allowable rung spacing for the cable tray shall be _____ .

A. 6 inches
B. 9 inches
C. 12 inches
D. 15 inches

14. The NEC® mandates the MAXIMUM length permitted for a flexible cord supplying a 208-volt, single-phase, room air-conditioner to be _____ .

A. 4 feet
B. 6 feet
C. 8 feet
D. 10 feet

15. In general, which of the following receptacle outlets in a commercial kitchen are required by the NEC® to be GFCI protected?

A. All 125-volt, 15- or 20-ampere receptacles.
B. All 125-volt, 15- or 20-ampere receptacles in wet locations only.
C. All receptacles.
D. All 125-volt countertop receptacles only.

16. When installing pendant mounted luminaires, the pendant conductors LONGER than _____ shall be twisted together where not cabled in a listed assembly.

A. 18 inches
B. 24 inches
C. 30 inches
D. 36 inches

17. Branch-circuit conductors supplying more than one motor shall have an ampacity of at LEAST_____ of the FLC of the highest rated motor in the group, and 100 percent of the FLC of the other motor(s) in the group.

A. 25 percent
B. 80 percent
C. 100 percent
D. 125 percent

18. What is the MINIMUM size equipment grounding conductor required for a 5 hp, 3-phase, 208-volt motor having 20 ampere rated overload protection and branch-circuit, short-circuit and ground-fault protection rated 30 amperes?

A. 10 AWG
B. 14 AWG
C. 12 AWG
D. 8 AWG

19. If a circuit breaker serves as the controller for a motor, and the motor is not in sight of the breaker, the NEC® requires which of the following?

A. The motor to be less than 2 hp.
B. The breaker be able to be locked in the open position.
C. The motor to be Code letter "E".
D. The breaker to be rated 25,000 AIC.

20. For nonshielded conductors of over 1000 volts, the conductors shall not be bent to a radius of LESS than _____ times the overall conductor diameter.

A. six
B. eight
C. ten
D. twelve

21. Where an ac electrical service is supplied with four (4) parallel sets of size 500 kcmil aluminum ungrounded conductors, what is the MINIMUM size copper grounding electrode conductor required when connected to the concrete encased reinforcing building steel?
(Assume the grounding electrode conductor does not extend to other types of electrodes.)

A. 4 AWG
B. 3/0 AWG
C. 250 kcmil
D. 2/0 AWG

22. Where an ac transformer arc welder has a 50 ampere rated primary current and a 60 percent duty cycle, the MINIMUM size 60 deg. C rated copper conductors the NEC® requires to supply this welder is _____ .

A. 6 AWG
B. 8 AWG
C. 10 AWG
D. 4 AWG

23. When installing wiring for sensitive electronic equipment, the MAXIMUM voltage to ground is required to be _____ .

A. 277 volts
B. 120 volts
C. 60 volts
D. 30 volts

24. In a health care facility, a patient bed location in a critical care area (Category 1) is required to have which of the following?

A. Four single receptacles or two duplex receptacles.
B. Fourteen single receptacles or seven duplex receptacles.
C. Six duplex receptacles or twelve single receptacles.
D. Eight single receptacles or four duplex receptacles.

25. Flexible cords and cables shall NOT be used _____ .

A. as elevator cables
B. when run through holes in walls
C. as data processing cables
D. to prevent transmission of vibration

END OF EXAM #3

JOURNEYMAN ELECTRICIAN'S EXAM PREP GUIDE
PRACTICE EXAM #3
ANSWER KEY

ANSWER	REFERENCE	NEC PG. #
1. B	210.11(C)(4), Exception	pg. 60
2. C	Table 430.250	pg. 322
3. D	324.10(B)(2)	pg. 185
4. B	210.8(A)(9)	pg. 59
5. D	376.56(A)	pg. 221
6. A	352.26	pg. 202
7. B	250.52(A)(5)(a)	pg. 113
8. D	350.12(1)	pg. 201
9. B	110.14(C)	pg. 45
	Table 310.15(B)(16)	pg. 150
	Table 310.15(B)(2)(a)	pg. 147

Size 3 AWG THHN ampacity before derating = 110 amperes (90ºC Column)
110 amperes x .96 (temperature correction) = 105.6 amperes
*NOTE: Size 3 AWG (60ºC Column) with an allowable ampacity of 85 amperes
 should be selected.

10. D	800.44(B)	pg. 639
11. B	Table 352.30	pg. 203
12. A	250.24(C)	pg. 107
13. B	392.10(B)(1)(a)	pg. 228
14. B	440.64	pg. 329
15. A	210.8(B)(2)	pg. 59
16. D	410.54(C)	pg. 270

17. D	430.24(1)&(2)	pg. 303
18. A	Table 250.122	pg. 125
19. B	430.102(B)(2),Exception	pg. 314
20. B	300.34	pg. 143
21. A	250.66(B)	pg. 115
22. B	Table 630.11(A)	pg. 519
	Table 310.15(B)(16)	pg. 150

.78 (duty cycle) x 50 amperes (primary current) = 39 amperes
*NOTE: Tbl. 310.15(B)(16) indicates size 8 AWG conductors should be selected.

23. C	647.1	pg. 532
24. B	517.19(B)(1)&(2)	pg. 422
25. B	400.12(2)	pg. 250

##

JOURNEYMAN ELECTRICIAN'S EXAM PREP GUIDE
EXAM #4

The following questions are based on the 2017 edition of the National Electrical Code® and are typical of questions encountered on most Journeyman Electricians' Licensing Exams. On each question select the best answer from the choices given and review your answers with the answer key included in this book. Typically, the only material permitted for use on this type of exam is a calculator, scratch paper and a current edition of the NEC® book. Each question on this test has a value of 4 points: a passing score is 70%. In order to pass, you therefore need to get 18 of the 25 questions correct.

ALLOTTED TIME: 75 minutes

1. Conductors installed in electrically heated floors in bathrooms, kitchens, and in hydromassage bathtub locations shall be provided with_____ protection.

A. ground-fault circuit interrupter (GFCI)
B. arc-fault circuit interrupter (AFCI)
C. heat-detecting circuit interrupter (HDCI)
D. all the above

2. Where electrical equipment containing overcurrent devices, rated at LEAST _____ or more, is installed in an equipment room, personnel door(s) located less than 25 feet from the nearest edge of the working space must open in the direction of egress and have listed panic hardware.

A. 600 amperes
B. 800 amperes
C. 1000 amperes
D. 2000 amperes

3. What is the MAXIMUM length of a flexible cord that may be used for a recirculating water-pump motor on a swimming pool at a dwelling?

A. 3 feet
B. 4 feet
C. 6 feet
D. 8 feet

4. Plate grounding electrodes shall be installed NOT less than _____ below the surface of the earth.

A. 12 inches
B. 18 inches
C. 24 inches
D. 30 inches

5. A disconnecting means shall be provided on the supply side of all fuses in circuits having a voltage of at LEAST _____ to ground.

A. 120 volts
B. 250 volts
C. 150 volts
D. 277 volts

6. Where an 80-ampere, 240-volt, single-phase load is located 200 feet from a panelboard and is supplied with size 3 AWG copper conductors with THWN insulation, what is the approximate voltage-drop on the circuit?
(K = 12.9)

A. 6.0 volts
B. 4.0 volts
C. 9.2 volts
D. 7.84 volts

7. Enclosures in a Class I, Division 1 location containing components that have arcing devices must have an approved seal located within at LEAST _____ of each conduit run entering or leaving such enclosures.

A. 12 inches
B. 18 inches
C. 24 inches
D. 4½ feet

8. The purpose of the NEC® is _____ .

A. to have an installation that is efficient
B. the practical safeguarding of persons and property
C. for future expansion of electrical use
D. to provide an installation that is adequate for good service

9. The NEC® considers the area around the motor fuel dispensing pumps of an automotive service station to be a hazardous location. This area extends a height of 18 inches above grade, and up to a horizontal distance of _____from the enclosure of the outdoor motor fuel dispensing pumps.

A. 5 feet
B. 10 feet
C. 16 feet
D. 20 feet

10. According to the National Electrical Code®, what are the three (3) separate branches of the essential electrical systems for hospitals?

A. The emergency branch, life safety branch and the standby branch.
B. The life safety branch, equipment branch and the critical branch.
C. The normal branch, life safety branch and the alternate branch.
D. The essential branch, the emergency branch and the equipment branch.

11. Type UF cable is NOT permitted to be used _____.

A. in an attic space
B. as a substitute for Type NM cable
C. as service-entrance cable
D. for solar photovoltaic systems

12. Where an office building has a 208Y/120-volt, 3-phase service with a balanced net computed load of 90 kVA, what is the current each ungrounded (phase) conductor will carry at full load?

A. 188 amperes
B. 250 amperes
C. 433 amperes
D. 750 amperes

13. When grounding the structural reinforcing steel of a swimming pool, what is the smallest size grounding conductor permitted for this installation?

A. 12 AWG
B. 10 AWG
C. 8 AWG
D. 6 AWG

14. For dwelling units, GFCI protection shall be provided for lighting outlets not exceeding 120 volts where installed in _____.

 I. crawl spaces
 II. bathrooms

A. I only
B. II only
C. both I and II
D. neither I nor II

15. Where a motor of more than 1 horsepower has a temperature rise of 50 deg. C indicated on the nameplate, for the purposes of selecting the overload device, this device shall be selected to trip at NO more than _____ of the motor's full-load ampere rating. (Assume modification of this value is not necessary.)

A. 100 percent
B. 115 percent
C. 125 percent
D. 130 percent

16. Where a size 14 AWG branch-circuit conductor protected by a 15 ampere rated circuit breaker supplies three (3) 20 ampere rated duplex receptacles, this branch circuit _____ .

A. would be in compliance with the NEC® if the wire was size 12 AWG
B. would be in compliance with the NEC® if the breaker was rated 20-amperes
C. is not in compliance with the NEC® because the receptacles have a 20 ampere rating
D. is in compliance with the NEC®

17. What is the MAXIMUM number of times a wire-type grounding electrode conductor is permitted to be spliced by use of listed split-bolt connectors?

A. one
B. two
C. three
D. none

18. Given: A metal junction box has a volume of 27 cubic inches and contains a total of six (6) size 12 AWG conductors, no grounding conductors, devices or fittings are contained in the box. Additional wires of size 10 AWG need to be added in the box. What is the MAXIMUM number of size 10 AWG conductors may be added to this box?

A. two
B. five
C. six
D. eight

19. For enclosing a mobile home supply cord, what is the MAXIMUM trade size conduit permitted between the branch circuit panelboard of a mobile home and the underside of a mobile home floor?

A. 1 in.
B. 1¼ in.
C. 1½ in.
D. 2 in.

20. Which of the following wiring methods is/are approved for use for fixed wiring in an area above Class I locations in a commercial garage?

A. Type MI cable
B. Type TC cable
C. Type MC cable
D. all of the above

21. Class II locations are those that are hazardous because of the presence of _____.

A. flammable gas
B. ignitible fibers
C. ignitible vapors
D. combustible dust

22. Branch-circuit conductors supplying a fixed storage-type electric water heater with a capacity of 120 gallons or less, shall have an ampacity of NOT less than _____ of the full-load current of the water heater.

A. 80 percent
B. 100 percent
C. 125 percent
D. 150 percent

23. Household-type appliances with surface heating elements having a MAXIMUM demand of more than _____ shall have its power supply subdivided into two (2) or more circuits.

A. 60 amperes
B. 50 amperes
C. 40 amperes
D. 30 amperes

24. When driving a ground rod and solid rock is encountered, the ground rod is permitted to be buried in a trench at LEAST _____ deep.

A. 3 feet
B. 4 feet
C. 24 inches
D. 30 inches

25. A total of ten (10) copper THW conductors are to be installed in a 20 foot run of intermediate metal conduit (IMC), five (5) size 1 AWG and five (5) size 3 AWG. What is the MINIMUM allowable trade size IMC required to contain these ten (10) conductors?

A. 1½ in.
B. 2 in.
C. 2½ in.
D. 3 in.

END OF EXAM #4

JOURNEYMAN ELECTRICIAN'S EXAM PREP GUIDE
PRACTICE EXAM #4
ANSWER KEY

ANSWER	REFERENCE	NEC PG. #
1. A	424.44(E)	pg. 284
2. B	110.26(C)(3)	pg. 48
3. A	680.21(A)(3)	pg. 545
4. D	250.53(H)	pg. 113
5. C	240.40	pg. 99
6. D	Chapter 9, Table 8 Voltage-drop formula	pg. 689

$$VD = \frac{2KID}{CM} \qquad VD = \frac{2 \times 12.9 \times 80 \text{ amps} \times 200 \text{ ft.}}{52,620 \text{ CM}} = 7.84 \text{ volts}$$

7. B	501.15(A)(1)	pg. 357
8. B	90.1(A)	pg. 30
9. D	Table 514.3(B)(1)	pg. 400
10. B	517.31(A)	pg. 424
11. C	340.12(1)	pg. 196
12. B	Trade & General Knowledge 3-Phase Current Formula	

$$I = \frac{kVA \times 1,000}{E \times 1.732} \qquad I = \frac{90 \times 1,000}{208 \times 1.732} = \frac{90,000}{360.25} = 250 \text{ amperes}$$

13. C	680.26(B) 680.26(B)(1)(a)	pg. 549 pg. 549
14. A	210.8(E)	pg. 159
15. B	430.32(A)(1)	pgs. 304 & 305
16. C	Table 210.24	pg. 64

17. D 250.64(C)(1) pg. 114

18. B Table 314.16(B) pg. 176

Size 12 AWG = 2.25 cu. in. x 6 (existing wire in box) = 13.5 cu. in.

27.0 cu. in. (allowable fill of box)
-13.5 cu. in. (existing wire in box)
13.5 cu. in. (remaining space available)

$\dfrac{13.5 \text{ cu. in. (remaining space)}}{2.5 \text{ cu. in. (#10)}}$ = 5.4 = 5 size 10 AWG wires may be added

19. B 550.10(G) pg. 456

20. D 511.7(A)(1) pg. 394

21. D 500.5(C) pg. 351

22. C 422.10(A) pg. 276
 422.13 pg. 277

23. A 422.11(B) pg. 276

24. D 250.53(G) pg. 113

25. C Chapter 9, Table 4 pg. 681
 Chapter 9, Table 5 pg. 685

Size 1 AWG THW = .1901 sq. in. x 5 = .9505 sq. in.
Size 3 AWG THW = .1134 sq. in. x 5 = .567 sq. in.
 Total = 1.5175 sq. in.

*NOTE: A trade size 2½ in. IMC with an allowable 40% fill of 2.054 sq. in. should
 Be selected.

##

JOURNEYMAN ELECTRICIAN'S EXAM PREP GUIDE
EXAM #5

The following questions are based on the 2017 edition of the National Electrical Code® and are typical of questions encountered on most Journeyman Electricians' Licensing Exams. On each question select the best answer from the choices given and review your answers with the answer key included in this book. Typically, the only material permitted for use on this type of exam is a calculator, scratch paper and a current edition of the NEC® book. Each question on this test has a value of 4 points: a passing score is 70%. In order to pass, you therefore need to get 18 of the 25 questions correct.

ALLOTTED TIME: 75 minutes

1. Where flexible cord is used as the wiring method to supply ac motors, the MINIMUM size of the conductors shall be selected in accordance with _____ of the NEC®.

A. Table 310.15(B)(16)
B. Table 310.15(B)(17)
C. Table 310.15(B)(18)
D. Section 400.5

2. When an industrial control panel is supplied from a 3-phase, 4-wire, delta-connected electrical system, the phase having the higher voltage to ground is _____ .

A. required to be the "A" phase
B. required to be the "B" phase
C. required to be the "C" phase
D. permitted to be any phase

3. When conductors having a voltage of not more than 1000 volts pass above a public driveway, they shall have a MINIMUM clearance of NOTless than _____ above finished grade.

A. 10 feet
B. 15 feet
C. 18 feet
D. 20 feet

4. Shore power for boats shall be provided by single receptacles rated NOT less than
_____.

A. 20 amperes
B. 30 amperes
C. 50 amperes
D. 60 amperes

5. Where a mobile home has the main service disconnecting means installed outdoors,
the disconnecting means shall be installed so the bottom of the enclosure is NOT less
than _____ above finished grade.

A. two feet
B. three feet
C. four feet
D. six feet

6. Determine the MAXIMUM allowable ampacity of a 3-conductor size 6 AWG XHHW
aluminum SER cable installed in the attic of a one-family dwelling where the ambient
temperature is 44 degrees C.

A. 41.2 amperes
B. 52.2 amperes
C. 47.9 amperes
D. 56.2 amperes

7. Unless specifically identified for a higher percentage of fill, the cross-sectional area of
the conductors in a conduit seal shall NOT exceed _____ of the cross-sectional area of
a rigid metal conduit of the same trade size.

A. 25 percent
B. 40 percent
C. 50 percent
D. 60 percent

8. Where a transformer is installed to supply a 243 ampere, 208-volt, 3-phase load the
transformer must have a kVA rating of at LEAST _____.

A. 300 kVA
B. 150 kVA
C. 112½ kVA
D. 90 kVA

9. Direct-buried cables or conductors located in a trench below two (2) inch thick concrete or equivalent, shall have a MINIMUM cover requirement of _____.

A. 6 inches
B. 12 inches
C. 18 inches
D. 24 inches

10. The MAXIMUM unsupported length of Type MC cable used to supply a luminaire in an accessible ceiling is permitted to be NOT more than _____ in length.

A. 10 feet
B. 6 feet
C. 4½ feet
D. 18 inches

11. For other than one- and two family dwellings, at least one 125-volt, single-phase, 15- or 20-ampere rated receptacle outlet shall be installed in an accessible location within at LEAST _____ of the indoor electrical service equipment.

A. 10 feet
B. 25 feet
C. 50 feet
D. 6 feet

12. Where a submersible water pump is located in a pond of a water treatment plant, the on land service equipment for the pump shall be NO closer than _____ horizontally from the shoreline.

A. 6 feet
B. 10 feet
C. 5 feet
D. 3 feet

13. When splicing existing underground service conductors to extend to a new service location, the NEC® requires _____ .

 I. the use of splice boxes
 II. the conductors to be protected with a covering of at
 least two (2) inches of concrete

A. I only
B. II only
C. either I or II
D. neither I nor II

14. Equipment supplied by Class 1 circuits such as fire alarm, control, and signaling circuits shall be grounded, UNLESS operating at less than _____ .

A. 25 volts
B. 120 volts
C. 50 volts
D. 150 volts

15. A single-phase, 120/240-volt, 18 kW rated home standby generator has a full-load current rating of _____ .

A. 75 amperes
B. 87 amperes
C. 100 amperes
D. 150 amperes

16. A premises wiring system supplied by a grounded ac electrical service, shall have a grounding electrode conductor connected to _____ .

A. the grounded service conductor
B. the service disconnect enclosure
C. the equipment grounding conductor
D. the meter socket enclosure

17. Intrinsically safe apparatus, associated apparatus, and other equipment shall be installed _____, unless the equipment is a simple apparatus that does not interconnect intrinsically safe circuits.

A. in accordance with the control drawings
B. in the electrical equipment room
C. on a backboard of at least 3/4 in. thick plywood
D. in a dedicated enclosure

18. When a retail furniture store has 80 continuous linear feet of display show window, the NEC® mandates at LEAST _____ 125-volt, single-phase 15- or 20-ampere rated receptacle outlets shall be provided within 18 inches of the top of the show window for the show window lighting.

A. six
B. seven
C. eight
D. nine

19. Single grounding type receptacles, with GFCI protection that provide power for water pump circulation motors of permanently installed swimming pools shall be located at LEAST ____ from the inside walls of the pool.

A. 5 feet
B. 10 feet
C. 20 feet
D. 6 feet

20. What MINIMUM size 75ºC copper feeder conductors are required to supply the following listed 3-phase, 230-volt motors?

 * one (1) 15 hp wound-rotor
 * one (1) 7½ hp induction-type
 * one (1) 3 hp induction-type

A. 4 AWG THWN
B. 4 AWG THHN
C. C. 3 AWG THW
D. 2 AWG THW

21. Which of the following is NOT required to be marked on the nameplate of a transformer?

A. kVA rating
B. manufacturer
C. voltage
D. overcurrent protection

22. In general, when current-carrying conductors are installed in parallel, the paralleled conductors in each phase shall _____.

 I. be the same size in circular mil area
 II. have the same insulation type

A. I only
B. II only
C. both I and II
D. neither I nor II

23. In compliance with the rules set forth by the NEC®, conductors with type _____ insulation are not permitted for use in wet locations such as, where installed underground in a conduit or outdoors exposed to the weather.

A. TW
B. THWN
C. THHN
D. XHHW

24. Where transformer vaults are not protected with an automatic fire-suppression system, they shall be constructed of materials that have a MINIMUM fire-resistance rating of _____.

A. 1 hour
B. 2 hours
C. 3 hours
D. 4 hours

25. In regard to new outdoor installations of permanently installed swimming pools, luminaires installed above the pool or within 5 feet horizontally from the inside wall of the pool, shall be installed at a height of NOT less than _____ above the maximum water level of the pool.

A. 10 feet
B. 12 feet
C. 15 feet
D. 8 feet

END OF EXAM #5

JOURNEYMAN ELECTRICIAN'S EXAM PREP GUIDE
PRACTICE EXAM #5
ANSWER KEY

ANSWER	REFERENCE	NEC PG. #
1. D	430.6	pg. 297
2. B	409.102(B)	pg. 267
3. C	225.18(4)	pg. 80
4. B	555.19(A)(4)	pg. 484
5. A	550.32(F)	pg. 462
6. C	Table 310.104(A)	pg. 168
	Table 310.15(B)(16)	pg. 150
	Table 310.15(B)(2)(a)	pg. 147

Size 6 AWG AL XHHW ampacity before derating = 55 amperes
55 amperes x .87 (temperature correction) = 47.85 amperes

7. A	501.15(C)(6)	pg. 358
8. D	3-phase Power Formula	

First find the VA: 208 volts x 1.732 x 243 amperes = 87,542 VA
87,542 ÷ 1000 = 87.5 kVA

9. C	Table 300.5, Column 1	pg. 137
10. B	330.30(D)(2)	pg. 189
11. C	210.64	pg. 66
12. C	682.11	pg. 556
13. D	300.5(E)	pg. 136
14. C	250.112(I)	pg. 121
15. A	Single-Phase Current Formula	

$$I = \frac{power}{volts} \quad I = \frac{18 \text{ kW} \times 1,000}{240 \text{ volts}} = \frac{18,000}{240} = 75 \text{ amperes}$$

16. A 250.24(A) pg. 107

17. A 504.10(A) pg. 372

18. B 210.62 pg. 66

$$\frac{80 \text{ ft. (show window)}}{12 \text{ ft. (per receptacle)}} = 6.7 = 7 \text{ receptacles}$$

19. D 680.22(A)(2) pg. 546

20. A 430.24(1)&(2) pg. 303
 Table 430.250 pg. 322
 Table 310.15(B)(16) pg. 150

 15 hp FLC - 42 amperes x 125% = 52.5 amperes
 7½ hp FLC - 22 amperes x 100% = 22.0 amperes
 3 hp FLC – 9.6 amperes x 100% = 9.6 amperes
 Total = 84.1 amperes

 *NOTE: Size 4 AWG THWN conductors with an allowable ampacity of 85
 amperes should be selected.

21. D 450.11 pg. 335

22. C 310.10(H)(2)(3)&(4) pg. 146

23. C Article 100 Definitions pg. 38
 300.38 pg. 143
 Table 310.104(A) pg. 167

24. C 450.42 pg. 337

25. B 680.22(B)(1) pg. 546

###

JOURNEYMAN ELECTRICIANS EXAM PREP GUIDE
EXAM #6

The following questions are based on the 2017 edition of the National Electrical Code® and are typical of questions encountered on most Journeyman Electricians' Licensing Exams. On each question select the best answer from the choices given and review your answers with the answer key included in this book. Typically, the only material permitted for use on this type of exam is a calculator, scratch paper and a current edition of the NEC® book. Each question on this test has a value of 4 points: a passing score is 70%. In order to pass, you therefore need to get 18 of the 25 questions correct.

ALLOTTED TIME: 75 minutes

1. According to Ohms Law, what is the electrical unit of current?

A. volt
B. ampere
C. ohm
D. watt

2. The NEC® definition of _____ is "connected to establish electrical continuity and conductivity".

A. bonded (bonding)
B. bonding jumper
C. Bonding jumper (main)
D. bonding jumper, equipment

3. In addition to the number of 120-volt, single-phase branch circuits required in other areas of a dwelling, at least one additional _____ branch circuit shall be provided to supply the laundry outlet in the laundry room.

A. 15-ampere
B. 20-ampere
C. 25-ampere
D. 30-ampere

4. Where rigid metal conduit (RMC) or intermediate metal conduit (IMC) is threaded in the field where corrosion protection is necessary, the threads shall be coated with a/an _____ compound.

A. oil and tar based
B. judged suitable-corrosion-resistant
C. corrosion-proof
D. approved electrically conductive, corrosion-resistant

5. Which of the following 3-phase systems would be allowed to be a high-impedance grounded neutral system where a resistor limits the ground-fault current to a low value?

A. 230 volts
B. 208Y/120 volts
C. 480 volts
D. 480Y/277 volts

6. Which of the following shall be permitted in the dedicated electrical space above a panelboard?

A. air-conditioning ducts
B. leak protection
C. piping
D. sprinkler protection

7. Motors shall be located so that adequate _____ is provided and so that maintenance, such as lubrication of bearings and replacing of brushes, can be readily accomplished.

A. ventilation
B. spacing
C. air-flow
D. dimensions

8. For bathtub and shower areas, no parts of cord-connected luminaires, lighting track or ceiling-suspended (paddle) fans shall be located within a zone measured _____ horizontally from the top of the bathtub rim or shower stall threshold.

A. 3 feet
B. 4 feet
C. 6 feet
D. 8 feet

9. After all demand factors have been taken into consideration, a one-family dwelling with a 120/240-volt, single-phase electrical system has a demand load of 35,000 VA. The MINIMUM size THWN copper phase conductors required for an underground installed service is _____.

A. 3/0 AWG
B. 2/0 AWG
C. 1/0 AWG
D. 1 AWG

10. In general, when sizing the overcurrent protection, disconnect size and the supply circuit conductors for a motor used in a continuous-duty application, they shall be sized based on the:

A. full-load running current of the motor given in the Tables of the NEC.
B. actual current marked on the motor nameplate.
C. locked-rotor current.
D. starting current of the motor.

11. Continuous-duty motors, more than one hp, with a marked service factor less than 1.15 shall have the MINIMUM running overload protection sized at _____ of the nameplate rating of the motor.

A. 140 percent
B. 125 percent
C. 130 percent
D. 115 percent

12. Mobile home service equipment shall be located in sight from and NOT more than _____ from the exterior wall of the mobile home it serves.

A. 25 feet
B. 30 feet
C. 50 feet
D. 100 feet

13. As a general rule, switches or circuit breakers shall _____.

A. not disconnect the grounded conductor of a circuit
B. be marked by means of a printed tag
C. be of the externally operable type
D. disconnect the grounded conductor of a circuit

14. A general-use switch with an ampere rating of NOT less than _____ shall be permitted as the motor controller for a single-phase, 2 hp, 230-volt motor.

A. 12 amperes
B. 15 amperes
C. 20 amperes
D. 24 amperes

15. Small gage conductors such as a single size 16 AWG conductor is permitted to carry continuous loads up to _____, as long as the conductor is protected by a fuse or circuit breaker.

A. 20 amperes
B. 15 amperes
C. 12 amperes
D. 8 amperes

16. The accessible portion of abandoned supply circuits and interconnecting cables located in an information technology equipment room shall be removed, UNLESS _____.

A. tagged and identified as abandoned
B. identified as Type CMP
C. contained in a raceway
D. disconnected from their supply source

17. Generally, in dwelling units, where one or more lighting outlets are installed for interior stairways, there shall be a wall switch at each floor level, and landing level that includes an entryway, to control the lighting outlets where the stairway between floor levels has at LEAST _____ risers or more.

A. four
B. five
C. six
D. eight

18. A receptacle installed outdoors in a location protected from the weather or in other damp locations shall have an enclosure for the receptacle that is _____ when the receptacle is covered (attachment plug cap not inserted and receptacle covers closed).

A. waterproof
B. weatherproof
C. raintight
D. watertight

19. As a general rule, the disconnecting means for motor circuits rated 1000 volts or less, shall have an ampacity of at LEAST _____ of the full-load current rating of the motor it disconnects.

A. 100 percent
B. 115 percent
C. 125 percent
D. 150 percent

20. Determine the current, in amperes, on the circuit conductors for a 208Y/120-volt, 3-phase system if each phase is balanced with a 2,500 VA load and the total load is 7,500 VA.

A. 12.01 amperes
B. 20.82 amperes
C. 36.05 amperes
D. 40.00 amperes

21. No overcurrent device shall be connected in series with any conductor that is intentionally grounded, unless the overcurrent device or circuit breaker _____.

A. simultaneously opens all conductors of the circuit
B. is corner-grounded, wye voltage systems
C. is part of a listed assembly for motor short-circuit and ground-fault protection
D. is red in color

22. For temporary wiring installations that have an assured equipment grounding conductor program, all required tests shall be performed at intervals NOT exceeding.

A. 1 month
B. 2 months
C. 3 months
D. 6 months

23. For continuous-duty motors, the motor nameplate current rating is used to determine the size of the _____ required for the motor.

A. short-circuit protection
B. branch-circuit conductors
C. disconnecting means
D. motor overload protection

24. GFCI protection for personnel is required where a 125-volt, single-phase, receptacle is located on a wet bar countertop if within _____ from the top inside edge of the bowl of the sink.

A. 6 feet
B. 10 feet
C. 12 feet
D. 15 feet

25. Boxes shall be closed by suitable covers securely fastened in place. An underground metal box cover that weighs over _____ shall be considered meeting this requirement.

A. 75 pounds
B. 80 pounds
C. 90 pounds
D. 100 pounds

END OF EXAM #6

JOURNEYMAN ELECTRICIAN'S EXAM PREP GUIDE
PRACTICE EXAM #6
ANSWER KEY

ANSWER	REFERENCE	NEC PG. #
1. B	Ohms Law I = voltage ÷ ohms = amperes	
2. A	Article 100 - Definitions	pg. 34
3. B	210.11(C)(2)	pg. 60
4. D	300.6(A)	pg. 138
5. C	250.36	pg. 111
6. D	110.26(E)(1)(a)&(c)	pg. 48
7. A	430.14(A)	pgs. 301 & 302
8. A	410.10(D)	pg. 268
9. D	Single-phase Current Formula I = P ÷ E 310.15(B)(7)(1) Table 310.15(B)(16)	pg. 149 pg. 150

$$I = \frac{36{,}000 \text{ VA}}{240 \text{ volts}} = 145.8 \text{ amperes} \times .83 = 121 \text{ amperes}$$

Size 1 AWG copper conductors with an ampacity of 130 amperes should be selected from Table 310.15(B)(16).

10. A	430.6(A)(1)	pg. 297
11. D	430.32(A)(1)	pgs. 304 & 305
12. B	550.32(A)	pg. 461
13. A	404.2(B)	pg. 254
14. D	Table 430.248 430.83(C)(1)	pg. 321 pg. 312

12 amperes x 2 = 24 amperes

15. D 240.4(D)(2)(1) pg. 94

16. C 645.5(G) pg. 527

17. C 210.70(A)(2)(c) pg. 67

18. B 406.9(A) pg. 260

19. B 430.110(A) pg. 315

20. B 3-phase current formula

$$I = VA \div volts \times 1.732$$

$$I = \frac{7,500 \ VA}{208 \times 1.732} = \frac{7,500}{360.25} = 20.82 \ amperes$$

21. A 240.22(1) pg. 98

22. C 590.6(B)(3)(a)(3)(d) pg. 487

23. D 430.6(A)(2) pg. 298

24. A 210.8(A)(7) pg. 59

25. D 314.72(E) pg. 182

###

JOURNEYMAN ELECTRICIANS EXAM PREP GUIDE
EXAM #7

The following questions are based on the 2017 edition of the National Electrical Code® and are typical of questions encountered on most Journeyman Electricians' Licensing Exams. On each question select the best answer from the choices given and review your answers with the answer key included in this book. Typically, the only material permitted for use on this type of exam is a calculator, scratch paper and a current edition of the NEC® book. Each question on this test has a value of 4 points: a passing score is 70%. In order to pass, you therefore need to get 18 of the 25 questions correct.

ALLOTTED TIME: 75 minutes

1. The branch-circuit conductors supplying a continuous-duty ac motor shall have an ampacity of NOT less than what percent of the motors full-load current rating?

A. 115 percent
B. 125 percent
C. 100 percent
D. 150 percent

2. Luminaires installed under metal-corrugated sheet roofing decking shall be installed and supported so there is NOT less than _____ clearance from the roof decking to the top of the luminaires.

A. 1 inch
B. 1¼ inches
C. 1½ inches
D. 1¾inches

3. For the purpose of calculating the general lighting load for a dwelling unit, the floor area should include all the following EXCEPT _____.

A. kitchens
B. bathrooms
C. an unfinished basement intended for future living space
D. an open porch not adaptable for future use

4. Where flexible cord is approved for use and used with a specific listed appliance, it shall be considered to be protected _____.

A. at 125% of the branch circuit rating
B. at 80% of the branch circuit rating
C. at 100% of the branch circuit rating
D. when applied within the appliance listing requirements

5. Electrical equipment, such as distribution panelboards, motor controllers, and motor control centers that are located in other than dwelling units, and are likely to require examination, adjustment, servicing, or maintenance while energized shall be field or factory marked to warn qualified persons of _____.

A. potential arc flash hazards
B. arcing parts
C. shock hazard warning
D. conductor ampacity corrections

6. Determine the MINIMUM required ampacity of the branch-circuit conductors to supply a continuous-duty, Design B, 3-phase, 208-volt, 10 hp, ac motor.

A. 30.8 amperes
B. 46.2 amperes
C. 38.5 amperes
D. 32.2 amperes

7. What is the MAXIMUM ampere rating permitted for a 125-volt, single-phase, receptacle having a cord-and-plug connected motor-load that does NOT have overload protection?

A. 10 amperes
B. 15 amperes
C. 20 amperes
D. 25 amperes

8. Which of the following 125-volt, single-phase, 15- and 20-ampere rated dwelling unit receptacles do NOT require GFCI protection for personnel?

A. A receptacle located outdoors.
B. A receptacle installed in a crawl space.
C. A receptacle behind the refrigerator in the kitchen, where more than 6 ft. from the sink.
D. A receptacle in the garage for a garage-door opener.

9. Fastened in place utilization equipment, other than luminaires, that is connected to a branch circuit with other loads shall NOT exceed _____ of the branch circuit rating.

A. 50 percent
B. 75 percent
C. 80 percent
D. 100 percent

10. In compliance with the NEC®, a 3 in. x 2 in. x 1½ in. metal device box may contain NO more than _____ size 12 AWG conductors.

A. three
B. four
C. five
D. six

11. The workspace in front of electrical equipment such as panelboards, switchboards and motor control centers rated 600 volts or less, shall be at LEAST _____ wide or the width of the equipment, whichever is greater.

A. 12 inches
B. 15 inches
C. 18 inches
D. 30 inches

12. Each receptacle of dc plugging boxes in motion picture studios shall be rated at NOT less than _____.

A. 50 amperes
B. 30 amperes
C. 15 amperes
D. 20 amperes

13. Fixed electric space-heating equipment and motors shall be considered as a _____ load when sizing branch circuits.

A. non-continuous
B. listed
C. continuous
D. consuming

14. The NEC® mandates specific branch-circuits, receptacle outlets and utilization equipment to be provided with a ground-fault circuit interrupter (GFCI); this device is intended _____.

A. to prevent overloading the conductors
B. to prevent overloading the circuit breakers
C. for the protection of equipment from overloads
D. for the protection of personnel

15. For a grounded electrical system, the equipment grounding conductor shall be sized in accordance with the _____.

A. ungrounded circuit conductors
B. overcurrent protective device
C. size of the service entrance conductors
D. grounding electrode length

16. Determine the MINIMUM size 75°C copper conductors permitted to supply a 30 hp, 230-volt, 3-phase, induction-type, continuous-duty motor.

A. 4 AWG THHN
B. 2 AWG THW
C. 4 AWG THWN
D. 3 AWG THW

17. Given: A rigid metal conduit (RMC) originates from a panelboard in an area that is unclassified, then passes through a Class I, Division 1 area, and then terminates in equipment that is also in an unclassified area. The RMC is without any connections or fittings except at the terminations. How many seal-off fittings are required in the RMC?

A. none
B. one
C. two
D. three

18. What is the MAXIMUM distance between conduit supports for trade size 2 in. rigid metal conduit?

A. 16 feet
B. 10 feet
C. 8 feet
D. 6 feet

19. Receptacles supplying power to freestanding-type office furnishings shall be located NOT more than _____ from the furnishing that is connected to it.

A. 6 feet
B. 3 feet
C. 1 foot
D. 8 feet

20. For the purpose of determining conductor fill in a device box, the NEC® mandates a switch to be counted as equal to two (2) conductors. The volume allowance for the two (2) conductors shall be based on the:

A. largest size wire in the box.
B. largest grounding conductor in the box.
C. largest size wire connect to the switch.
D. the number of clamps in the box.

21. A device or group of devices that serves to govern, in some predetermined manner, the electric power delivered to the apparatus to which it is connected is a _____.

A. panelboard
B. governor
C. generator
D. controller

22. Which of the following type motors are NOT approved for use in a Class, I Division 1 location?

A. Totally enclosed fan cooled motors.
B. Submerged motors in a liquid that is flammable only when vaporized.
C. Totally enclosed motors with positive ventilation.
D. Totally enclosed motors filled with inert gas.

23. Unless listed and identified otherwise, terminations and conductors of circuits rated 100 amperes or larger, shall be rated for _____.

A. 60°C
B. 75°C
C. 90°C
D. 100°C

24. Determine the conductor ampacity where given the following related information:

- conductors are size 500 kcmil THWN copper
- ambient temperature is 125°F
- eight (8) current-carrying conductors are in the raceway

A. 178.2 amperes
B. 199.5 amperes
C. 294.6 amperes
D. 380.0 amperes

25. Receptacles incorporating an isolated grounding conductor connection intended for the reduction of electrical noise, shall be identified by a/an _____ located on the face of the receptacle.

A. red dot
B. orange dot
C. yellow happy face
D. orange triangle

END OF EXAM #7

JOURNEYMAN ELECTRICIAN'S EXAM PREP GUIDE
PRACTICE EXAM #7
ANSWER KEY

ANSWER	REFERENCE	NEC PG. #
1. B	430.22	pg. 302
2. C	410.10(F)	pg. 268
3. D	220.12	pg. 70
4. D	240.5(B)(1)	pg. 95
5. A	110.16	pg. 45
6. C	Table 430.250 430.22	pg. 322 pg. 302

FLC of motor = 30.8 amperes amperes x 125% = 38.5 amperes

7. B	430.42(C)	pg. 307
8. C	210.8(A)(1)-(7)	pg. 59
9. A	210.23(A)(2)	pg. 63
10. A	Table 314.16(A)	pg. 176
11. D	110.26(A)(2)	pg. 47
12. B	530.14	pg. 448
13. C	424.3(B)	pg. 280
14. D	Article 100 - Definitions	pg. 37
15. B	250.32(B)(1) Table 250.122	pg. 110 pg. 125
16. D	Table 430.250 430.22 Table 310.15(B)(16)	pg. 322 pg. 302 pg. 150

FLC of motor – 80 amperes x 125% = 100 amperes
Size 3 AWG conductors with an ampacity of 100 amperes should be selected from Table 310.15(B)(16).

17. A 501.15(A)(4), Exception 1 pg. 357

18. A Table 344.30(B)(2) pg. 199

19. C 605.9(B) pg. 496

20. C 314.16(B)(4) pg. 176

21. D Article 100 – Definitions pg. 35

22. A 501.125(A)(1)-(4) pg. 362

23. B 110.14(C)(1)(b)(1) pg. 45

24. A Table 310.15(B)(16) pg. 150
Table 310.15(B)(2)(a) pg. 147
Table 310.15(B)(3)(a) pg. 148

500 kcmil THWN copper ampacity before derating = 380 amperes
380 amps x .67 (temp. correction) x .7 adj. factor = 178.22 amperes

25. D 406.3(D) pg. 258

##

JOURNEYMAN ELECTRICIANS EXAM PREP GUIDE
EXAM #8

The following questions are based on the 2017 edition of the National Electrical Code® and are typical of questions encountered on most Journeyman Electricians' Licensing Exams. On each question select the best answer from the choices given and review your answers with the answer key included in this book. Typically, the only material permitted for use on this type of exam is a calculator, scratch paper and a current edition of the NEC® book. Each question on this test has a value of 4 points: a passing score is 70%. In order to pass, you therefore need to get 18 of the 25 questions correct.

ALLOTTED TIME: 75 minutes

1. When determining the initial standard size time-delay fuses for branch-circuit, short-circuit and ground-fault protection for a three-phase, continuous-duty, squirrel cage, ac motor, the fuses shall have a rating of _____ of the full-load current of the motor. When the value determined does not correspond to a standard ampere rating, the next higher standard rating shall be permitted.

A. 175 percent
B. 150 percent
C. 225 percent
D. 250 percent

2. A junction box to be installed will contain five (5) size 12 AWG conductors and six (6) size 10 AWG conductors. The junction box is required to have a volume of at LEAST _____.

A. 21.00 cu.in.
B. 22.75 cu. in.
C. 24.75 cu. in.
D. 26.25 cu. in.

3. Neon sign equipment having an open circuit voltage exceeding how many volts shall NOT be installed in or on dwelling occupancies?

A. 1000 volts
B. 300 volts
C. 250 volts
D. 125 volts

4. What MINIMUM size equipment grounding conductor is required for a 240-volt, single-phase, 10 kW residential electric range?

A. 10 AWG
B. 8 AWG
C. 12 AWG
D. 6 AWG

5. Where the NEC® specifies that one equipment shall be within sight of another equipment, the specified equipment is to be visible and NOT more than _____ distant from the other.

A. 100 feet
B. 50 feet
C. 10 feet
D. 25 feet

6. All 125-volt, single-phase, 15- and 20-ampere receptacle outlets in a dwelling must be installed in habitable rooms so that no point along the floor line is further from an outlet than _____.

A. 5 feet
B. 4½ feet
C. 6 feet
D. 12 feet

7. Luminaires mounted in walls of permanently installed swimming pools shall be installed with the top of the luminaire lens NOT less than _____ below the normal water level of the pool, unless the luminaire is listed and identified for use at lesser depths.

A. 18 inches
B. 6 inches
C. 24 inches
D. 12 inches

8. Where there is no overcurrent protection on the secondary side of a 480-volt transformer with a primary current of 100 amperes, the rating of the primary overcurrent protective device should NOT exceed _____.

A. 100 amperes
B. 250 amperes
C. 125 amperes
D. 80 amperes

9. For the purpose of maintaining and servicing a 3-phase, 208Y/120-volt switchboard, a MINIMUM clear depth distance of _____ must be maintained in front of the switchboard.

A. 4 feet
B. 3½ feet
C. 2 feet
D. 3 feet

10. Where a permanently installed generator is installed as a separately derived system, which of the following must be provided?

A. main bonding jumper
B. system bonding jumper
C. one grounding electrode only
D. multiple grounding electrodes

11. Type AC cable shall provide an adequate path for _____.

A. water drainage
B. a grounding electrode
C. fault-current
D. grounding conductors

12. Mandatory rules of the NEC® are those that identify actions that are specifically required or prohibited are characterized by the use of the terms _____.

A. shall or shall not
B. may or may not
C. will or will not
D. all of these terms apply

13. For a direct burial feeder cable to a water well pump located 50 feet from a dwelling, which of the following listed wiring methods is approved for such use?

A. Type NM cable
B. Type AC cable
C. Type TC cable
D. Type UF cable

14. All of the following wiring methods are permitted in a ceiling space used as a return-air plenum EXCEPT:

A. Type AC cable.
B. rigid PVC conduit.
C. intermediate metal conduit (IMC).
D. Type MI cable.

15. A 240-volt, single-phase 10 kW commercial dishwasher will draw _____ of current.

A. 21 amperes
B. 24 amperes
C. 42 amperes
D. 30 amperes

16. A type of fuse NOT permitted for new installations and shall be used only for replacements in existing installations is a/an _____ fuse.

A. Edison-base
B. Class K
C. Class CC
D. time-delay

17. Which of the following listed flexible cords shall be permitted to be immersed in water to supply a permanently installed fountain located at an amusement park?

A. Type SJOW
B. Type SOO
C. Type SJ
D. Type SOW

18. Where cord-and-plug connected appliances are likely to be used simultaneously, each _____ or fraction thereof of fixed multioutlet assemblies used in other than dwelling units, shall be considered as an outlet of not less than 180 volt-amperes.

A. 24 inches
B. 6 inches
C. 48 inches
D. 12 inches

19. All 15- and 20-ampere, single-phase, 125-volt receptacles located within at LEAST _____ of the inside walls of a permanently installed swimming pool must be provided with GFCI protection.

A. 10 feet
B. 15 feet
C. 25 feet
D. 20 feet

20. A point on a wiring system at which current is taken to supply fixtures, lamps, heaters, motors and similar current-consuming equipment is considered a/an _____.

A. outlet
B. service
C. receptacle
D. circuit breaker

21. The MINIMUM number of 120-volt, 15-ampere, general lighting branch circuits required for a dwelling with 70 feet by 30 feet of livable space is _____.

A. two
B. three
C. four
D. five

22. Given: A branch circuit supplies a single hermetic refrigerant motor-compressor, with a FLC rating of 18 amperes, for an air conditioning unit on a dwelling unit. If 30-

ampere fuses used as overcurrent protection will not carry the starting current of the unit, the rating of the fuses may be increased to a MAXIMUM value of _____.

A. 35 amperes
B. 40 amperes
C. 45 amperes
D. 50 amperes

23. The NEC® requires branch circuits be rated in accordance with the overcurrent protective device. Therefore, which of the following combinations of loads are permitted for lighting branch-circuits?

A. 20, 30, 40, 50 and 70 amperes
B. 20, 30, 40, 50 and 60 amperes
C. 15, 25, 35, 45 and 50 amperes
D. 15, 20, 30, 40 and 50 amperes

24. Generally, outside open conductors on insulators, of 600 volts or less, must be covered or insulated when they are within _____ of a building.

A. 10 feet
B. 12 feet
C. 15 feet
D. 25 feet

25. Disregarding exceptions, the NEC® mandates the MINIMUM size overhead service conductors to be _____.

A. 1 AWG copper or 2 AWG aluminum
B. 6 AWG copper or 4 AWG aluminum
C. 8 AWG copper or 6 AWG aluminum
D. 1/0 AWG copper or 2/0 AWG aluminum

END OF EXAM #8

JOURNEYMAN ELECTRICIAN'S EXAM PREP GUIDE
PRACTICE EXAM #8
ANSWER KEY

ANSWER	REFERENCE	NEC PG. #
1. A	Table 430.52	pg. 308
	430.52(C)(1), Exception 1	pg. 307
2. D	Table 314.16(B)	pg. 176

Size 12 AWG – 2.25 cu. in x 5 wires = 11.25 cu. in.
Size 10 AWG - 2.50 cu. in. x 6 wires = 15.00 cu. in.
TOTAL = 26.25 cu. in.

3. A	600.32(I)	pg. 492
4. A	Table 220.55, Column C	pg. 74
	210.19(A)(3)	pg. 62
	Table 250.122	pg. 125
5. B	Article 100 - Definitions	pg. 38
6. C	210.52(A)(1)	pg. 64
7. A	680.23(A)(5)	pg. 547
8. C	450.3(B)	pg. 332
	Table 450.3(B)	pg. 333

100 amperes x 125% = 125 amperes

9. D	Table 110.26(A)(1)	pg. 47
10. B	250.35(A)	pg. 111
	250.30(A)(1)	pg. 108
11. C	320.108	pg. 183
12. A	90.5(A)	pg. 31
13. D	340.10(1)	pg. 195
14. B	300.22(C)(1)	pg. 142

15. C Single-phase current formula
$$I = power \div volts$$

$$I = \frac{10{,}000 \text{ watts}}{240 \text{ volts}} = 41.6 \text{ amperes}$$

16. A 240.51(B) pg. 99

17. D 680.56(B) pg. 554
 Table 400.4 pg. 245

18. D 220.14(H)(2) pg. 71

19. D 680.22(A)(4) pg. 546

20. A Article 100 – Definitions pg. 39

21. C Table 220.12 pg. 71

70 ft. x 30 ft. = 2100 sq. ft. x 3 VA = 6300 VA (house load)
120 volts x 15 amperes = 1800 VA (one circuit)

$$\frac{6300 \text{ VA (load)}}{1800 \text{ VA (circuit)}} = 3.5 = 4 \text{ general lighting circuits}$$

22. B 440.22(A) pg. 327

18 amperes x 225 % = 40.5 amperes

23. D 210.18 pg. 61

24. A 225.4 pg. 78

25. C 230.23(B) pg. 85

##

JOURNEYMAN ELECTRICIANS EXAM PREP GUIDE
EXAM #9

The following questions are based on the 2017 edition of the National Electrical Code® and are typical of questions encountered on most Journeyman Electricians' Licensing Exams. On each question select the best answer from the choices given and review your answers with the answer key included in this book. Typically, the only material permitted for use on this type of exam is a calculator, scratch paper and a current edition of the NEC® book. Each question on this test has a value of 4 points: a passing score is 70%. In order to pass, you therefore need to get 18 of the 25 questions correct.

ALLOTTED TIME: 75 minutes

1. Every panelboard circuit and circuit modification shall be:

A. legibly identified at the panelboard.
B. copper conductors only.
C. marked before insulating.
D. identified by orange in color.

2. Installation of direct-buried cables in an area that is subject to movement by frost or settlement shall be _____.

A. prohibited
B. pre-tensioned prior to cover
C. placed with "S" loops or adequate allowance for movement
D. placed on running boards of pressure-treated wood or PVC type boards

3. As a general rule, the disconnecting means for an air-conditioning or refrigerating unit is required to be a MINIMUM rating of _____ of its nameplate rated-load current.

A. 100%
B. 115%
C. 125%
D. 150%

4. Electrical equipment rooms or enclosures housing electrical apparatus that are controlled by a lock(s) shall be considered accessible to _____.

A. qualified persons only
B. electricians only
C. the building management
D. the authority having jurisdiction

5. What MINIMUM size copper THW conductors are required to supply a single-phase, 240-volt, 5 hp motor and a single-phase, 240-volt, 1kW, non-continuous non-motor load?

A. 10 AWG
B. 6 AWG
C. 4 AWG
D. 8 AWG

6. When buried, rigid metal conduit shall have a MINIMUM ground cover of _____.

A. 24 inches
B. 18 inches
C. 12 inches
D. 6 inches

7. Cable splices made and insulated by approved methods shall be permitted to be located within a cable tray, provided they are _____.

A. well insulated from physical damage
B. performed with only copper conductors
C. accessible
D. non-accessible

8. Metallic surface-type cabinets for electrical equipment in damp or wet locations shall be mounted so there is at LEAST _____ air space between the cabinet and the wall or other supporting surface.

A. 1/8 in.
B. 1/4 in.
C. 3/8 in.
D. 1/2 in.

9. Given: An equipment disconnecting means is mounted at a height of 6 feet on a remote wall in an aircraft storage and maintenance hangar. The disconnect switch is 10 feet away from any aircraft fuel tanks. The disconnect switch is located in a/an _____ area.

A. Class II, Division 1
B. Class I, Division 2
C. Class I, Division 1
D. unclassified

10. The size of an equipment grounding conductor is most dependent upon _____.

A. line voltage
B. line resistance
C. line inductance
D. available fault-current

11. Busways shall be securely supported at intervals NOT exceeding _____ unless the raceway is otherwise designed and marked.

A. 6 feet
B. 5 feet
C. 8 feet
D. 4 feet

12. Given: You are to install an underground 50 ft. run of Schedule 40 PVC conduit that will contain three (3) size 2 AWG THWN circuit conductors and one (1) size 8 AWG THWN equipment grounding conductor. In compliance with the NEC®, what is the MINIMUM trade size PVC required for this installation?

A. 2 in.
B. 1 in.
C. 1¼ in.
D. 1½ in.

13. A single-phase, 125-volt, 15- or 20-ampere receptacle outlet shall be installed at each residential kitchen countertop and work surface that is at LEAST _____ or wider.

A. 48 inches
B. 23 inches
C. 24 inches
D. 12 inches

14. The short-circuit and ground-fault protective device protecting an air-conditioner motor-compressor branch circuit shall have sufficient _____ to permit the motor-compressor and other motors to start and accelerate their loads.

A. time delay
B. overcurrent protection
C. load
D. rating

15. In an outdoor swimming pool area, ceiling-suspended (paddle) fans installed above the pool or the area extending 5 ft. horizontally from the inside walls of the pool, shall be installed at a height NOT less than _____ above the pool water level.

A. 12 feet
B. 10 feet
C. 8 feet
D. 13 feet

16. At least one 15-volt, single-phase, 15- or 20-ampere-rated receptacle outlet is required to be installed within 18 in. of the top of a show window for each _____ linear feet or major fraction thereof of horizontal show window area.

A. 10 feet
B. 12 feet
C. 15 feet
D. 18 feet

17. Where junction or pull boxes enclose conductors of size 4 AWG or larger the boxes are to be sized by the raceway(s) entering the box and not by the size of the conductors contained in the box. Where splices, angle or U-pulls are made, the distance between each raceway entry in the box and opposite wall of the box shall NOT be less than _____ times the largest raceway in a row plus the sum of the additional raceways in the row.

A. eight
B. ten
C. six
D. seven

18. Circuit protection must be designed and capable of disconnecting motors and their controllers from the circuit. The disconnecting means of motors and their controllers shall open _____ conductor(s) of the circuit.

A. the neutral
B. the A phase
C. the B phase
D. simultaneously all ungrounded phase

19. A feeder tap less than 25 feet long does not require overcurrent protection at the tap if the ampacity of the tap conductor is at LEAST _____ of the rating of the overcurrent device protecting the feeder conductor.

A. one-half
B. 40%
C. one-third
D. 25%

20. As a general rule, overhead spans of open conductors and multiconductor cables, of not over 1000 volts, shall have a vertical clearance of NOT less than _____ above the roof surface of a building or structure.

A. 8 feet
B. 10 feet
C. 6 feet
D. 8½ feet

21. Given: A 75 kVA transformer will supply a 225 ampere rated panelboard with size 4/0 AWG THWN copper conductors. What MINIMUM size copper system bonding jumper is required for the transformer?

A. 1/0 AWG
B. 2 AWG
C. 4 AWG
D. 6 AWG

22. In a Class I, Division 1 location, each conduit entry into an explosionproof enclosure shall have a conduit seal installed within _____ from the enclosure.

A. 24 inches
B. 30 inches
C. 36 inches
D. 18 inches

23. Each commercial building accessible to pedestrians shall have an outside electric sign circuit rated at LEAST _____ that supplies no other load.

A. 15 amperes
B. 20 amperes
C. 25 amperes
D. 30 amperes

24. As a general rule, overhead service conductors, installed as open conductors, must have a clearance of at LEAST _____ laterally (to the side) from windows that are designed to be opened, doors, ladders, stairs and porches.

A. 3 feet
B. 4 feet
C. 6 feet
D. 8 feet

25. Given: A 240-volt, single-phase motor has the following marked on the nameplate:
 FLA 18 amperes
 Temperature rise 40°C
 Service factor 1.15

The overloads have a setting of 22.5 amperes however, the overload devices trip and do not allow the motor to start. The NEC® allows modification of this value and a higher setting of NOT larger than _____ is permitted for the overloads.

A. 26.4 amperes
B. 23.4 amperes
C. 25.2 amperes
D. 28.6 amperes

END OF EXAM #9

JOURNEYMAN ELECTRICIAN'S EXAM PREP GUIDE
PRACTICE EXAM #9
ANSWER KEY

ANSWER	REFERENCE	NEC PG. #
1. A	408.4(A)	pg. 263
2. C	300.5(J)(IN)	pg. 138
3. B	440.12(A)(1)	pg. 325
4. A	110.26(F)	pg. 49
5. D	Table 430.248	pg. 321
	430.24	pg. 303
	Single-phase current formula	
	Table 310.15(B)(16)	pg. 150

FLC of motor = 28 amperes x 125% = 35.0 amperes
Non-motor load I = P÷E I = 1000 ÷ 240 = 4.1 amperes
 Total load = 39.1 amperes

Size 8 AWG conductors with an ampacity of 50 amperes should be selected from Table 310.15(B)(16).

6. D	Table 300.5, Column 2	pg. 137
7. C	392.56	pg. 232
8. B	312.2	pg. 171
9. D	513.3(C)(1)	pg. 396
10. D	250.4(A)(5)	pg. 104
11. B	368.30	pg. 216

12. C Chapter 9, Table 5 pg. 685
 Chapter 9, Table 4 pg. 683

Size 2 AWG THWN = 0.1158 sq. in. x 3 wires = 0.3474 sq. in.
Size 8 AWG THWN = 0.0366 sq. in. x 1 wire = 0.0366 sq. in.
 Total = 0.3840 sq. in.

The 40% Column of Table 4 shows a trade size 1¼ in. PVC with a permitted fill of 0.581 sq. in. should be selected.

13. D 210.52(C)(1) pg. 65

14. A 440.54(B) pg. 329

15. A 680.22(B)(1) pg. 546

16. B 210.62 pg. 66

17. C 314.28(A)(2) pg. 180

18. D 430.103 pg. 314

19. C 240.21(B)(2)(1) pg. 96

20. D 225.19(A) pg. 80

21. B 250.30(A)(1) pg. 108
 250.28(D)(1) pg. 108
 Table 250.102(C)(1) pg. 119

22. D 501.15(A)(1) pg. 357

23. B 600.5(A) pg. 488

24. A 230.9(A) pg. 85

25. C 430.32(A)(1) pg. 304
 430.32(C) pg. 305

18 amperes x 140% = 25.2 amperes

##

JOURNEYMAN ELECTRICIANS EXAM PREP GUIDE
EXAM #10

The following questions are based on the 2017 edition of the National Electrical Code® and are typical of questions encountered on most Journeyman Electricians' Licensing Exams. On each question select the best answer from the choices given and review your answers with the answer key included in this book. Typically, the only material permitted for use on this type of exam is a calculator, scratch paper and a current edition of the NEC® book. Each question on this test has a value of 4 points: a passing score is 70%. In order to pass, you therefore need to get 18 of the 25 questions correct.

ALLOTTED TIME: 75 minutes

1. Where exceptions are not applicable, when a metal pole supports a luminaire, the pole shall be provided with an accessible handhole NOT of less than _____ near the base of the pole.

A. 2 in. x 6 in.
B. 3 in. x 4 in.
C. 2 in. x 4 in.
D. 4 in. x 6 in.

2. What is the MINIMUM wire bending space required at the top and bottom of a panelboard that has one (1) size 3/0 AWG conductor connected to each busbar in the panelboard?

A. 6½ inches
B. 8 inches
C. 7½ inches
D. 6 inches

3. A type of conductor insulation approved for use in both dry and wet locations is _____.

A. TFE
B. THHN
C. THWN
D. SA

4. Equipment or materials to which has been attached a symbol or other identifying mark of an organization that is acceptable to the authority having jurisdiction is defined as _____.

A. listed
B. labeled
C. approved
D. acceptable

5. Disregarding exceptions, the MAXIMUM distance permitted for seven (7) current-carrying multiconductor cables to be bundled together without requiring the ampacity of the conductors to be derated and adjustment factors be applied is _____.

A. 6 inches
B. 12 inches
C. 18 inches
D. 24 inches

6. The cut ends of electrical metallic tubing (EMT) are required to be _____.

 I. reamed
 II. threaded

A. I only
B. II only
C. both I and II
D. neither I nor II

7. Unless permitted by local code regulations, Type AC cable shall be secured within _____ of every box, cabinet, or fitting and at intervals not exceeding 4½ feet where installed on or across framing members.

A. 12 inches
B. 18 inches
C. 24 inches
D. 30 inches

8. Given: A 120/240-volt, single-phase, one-family dwelling service has a metal chain link fence opposite exposed live parts of the service equipment. The required depth of the clear working space in front of the service equipment must be at LEAST _____.

A. 2 ft. 6 in.
B. 3 ft.
C. 3 ft. 6 in.
D. 4 ft.

9. Branch circuits servicing patient bed locations in the general care (category 2) spaces of hospitals shall _____.

A. provide a minimum of 4 receptacles
B. have isolated-ground receptacles
C. have GFCI protected receptacles
D. not be part of a multiwire branch circuit

10. What MINIMUM size ungrounded (phase) THWN copper service entrance conductors are required for a 208Y/120-volt, three-phase commercial service with a demand load 72,000 VA?

A. 250 kcmil
B. 2/0 AWG
C. 3/0 AWG
D. 4/0 AWG

11. Given: A retail jewelry store has two (2) large show windows having a length of 15 feet each. One show window is on each side of the front entry/exit door. How many single-phase, 125-volt, 15- or 20-ampere rated receptacles must be provided for the show window lighting?

A. one per window
B. two per window
C. three per window
D. four per window

12. Type NM cable is permitted to be used under all the following conditions or locations EXCEPT:

A. as a feeder.
B. in Type V construction.
C. in a wet or damp location.
D. in multifamily dwellings.

13. What size copper grounding electrode conductor is required for service where size 350 kcmil copper conductors are used as the service entrance conductors?

A. 3 AWG
B. 1/0 AWG
C. 4 AWG
D. 2 AWG

14. In kitchens of dwelling units, receptacle outlets serving each wall countertop and work surface shall be installed so that no point along the wall line is more than _____ measured horizontally from a receptacle outlet in that space.

A. 24 inches
B. 6 feet
C. 4 feet
D. 8 feet

15. Where portions of a raceway are known to be subjected to different temperatures and where condensation is known to be a problem, the raceway shall be _____.

A. protected by enamel
B. of nonmetallic material
C. coated with an approved corrosion-resistant material
D. filled with an approved material to prevent the circulation of air

16. Determine the ampacity of six (6) current-carrying size 4/0 AWG XHHW aluminum conductors where installed underground in a PVC conduit.

A. 135 amperes
B. 144 amperes
C. 185 amperes
D. 210 amperes

17. Given: A six (6) foot high chain-link fence topped with razor-wire, used to deter access by persons who are not qualified, encloses an outdoor installation of electrical apparatus rated 12 kV. The razor-wire above the chain-link fence shall be at LEAST _____ in height to comply with the NEC® standards.

A. 12 inches
B. 18 inches
C. 6 inches
D. 24 inches

18. Where electrical metallic tubing (EMT) is installed under metal-corrugated sheet roof decking, the EMT shall be installed so there is NOT less than _____ clearance from the lowest surface of the roof decking to the top of the EMT.

A. 1 in.
B. 1¼ in.
C. 1½ in.
D. 2 in.

19. Remote disconnecting controls shall not be required for critical operations data systems when _____.

A. an approved fire suppression system suitable for the application is in place
B. wiring is grouped and identified
C. wiring is in metal raceways
D. wiring is under raised floors

20. Unless listed and identified otherwise, terminations and conductors of circuits rated 100 amperes or less, or marked for conductor sizes 14 AWG through 1 AWG, shall be considered rated for _____.

A. 60°C
B. 75°C
C. 90°C
D. 30°C

21. Service equipment with two or three single-pole circuit breakers shall be permitted on multiwire branch-circuits, provided they are equipped with _____.

A. proper UL listing
B. proper label affixed on circuit breakers
C. a metal rod extending through all the holes in the circuit breaker handles
D. identified handle ties

22. The NEC® requires a MAXIMUM spacing between supports for trade size 4 in. rigid polyvinyl chloride conduit (PVC) to be _____

A. 4 feet
B. 6 feet
C. 10 feet
D. 7 feet

23. Determine the MINIMUM size copper branch-circuit conductors required to supply a 5.0 kW, 240-volt, single-phase storage-type residential electric water heater. Use Type NM cable and consider all terminations to be rated 60°C.

A. 12 AWG
B. 10 AWG
C. 8 AWG
D. 6 AWG

24. As indicated in the NEC®, all of the following listed locations of dwelling units require AFCI protection on the 120-volt, single-phase, 15- and 20-ampere branch circuits supplying outlets or devices EXCEPT _____.

A. parlor, library and den
B. sunroom, closet and hallway
C. bathrooms and garages
D. dining room, living room and multimedia room

25. Where a 240-volt, single-phase residential branch-circuit using copper Type NM cable, supplies a 8 kW rated counter-mounted cooking unit and a wall-mounted oven rated 6 kW, what MINIMUM size NM cable is required?

A. 6/3 AWG with ground
B. 8/3 AWG with ground
C. 4/3 AWG with ground
D. 10/3 AWG with ground

END OF EXAM #10

JOURNEYMAN ELECTRICIAN'S EXAM PREP GUIDE
PRACTICE EXAM #10
ANSWER KEY

ANSWER	REFERENCE	NEC PG. #
1. C	410.30(B)(1)	pg. 269
2. A	Table 312.6(B), Column 1	pg. 174
3. C	Table 310.104(A)	pg. 167
	310.10(B)&(C)(2)	pg. 145
4. B	Article 100 - Definitions	pg. 38
5. D	310.15(B)(3)(a)	pg. 147
6. A	358.28(A)&(B)	pg. 210
7. A	320.30(B)	pg. 183
8. B	Table 110.26(A)(1)	pg. 47
9. D	517.18(A)	pg. 422
10. C	3-phase current formula	
	Table 310.15(B)(16)	pg. 150

$$I = P \div E \times 1.732 \quad I = \frac{72,000 \text{ VA}}{208 \times 1.732} = \frac{72,000}{360.25} = 199.8 \text{ amperes}$$

Size 3/0 AWG THWN conductors with an allowable ampacity of 200 amperes should be selected.

11. B	210.62	pg. 66

One receptacle is required for each 12 ft. of show window or major fraction thereof therefore, 2 receptacles are required for each 15 ft. show window.

12. C	334.12(B)(4)	pg. 191
13. D	250.66	pg. 115
	Table 250.66	pg. 116

14. A 210.52(C)(1) pg. 65

15. D 300.7(A) pg. 138

16. B Table 310.104(A) pg. 168
 Table 310.15(B)(16) pg. 150
 Table 310.15(B)(3)(a) pg. 148

Size 4/0 AWG XHHW AL – (75°C ampacity, wet location) = 180 amperes
180 amperes x .8 (adjustment factor) = 144 amperes

17. A 110.31 pg. 49

18. C 300.4(E) pg. 135

19. A 645.10(B)(4) pg. 527

20. A 110.14(C)(1)(a) pg. 45

21. D 230.71(B) pg. 89

22. D Table 352.30 pg. 203

23. B 422.13 pg. 277
 422.10(A) pg. 276
 Single-phase current formula
 Table 310.15(B)(16) pg. 150

$I = P \div E$ $I = \dfrac{5 \text{ kW} \times 1000}{240 \text{ volts}} = \dfrac{5000}{240} = 20.8$ amperes x 1.25 = 26 amperes

Size 10 AWG conductors with an ampacity of 30 amperes should be selected.

24. C 210.12(A) pg. 60

25. B 334.80 pg. 192
 Table 220.55, Notes 1 & 4 pg. 74
 Single-phase current formula
 Table 310.15(B)(16) pg. 150

8 kW + 6 kW = 14 kW (treat as one range)
14 kW – 12 kW = 2 kW x 5% = 10% increase in Column C
8 kW (column C) x 110% = 8.8 kW

$I = P \div E$ $I = \dfrac{8.8 \text{ kW} \times 1000}{240 \text{ volts}} = \dfrac{8800}{240} = 36.7$ amperes

Size 8 AWG conductors with an ampacity of 40 amperes should be selected from the 60°C column of Table 310.15(B)(16).

##

JOURNEYMAN ELECTRICIANS EXAM PREP GUIDE
EXAM #11

The following questions are based on the 2017 edition of the National Electrical Code® and are typical of questions encountered on most Journeyman Electricians' Licensing Exams. On each question select the best answer from the choices given and review your answers with the answer key included in this book. Typically, the only material permitted for use on this type of exam is a calculator, scratch paper and a current edition of the NEC® book. Each question on this test has a value of 4 points: a passing score is 70%. In order to pass, you therefore need to get 18 of the 25 questions correct.

ALLOTTED TIME: 75 minutes

1. Where used outdoors, aluminum or copper-clad aluminum grounding conductors shall NOT be installed or terminated within _____ of the earth.

A. 36 inches
B. 24 inches
C. 18 inches
D. 12 inches

2. A wall-mounted central vacuum assembly connected to a single receptacle located in an attached garage shall be provided with _____ protection.

A. AFCI
B. GFCI
C. LCDI
D. both AFCI and GFCI

3. Where a building or structure is supplied by more than one service:

A. a fire pump shall be installed.
B. an emergency system shall be installed.
C. an optional standby system shall be installed.
D. a permanent plaque shall be installed at each service disconnect.

4. Direct and alternating current differ in that alternating current _____.

A. reverses at intervals
B. travels in one direction
C. is intermittent
D. is asynchronous

5. As a general rule and under normal operating conditions, regardless of the type of insulation, size 12 AWG copper conductors are permitted to be protected by an overcurrent protective device with a standard rating of NOT more than _____.

A. 15 amperes
B. 20 amperes
C. 25 amperes
D. 30 amperes

6. For the purpose of service load calculations in dwelling units, each two (2) wire small appliance branch circuit shall be calculated at _____.

A. 1,000 VA
B. 1,200 VA
C. 1,500 VA
D. 2,000 VA

7. The disconnecting means for a permanently connected appliance, rated not over 300 VA or _____, is permitted to be the branch circuit overcurrent protective device where the switch or circuit breaker is within sight from the appliance or is lockable.

A. 1/8 hp
B. 1/16 hp
C. 1/4 hp
D. 1/2 hp

8. Where a straight run of trade size 4 in. conduit containing size 2/0 AWG conductors enters and exits a pull-box and no terminations or splices are made, what is the MINIMUM required length of the pull-box?

A. 20 inches
B. 24 inches
C. 32 inches
D. 36 inches

9. Where the design and operation of a generator does not prevent overloading, the ampacity of the conductors from the generator terminals to the first overcurrent protection device shall NOT be less than _____ of the nameplate current rating of the generator.

A. 115 percent
B. 125 percent
C. 130 percent
D. 150 percent

10. All single-phase cord-and-pug connected room air conditioners shall be provided with _____.

A. a cord not more than 6 ft. in length
B. a cord with conductors not smaller than 12 AWG
C. factory-installed GFCI protection
D. factory-installed AFCI, HCDI, or LCDI protection

11. The NEC® requires an equipment bonding jumper to be _____.

A. insulated
B. non-insulated
C. continuous
D. reliable

12. For Type MI cable with an outer sheath made of steel, a separate _____ shall be provided.

A. steel conductor
B. grounded conductor
C. ungrounded conductor
D. equipment grounding conductor

13. Luminaires shall be installed or constructed so that adjacent combustible materials will not be subject to temperatures in excess of _____.

A. 60°C
B. 90°C
C. 75°C
D. 30°C

14. Luminaires containing a metal halide lamp (other than a thick-glass PAR lamp) shall be provided with a containment barrier that encloses the lamp, or shall be provided with a physical means that only allow the use of a _____.

A. lamp that is Type O
B. mogul base lamp
C. lamp that is Type CB
D. lamp that is listed as explosion proof

15. Unless GFCI protection is provided, luminaires and ceiling fans located over or within 5 ft. horizontally from the inside walls of an indoor installed spa or hot tub shall have a mounting height of NOT less than _____ above the maximum water level of the spa or hot tub.

A. 6 feet
B. 8 feet
C. 10 feet
D. 12 feet

16. Which of the following wiring methods is approved for use under the accessible raised floor area of an information technology equipment room?

A. Type AC cable
B. rigid nonmetallic conduit
C. Type MC cable
D. all of these

17. The ampacity adjustment factors for conductors in Section 310.15(B)(3)(a) of the NEC® are not required to be applied when the conductors are installed in a metal wireway unless, the number of current-carrying conductors within the wireway exceeds _____.

A. 20
B. 30
C. 40
D. 50

18. The voltage at the line terminals of a fire pump motor controller shall NOT drop more than _____ below the controller's nominal rated voltage under motor-starting conditions. This limitation shall not apply for emergency run mechanical starting.

A. 5 percent
B. 10 percent
C. 15 percent
D. 20 percent

19. Where a size 1/0 AWG THWN aluminum conductor is installed outdoors in a raceway with two (2) other current-carrying conductors of the same size and the ambient temperature reaches 110°F, the conductor has an allowable ampacity of _____.

A. 100 amperes
B. 90 amperes
C. 98 amperes
C. 104 amperes

20. Ceiling suspended (paddle) fans weighing MORE than _____ shall be supported independently of the outlet box.

A. 35 pounds
B. 50 pounds
C. 30 pounds
D. 70 pounds

21. Inverse-time circuit breakers rated at _____ or less and 1000 volts or less shall have the ampere rating molded, stamped, etched or similarly marked into their handles or escutcheon areas.

A. 200 amperes
B. 100 amperes
C. 400 amperes
D. 600 amperes

22. Where the service of a building is provided with ground-fault protection, the MAXIMUM trip time delay shall be _____ for ground-fault currents equal to or greater than 3,000 amperes.

A. one second
B. five seconds
C. 30 seconds
D. 60 seconds

23. Conductor ampacity adjustment factors shall not apply to conductors in raceways having a length NOT exceeding _____.

A. 12 inches
B. 24 inches
C. 18 inches
D. 36 inches

24. The connection between the grounded circuit conductor and the equipment grounding conductors at the electrical service is recognized as the _____ in the NEC®.

A. main bonding jumper
B. grounding electrode conductor
C. equipment bonding jumper
D. neutral conductor

25. Appliances require a separate disconnecting means or a unit switch with a marked "OFF" position, that is part of the appliance and will disconnect all _____.

A. circuit conductors
B. grounded conductors
C. ungrounded conductors
D. conductors including the grounding conductor

END OF EXAM #11

JOURNEYMAN ELECTRICIAN'S EXAM PREP GUIDE
PRACTICE EXAM #11
ANSWER KEY

ANSWER	REFERENCE	NEC PG. #
1. C	250.64(A)	pg. 114
2. B	210.8(A)(2)	pg. 59
3. D	230.2(E)	pg. 84
4. A	Trade knowledge	
5. B	240.4(D)(5)	pg. 94
6. C	220.52(A)	pg. 73
7. A	422.31(A)	pg. 278
8. C	314.28(A)(1)	pg. 180

4 in. (conduit) x 8 = 32 inches

9. A	445.13	pg. 330
10. D	440.65	pg. 329
11. C	250.102(D)	pg. 119
12. D	332.108	pg. 190
13. B	410.11	pg. 268
14. A	410.130(F)(5)	pg. 273
15. D	680.43(B)(1)(A)	pg. 552
16. D	645.5(E)(1)(b)	pg. 526
17. B	376.22(B)	pg. 220
18. C	695.7(A)	pg. 579

| 19. C | Table 310.15(B)(16) | pg. 150 |
| | Table 310.15(B)(2)(a) | pg. 147 |

1/0 AWG AL ampacity before derating = 120 amperes
120 amperes x .82 (temperature correction factor) = 98.4 amperes

20. D	314.27(C)	pg. 179
21. B	240.83(B)	pg. 100
22. A	230.95(A)	pg. 91
23. B	310.15(B)(3)(a)(2)	pg. 147
24. A	Article 100 – Definitions	pg. 34
25. C	422.34	pg. 279

###

JOURNEYMAN ELECTRICIANS EXAM PREP GUIDE
EXAM #12

The following questions are based on the 2017 edition of the National Electrical Code® and are typical of questions encountered on most Journeyman Electricians' Licensing Exams. On each question select the best answer from the choices given and review your answers with the answer key included in this book. Typically, the only material permitted for use on this type of exam is a calculator, scratch paper and a current edition of the NEC® book. Each question on this test has a value of 4 points: a passing score is 70%. In order to pass, you therefore need to get 18 of the 25 questions correct.

ALLOTTED TIME: 75 minutes

1. Which of the following is a correct NEC® provision for an equipment bonding jumper?

A. An equipment bonding jumper is permitted to be a wire, bus, or screw.
B. The bonding jumper shall be of the same size and of the same material as the ungrounded conductors in the raceway.
C. The size of an equipment bonding jumper on the load side of the service is based on the size of the largest ungrounded service-entrance conductor.
D. The maximum length of an equipment bonding jumper is 10 feet.

2. Where a 15- or 20-ampere rated branch circuit supplies three (3) 15-ampere rated receptacles, the MAXIMUM load any one receptacle is permitted to carry is _____.

A. 10 amperes
B. 15 ampere
C. 12 amperes
D. 8 amperes

3. Where a surface-mounted luminaire containing a ballast or transformer is to be located on combustible low-density cellulose fiberboard, the ballast or transformer shall be marked for this condition or shall be spaced NOT less than _____ from the surface of the fiberboard.

A. 1 in.
B. 1½ in.
C. 1¾ in.
D. 1¼ in.

4. A metal device box to be installed will contain one (1) duplex receptacle, two (2) internal cable clamps and two (2) size 12/2 with ground nonmetallic sheathed cables. To comply with NEC® standards the device box must have a volume, in cubic inches, of at LEAST _____.

A. 13.50 cubic inches
B. 15.75 cubic inches
C. 16.00 cubic inches
D. 18.00 cubic inches

5. On a 4-wire delta-connected system, the conductor having the higher phase voltage to ground shall be durably and permanently marked by an outer finish that is _____ in color or by other effective means.

A. red
B. black
C. white
D. orange

6. Resistance-type hating elements in electric space heating equipment shall be subdivided into loads NOT exceeding _____.

A. 60 amperes
B. 50 amperes
C. 48 amperes
D. 40 amperes

7. When a receptacle outlet is removed from an underfloor raceway, the conductors supplying the outlet _____.

A. shall be capped with an approved insulating material
B. shall be taped off and identified with red colored phase tape
C. are permitted to be marked, identified and remain in the raceway
D. shall be removed from the raceway

8. For other than listed low-voltage luminaires not requiring grounding, wet-niche luminaires installed in permanently installed swimming pools shall be connected to an insulated copper equipment grounding conductor NOT smaller than _____.

A. 12 AWG
B. 10 AWG
C. 14 AWG
D. 8 AWG

9. Disregarding exceptions, the MINIMUM size grounded or ungrounded conductors permitted to be connected in parallel (electrically joined at both ends) is _____.

A. 6 AWG
B. 1 AWG
C. 1/0 AWG
D. 2/0 AWG

10. For track lighting located in other than dwelling units, or guest rooms or suites of hotels or motels, a load of _____ shall be calculated for every two (2) feet of lighting track or fraction thereof.

A. 150 VA
B. 180 VA
C. 120 VA
D. 200 VA

11. Branch circuits supplying one or more information technology units or data processing units shall have an ampacity (current-carrying capacity) of NOT less than _____ of the total connected load.

A. 115%
B. 125%
C. 100%
D. 150%

12. Where installed in an ambient temperature of not more than 86°F, Type SRD multiconductor cable consisting of size 8 AWG conductors and only two (2) conductors in the cable are current-carrying, the allowable ampacity of the conductors is _____.

A. 25 amperes
B. 30 amperes
C. 40 amperes
D. 35 amperes

13. A fifty (50) ft. run of Schedule 40 PVC conduit is to contain the following copper conductors:

• four (4) size 1 AWG XHHW
• one (1) size 6 AWG bare

Determine the MINIMUM trade size PVC required as per the NEC®.

A. 2 in.
B. 1½in.
C. 1¼ in.
D. 1 in.

14. For circuits over _____ to ground, the electrical continuity of rigid metal conduit (RMC) that contain any conductor, other than service conductors, shall be insured with two (2) locknuts, one inside and one outside of boxes and cabinets.

A. 120 volts
B. 150 volts
C. 240 volts
D. 250 volts

15. In regard to dwelling units, at least one _____ branch circuit shall be provided to supply the laundry receptacle outlet(s).

A. 15 ampere
B. 20 ampere
C. 25 ampere
D. 30 ampere

16. Given: An 18 cubic inch Type FS device box that contains a receptacle is supported only by two (2) underground installed rigid metal conduits that are made-up wrench-tight into the box. Each conduit shall be secured within at LEAST _____ of the box.

A. 18 inches
B. 12 inches
C. 24 inches
D. 8 inches

17. Where a conductor is marked *RHW-2* on the insulation, what does the *-2* represent?

A. The cable has two conductors.
B. The conductor is double insulated.
C. The conductor has a nylon outer jacket.
D. The conductor has a maximum operating temperature of 90°C.

18. Drywall or plasterboard surfaces that are damaged around boxes having a flush-type cover or faceplate shall be repaired so there will be no gaps greater than _____ at the edge of the box.

A. 1/8 in.
B. 1/4 in.
C. 3/8 in.
D. 1/2 in.

19. All electrical equipment including boxes, cabinets and raceways installed in Class I, Division 1 locations shall be _____ equipment.

A. explosion resistant
B. dust-tight
C. dust-proof
D. explosionproof

20. Where the service-entrance conductors for a commercial occupancy are size 350 kcmil aluminum, what size copper grounding electrode conductor would be required? (Assume the grounding conductor extends to multiple electrodes.)

A. 6 AWG
B. 4 AWG
C. 2 AWG
D. 1/0 AWG

21. Equipment grounding conductors for photovoltaic source and photovoltaic output circuits shall NOT be smaller than _____.

A. 14 AWG
B. 12 AWG
C. 10 AWG
D. 8 AWG

22. What is the approximate horsepower rating of a 240-volt, single-phase motor that draws 18.5 amperes of current, with an efficiency of 85 percent?

A. 3½ hp
B. 5 hp
C. 10 hp
D. 7½ hp

23. Where exposed Type NM cable passes through a floor, the cable shall be protected from physical damage by an approved means extending at LEAST _____ above the floor.

A. 4 inches
B. 6 inches
C. 8 inches
D. 10 inches

24. Branch circuit outlets supplying 120-volt, single phase, swimming pool pump motors for a permanently installed swimming pool shall be provided with GFCI protection for personnel when _____.

I. cord-and-plug connected to a receptacle
II. direct connected (hard-wired)

A. I only
B. II only
C. either I or II
D. neither I nor II

25. Recessed luminaires installed in suspended ceilings shall:

A. be supported independently of the ceiling grid.
B. not be attached to the ceiling framing members.
C. be attached to the building structural support framing members.
D. be attached to the ceiling framing members by clips, screws or rivets listed and identified for use with the luminaire and ceiling framing members.

END OF EXAM #12

JOURNEYMAN ELECTRICIAN'S EXAM PREP GUIDE
PRACTICE EXAM #12
ANSWER KEY

ANSWER	REFERENCE	NEC PG. #
1. A	250.102(A)	pg. 118
2. C	Table. 210.21(B)(2)	pg. 63
3. B	410.136(B)	pg. 274
4. D	314.16(B)(1),(2),(4)&(5) Table 314.16(B)	pgs. 175 & 176 pg. 176

 2 ungrounded conductors = 2 x 2.25 cu. in. = 4.50 cubic inches
 2 grounded conductors = 2 x 2.25 cu. in. = 4.50 cubic inches
 2 grounding conductors = 1 x 2.25 cu. in. = 2.25 cubic inches
 2 cable clamps = 1 x 2.25 cu. in. = 2.25 cubic inches
 1 device = 2 x 2.25 cu. in. = 4.50 cubic inches
 Total = 18.00 cubic inches

5. D	110.15	pg. 45
6. C	424.22(B)	pg. 282
7. D	390.8	pg. 228
8. A	680.23(F)(2)	pg. 548
9. C	310.10(H)(1)	pg. 146
10. A	220.43(B)	pg. 72
11. B	645.5(A)	pg. 526
12. C	Table 400.5(A)(1), Column B	pg. 248

13. B Chapter 9, Table 5 pg. 687
 Chapter 9, Table 8 pg. 689
 Chapter 9, Table 4 pg. 683

Size 1 AWG XHHW = .1534 sq. in. x 4 wires = .6136 sq. in.
Size 6 AWG bare = .0270 sq. in.
 Total = .6406 sq. in.

A trade size 1½ in. Schedule 40 PVC with an allowable fill of .794 sq. in. should be selected.

14. D 250.97, Exception 2 pg. 118

15. B 210.11(C)(2) pg. 60

16. A 314.23(F) pg. 178

17. D Table 310.104(A) pg. 166

18. A 314.21 pg. 177

19. D 500.7(A) pg. 352

20. C Table 250.66 pg. 116

21. A 690.45 pg. 566

22. B horsepower formula

$$HP = \frac{I \times E \times Eff.}{746 \text{ watts}} \qquad \text{*NOTE} - 1 \text{ hp} = 746 \text{ watts}$$

$$HP = \frac{18.5 \text{ amps} \times 240 \text{ volts} \times .85 \text{ eff.}}{746 \text{ watts}} = \frac{3{,}774}{746} = 5.05 \text{ hp}$$

23. B 334.15(B) pg. 191

24. C 680.21(C) pg. 546

25. D 410.36(B) pg. 269

###

JOURNEYMAN ELECTRICIAN'S EXAM PREP GUIDE
FINAL EXAM #1

The following questions are based on the 2017 edition of the National Electrical Code® and are typical of questions encountered on most Journeyman Electricians' Licensing Exams. On each question select the best answer from the choices given and review your answers with the answer key included in this book. A passing score on this exam is 70%, and the exam consists of 80 questions valued at 1.25 points each. You therefore must answer 56 questions correctly for a passing score. If you do not score at least 70%, try again and keep studying. GOOD LUCK.

ALLOTTED TIME: 4 hours

1. Where not in excess of 1000 volts, the MINIMUM permitted height of service-drop conductors installed over an apple orchard or orange grove is _____ above ground.

A. 12 feet
B. 15 feet
C. 21 feet
D. 18 feet

2. The purpose of the NEC® is _____.

A. to have an installation that is efficient
B. the practical safeguarding of persons and property
C. for future expansion of electrical use
D. to provide an installation that is adequate for good service

3. For the purpose of maintaining electrical equipment such as panelboards, switchboards, motor control centers and switchgear of 600 volts or less, the width of the working space in front of the equipment shall be the width of the equipment or NOT less than _____, whichever is greater.

A. 24 inches
B. 48 inches
C. 30 inches
D. 36 inches

4. All 15- and 20-ampere 125-volt, single-phase straight blade-type receptacles located in _____ shall be listed as tamper-resistant.

A. dormitories
B. waiting rooms of dental offices
C. elementary schools
D. all of these

5. When wiring motor fuel dispensing pumps, the first fitting that should be installed in the raceway that emerges from below ground or concrete into the base of the gasoline dispenser is a/an:

A. automatic cut-off breakaway valve.
B. disconnect.
C. sealing fitting.
D. no fittings of any kind are permitted in this location.

6. One kVA is equal to _____.

A. one hundred watts
B. one thousand volt-amps
C. one hundred kilo-watts
D. one hundred volt-amps

7. A 15 kW, 208-volt, single-phase heat-pump has a full-load current rating of _____.

A. 42 amperes
B. 125 amperes
C. 65 amperes
D. 72 amperes

8. When sizing the overcurrent protection for a single non-motor operated appliance such as a storage-type water heater, cooktop or range, which of the following need NOT to be taken into consideration?

A. The length of time the appliance operates.
B. The full-load current marked on the appliance.
C. The voltage rating of the appliance.
D. Where the overcurrent protection device selected is not a standard size.

9. When installed, a metal junction box will contain the following conductors:

 * three - 6 AWG wires, 2 ungrounded & 1 grounded
 * one - 8 AWG equipment grounding conductor
 * two - internal clamps
 * one - pigtail

Determine the MINIMUM size box, in cubic inches, the NEC® requires.

A. 16 cubic inches
B. 18 cubic inches
C. 20 cubic inches
D. 23 cubic inches

10. Round access openings in a manhole shall NOT be less than _____ in diameter.

A. 24 inches
B. 26 inches
C. 30 inches
D. 36 inches

11. Strut-type channel raceways shall be permitted to be suspension mounted in air with identified methods at intervals NOT to exceed _____.

A. 6 feet
B. 10 feet
C. 12 feet
D. 8 feet

12. On land, the service equipment for floating structures and submersible electrical equipment shall be located NO closer than _____ horizontally from the shoreline.

A. 5 feet
B. 10 feet
C. 15 feet
D. 20 feet

13. Determine the MINIMUM size 75 deg. C rated copper conductors required to supply a fixed electric space heating unit with heating elements having a full-load current rating of 125 amperes and a blower motor having a full-load current rating of 2.5 amperes.

A. 1 AWG
B. 2 AWG
C. 2/0 AWG
D. 3/0 AWG

14. Where a thermal protector is integral with the motor, the ultimate trip current of a thermally protected 2 horsepower, single-phase, 240-volt motor shall NOT exceed _____ of the full-load current of the motor.

A. 115 percent
B. 125 percent
C. 140 percent
D. 156 percent

15. Under which one of the following conditions are you required to use an approved electrically conductive corrosion resistance compound on metal conduit threads?

A. In Class I Division 1 locations.
B. In Class II Division 1 locations.
C. On field cut threads for indoor locations.
D. On field cut threads in corrosive locations.

16. Disregarding exceptions, each patient bed location in general care (category 2) spaces of hospitals shall be provided with a MINIMUM of _____ "hospital grade" receptacles.

A. eight
B. ten
C. twelve
D. fourteen

17. Where a receptacle outlet is installed for a specific appliance, such as a washing machine located in a laundry room, the outlet shall be installed within at LEAST _____ of the intended location of the appliance.

A. 4 feet
B. 6 feet
C. 5 feet
D. 8 feet

18. In general, overhead service-drop conductors shall NOT be smaller than size _____.

A. 8 AWG copper
B. 6 AWG copper
C. 8 AWG aluminum
D. 2 AWG aluminum

19. What MINIMUM size bonding conductor must bond all metal parts associated with a hot tub?

A. 12 AWG
B. 10 AWG
C. 8 AWG
D. 6 AWG

20. When installing galvanized rigid metal conduit (RMC), where structural members readily permit fastening, the conduit is required to be fastened within at LEAST _____ of a junction box, panelboard or cabinet.

A. 3 feet
B. 5 feet
C. 6 feet
D. 10 feet

21. In general, the disconnecting means for motor circuits rated 1000 volts or less, shall have an ampere rating of at LEAST what percent of the full-load current rating of the motor supplied?

A. 80 percent
B. 100 percent
C. 115 percent
D. 125 percent

22. Given: A 240-volt wye-connected motor derives power from a converted single-phase source. It is desired to connect a 120/240-volt transformer for control of the motor on the load side of the converter. The control transformer must _____ .

A. be connected to the manufactured phase
B. be disconnected after start-up of the motor
C. have separate overcurrent protection
D. not be connected to the manufactured phase

23. What is the MAXIMUM size overcurrent protection device required to protect size 14 AWG conductors used for the pump motor control-circuit that is protected by the motor branch circuit protection device and extends beyond the enclosure?

A. 15 amperes
B. 20 amperes
C. 45 amperes
D. 100 amperes

24. Where raceways are installed above grade outdoors and exposed to the weather, the interior of these raceways shall be considered to be a _____ location.

A. damp
B. moist
C. dry
D. wet

25. In dwelling units, hallways of at LEAST _____ or more in length shall be provided with at least one 125-volt, 15- or 20-ampere rated receptacle.

A. 10 feet
B. 12 feet
C. 15 feet
D. 20 feet

26. A motor overload device functions in direct response to _____.

A. voltage
B. motor current
C. temperature rise of the motor
D. ambient temperature

27. When a cord-and-plug connected water softener is wired to a 20 ampere rated branch-circuit, the SMALLEST size flexible cord to supply the water softener as permitted by the NEC® is size _____.

A. 18 AWG
B. 16 AWG
C. 14 AWG
D. 20 AWG

28. When twenty (20) size 10 AWG copper current-carrying conductors with THHN insulation are installed in a 50 feet run of trade size 1½ in. electrical metallic tubing (EMT), what is the allowable ampacity rating of each conductor?

A. 15 amperes
B. 20 amperes
C. 25 amperes
D. 30 amperes

29. Flexible metal conduit (FMC) is permitted for use in wet locations _____.

A. when the conductors within the FMC have a temperature rating of not less than 90 deg. C
B. when the conductors contained within the FMC are approved for use in wet locations
C. where the length of the FMC is not more than six (6) feet
D. under no circumstances

30. The MINIMUM size copper wire that may be used for grounding the secondary of an instrument transformer is _____.

A. 6 AWG
B. 8 AWG
C. 10 AWG
D. 12 AWG

31. In general, which one of the following statements is TRUE regarding the required disconnecting means for a fluorescent luminaire.

A. Only the ungrounded conductor to the ballast is required to be disconnected when connected to multiwire branch circuits.
B. The disconnecting means shall not be external to the luminaire.
C. The disconnecting means shall simultaneously break all supply conductors to the ballast, when connected to a multiwire branch circuit.
D. The disconnecting means shall be external to the luminaire.

32. Class 1 control-circuit conductors and motor branch-circuits are permitted by the NEC® to occupy the same raceway, if the control circuit conductors _____.

A. carry no more than 24 volts
B. have a voltage to ground not to exceed 150 volts
C. have a voltage to ground not to exceed 277 volts
D. are functionally associated with the motor system

33. In guest rooms and guest suites of hotels and motels, at LEAST _____ single-phase, 125-volt, 15- or 20-ampere rated receptacle outlet(s) shall be readily accessible.

A. one
B. two
C. three
D. four

34. A feeder supplying two (2) continuous-duty, 208-volt, 3-phase motors, one 10 hp and one 7½ hp shall have a MINIMUM ampacity of _____ amperes.

A. 55.00
B. 68.75
C. 62.70
D. 38.50

35. The reason the NEC® requires all phase conductors of the same circuit to be in the same ferrous metal raceway is to reduce _____.

A. expense
B. inductive heat
C. voltage drop
D. resistance

36. Which of the following conductor insulation types, if any, is/are acceptable for wiring in a fluorescent luminaire when the branch circuit conductor passes within three (3) inches of the ballast?

 I. THW
 II. THWN

A. I only
B. II only
C. both I and II
D. neither I nor II

37. Where practicable, a separation of at LEAST _____ shall be maintained between communications wires and cables on buildings and lightning conductors.

A. 18 inches
B. 24 inches
C. 4 feet
D. 6 feet

38. A fluorescent luminaire shall be permitted to be cord connected _____ .

A. where the flexible cord is contained in an approved raceway
B. where the flexible cord is visible for its entire length
C. where the flexible cord is at least size 12 AWG
D. never

39. Wiring located above heated ceilings shall be spaced at not less than 2 inches above the heated ceiling and shall be considered as operating at an ambient temperature of _____.

A. 50°C
B. 99°F
C. 60°C
D. 75°C

40. An equipotential bonding grid must be installed in the deck around a permanently installed swimming pool; the bonding grid shall extend for at LEAST _____ horizontally beyond the inside walls of the pool.

A. 3 feet
B. 5 feet
C. 6 feet
D. 10 feet

41. Where not in excess of 1000 volts, open overhead service conductors over public driveways are required to maintain a vertical clearance of NOT less than _____ from final grade.

A. 10 feet
B. 12 feet
C. 15 feet
D. 18 feet

42. All spa and hot tub equipment installed in non-dwelling occupancies shall be provided with an emergency shutoff or control switch within sight of the unit(s), and located NOT less than _____ from the inside wall of the spa or hot tub.

A. 6 feet
B. 10 feet
C. 5 feet
D. 12 feet

43. Feeders to floating buildings are permitted to be installed in _____ where flexible connections are required.

A. MC cable
B. AC cable
C. NMC cable
D. portable power cable

44. Where a building or structure is supplied with a 3-phase, 480Y/277-volt service, each disconnecting means rated at LEAST _____ or more shall be provided with ground-fault protection.

A. 1000 amperes
B. 1200 amperes
C. 1500 amperes
D. 2000 amperes

45. In a marina, the disconnecting means for a boat receptacle must be readily accessible and NOT more than _____ from the receptacle.

A. 6 feet
B. 10 feet
C. 30 inches
D. 50 feet

46. Branch circuit conductors supplying a varying duty motor with a 30 minute and/or 60 minute rating shall have an ampacity of at LEAST _____ of the nameplate rating of the motor to be supplied.

A. 85 percent
B. 110 percent
C. 120 percent
D. 150 percent

47. Cablebus shall be installed only for _____ locations.

A. exposed
B. commercial
C. concealed
D. hazardous

48. Solar photovoltaic system dc circuits on or in one- and two-family dwellings shall be permitted to have a MAXIMUM voltage of _____ or less.

A. 120 volts
B. 250 volts
C. 600 volts
D. 50 volts

49. A hospital conference room is considered to be an assembly occupancy when designed for the assembly of at LEAST _____ or more persons.

A. 25
B. 50
C. 75
D. 100

50. Determine the MINIMUM required size 75 deg. C rated copper conductors to supply a demand load of 200 amperes where installed in an area with an expected ambient temperature of 120 deg. F.

A. 3/0 AWG
B. 4/0 AWG
C. 300 kcmil
D. 250 kcmil

51. Where concrete encased, raceways approved for burial only shall require a concrete envelope NOT less than _____ thick.

A. 2 inches
B. 4 inches
C. 6 inches
D. 8 inches

52. Overhead communications wires and cables shall have a separation of at LEAST _____ from supply service-drops of 0-750 volts at any point in the span.

A. 30 inches
B. 24 inches
C. 12 inches
D. 18 inches

53. In general, electrical nonmetallic tubing (ENT) shall be securely fastened in place within at LEAST _____ of each outlet box, junction box, or panelboard.

A. 12 inches
B. 18 inches
C. 24 inches
D. 36 inches

54. Where flexible cord has one conductor identified by a ridge on the exterior of the cord, this conductor is identified as a/an _____ conductor.

A. ungrounded
B. grounded
C. phase
D. equipment grounding

55. Where a raceway enters a building or structure from an outside underground distribution system, it shall be _____.

A. sealed
B. marked
C. Schedule 40 PVC only
D. provided with a drain hole

56. Equipment grounding conductors used for systems over 1 kV that are not an integral part of a cable assembly shall NOT be smaller than _____ copper.

A. 8 AWG
B. 6 AWG
C. 4 AWG
D. 2 AWG

57. What is the MAXIMUM number of size 4 AWG THHN copper conductors permitted to be installed in a trade size 1¼ in. electrical metallic tubing (EMT) having a length of 18 inches?

A. 10
B. 11
C. 12
D. 13

58. What is the MINIMUM size 75 deg. C copper ungrounded (phase) service entrance conductors permitted for a 200-ampere rated commercial service?

A. 4/0 THW
B. 2/0 THW
C. 3/0 THHN
D. 3/0 THW

59. Where a surfaced-mounted luminaire containing a ballast, transformer, LED driver, or power supply is to be installed on combustible low-density cellulose fiberboard, it shall be marked for this condition or shall be spaced NOT less than _____ from the surface of the fiberboard.

A. 3/4 in.
B. 1 in.
C. 1¼ in.
D. 1½ in.

60. Which of the following listed cables have an overall covering that is fungus resistant?

A. Type NM
B. Type NMS
C. Type NMC
D. Type NM-B

61. The conductors in multiconductor portable cables of over 600 volts, used to connect mobile equipment and machinery, shall be at LEAST size _____ copper or larger and employ flexible stranding.

A. 14 AWG
B. 12 AWG
C. 10 AWG
D. 8 AWG

62. Where installed for a temporary electrical service in a wet location at a construction site, all _____ receptacles shall be listed as weather-resistant.

A. 125-volt, 30-ampere, straight-blade
B. 250-volt, 20-ampere, straight-blade
C. 125-volt, 30-ampere, twist-lock
D. 250-volt, 15-ampere, twist-lock

63. Given: Conductors of not over 25 ft. long are to be tapped from a service where two (2) parallel size 500 kcmil copper conductors per phase are protected by an 800 ampere overcurrent protection device. The tap conductors will terminate in a single circuit breaker. What MINIMUM size THW copper conductors are required for the tap conductors?

A. 500 kcmil
B. 400 kcmil
C. 300 kcmil
D. 250 kcmil

64. As a general rule, gas or oil central space heating equipment shall be _____.

A. supplied from an individual branch circuit
B. provided with GFCI protection
C. provided with LCDI protection
D. permitted to be supplied from a general-use branch circuit supplying other equipment

65. Given: A 12 unit condo will have an 8 kW electric range in each unit; apply the optional method of calculation for multifamily dwellings and calculate the demand load, in kW, on the ungrounded (line) service entrance conductors for the electric ranges.

A. 39.4 kW
B. 30.7 kW
C. 25.9 kW
D. 32.0 kW

66. A designated information technology equipment room is required to be _____.

A. sound-proofed
B. provided with at least two exit doors
C. equipped with walls at least 6 inches thick
D. separated from other occupancies by fire-resistant-rated walls, floors and ceilings

67. The classification of hazardous areas and zones is to be determined by _____ .

A. engineers
B. licensed electricians
C. qualified persons
D. the local authority having jurisdiction

68. When installing border lighting for stages in theaters, the luminaires shall be arranged so that no branch circuit will carry a load to exceed _____ .

A. 10 amperes
B. 20 amperes
C. 15 amperes
D. 30 amperes

69. Where a single device wider than two (2) inches is installed in a 2-gang device box, the device is to be counted as equal to _____ conductor(s).

A. one
B. two
C. three
D. four

70. The allowable ampacity of size 22 AWG conductors of instrumentation tray cable shall be _____.

A. 3 amperes
B. 5 amperes
C. 7 amperes
D. 10 amperes

71. Type AC cable shall be permitted _____.

A. for feeders
B. in wet locations
C. in damp locations
D. where exposed to physical damage

72. Where the outer sheath of Type MI cable is made of steel _____.

A. it shall provide an adequate path to serve as an equipment grounding conductor
B. a separate equipment grounding conductor shall be provided
C. the grounding and grounded conductors shall be connected together
D. it shall not be longer than 6 feet

73. Where electrical metallic tubing (EMT) is installed under metal-corrugated sheet roof decking, a clearance of at LEAST _____ must be maintained between the tubing and the surface of the roof decking.

A. 1 in.
B. 1¼ in.
C. 1½ in.
D. 2 in.

74. A neutral conductor is always _____.

A. a grounded conductor not intended to carry current
B. an ungrounded conductor
C. green in color
D. the conductor connected to the neutral point of a system that is intended to carry current under normal conditions

75. Given: A one-family dwelling supplied by a single-phase, 120/240-volt system has a calculated demand load of 42,000 VA. What MINIMUM size XHHW aluminum conductors are required for the ungrounded (line) service-entrance conductors?

A. 1/0 AWG
B. 2/0 AWG
C. 3/0 AWG
D. 4/0 AWG

76. The insulated conductors of Type TC cables shall be in sizes _____ to 1000 kcmil copper, nickel, or nickel-coated copper.

A. 18 AWG
B. 16 AWG
C. 14 AWG
D. 12 AWG

77. In general, all panelboards are required to have overcurrent protection, an EXCEPTION to this rule is _____.

A. panelboards containing less than 42 overcurrent devices
B. panelboards containing only single-pole overcurrent devices
C. panelboards that supply a second bus structure within the same panelboard
D. for existing panelboards used as service equipment in a one-family dwelling

78. Where a motor controller that is not an inverse time circuit breaker or molded case switch, controls a 120 hp, continuous-duty, ac motor of not over 600 volts, the controller shall have a horsepower rating of NOT less than _____.

A. 120 hp
B. 150 hp
C. 175 hp
D. 200 hp

79. Overload relays and other devices for motor overload protection that are NOT capable of opening short-circuits or ground-faults shall be protected by a motor short-circuit protector or by _____.

A. an instantaneous trip circuit breaker only
B. fuses or circuit breakers
C. Class CC fuses only
D. a ground-fault circuit interrupter

80. An electrical system comprised of multiple power sources is known as a/an _____.

A. emergency system
B. optional standby system
C. hybrid system
D. legally required standby system

END OF JOURNEYMAN ELECTRICIANS FINAL EXAM #1

JOURNEYMAN ELECTRICIAN'S EXAM PREP GUIDE
FINAL EXAM #1
ANSWER KEY

ANSWER	REFERENCE	NEC PG. #
1. D	230.24(B)(4)	pg. 86
2. B	90.1(A)	pg. 30
3. C	110.26(A)(2)	pg. 47
4. D	406.12(B)(1)-(7)	pg. 261
5. C	514.9(A)	pg. 403
6. B	Trade Knowledge	
7. D	Single-Phase Current Formula	

$$I = \frac{Power}{volts} \quad I = \frac{15 \text{ kW} \times 1,000}{240 \text{ volts}} = \frac{15,000}{240} = 72.1 \text{ amperes}$$

8. A	422.11(E)(3)	pg. 277
9. D	314.16(B)	pg. 175
	314.16(B)(1),(2)&(5)	pgs. 175 & 176
	Table 314.16(B)	pg. 176

```
2 - 6 AWG ungrounded conductors = 2 x 5.00 cu. in. = 10 cu. in.
1 - 6 AWG grounded conductor   = 1 x 5.00 cu. in. =  5 cu. in.
1 - 8 AWG equipt. grounding    = 1 x 3.00 cu. in. =  3 cu. in.
2 - internal clamps            = 1 x 5.00 cu. in. =  5 cu. in.
1 - pigtail                    =     -0-          =  0 cu. in.
                                      TOTAL    =  23 cu. in.
```

10. B	110.75(A)	pg. 53
11. B	384.30(B)	pg. 225
12. A	682.11	pg. 556

13. C 424.3(B) pg. 280
 210.19(A)(1)(a) pg. 62
 Table 310.15(B)(16) pg. 150

[125 amperes + 2.5 amperes] x 125% = 159 amperes

*NOTE: Size 2/0 AWG conductors with an allowable ampacity of 175 amperes
should be selected.

14. D Table 430.248 pg. 321
 430.32(A)(2) pg. 305

15. D 300.6(A) pg. 138

16. A 517.18(B) pg. 422

17. B 210.50(C) pg. 64

18. A 230.23(B) pg. 85

19. C 680.43(E)(3) pg. 553

20. A 344.30(A)(1) pg. 198

21. C 430.110(A) pg. 315

22. D 455.9 pg. 339

23. C 430.72(B)(2) pg. 311
 Table 430.72, Column B pg. 311

24. D 300.9 pg. 139

25. A 210.52(H) pg. 66

26. B 430.32(A)(1) pg. 304

27. B 240.5(B)(4) pg. 95

28. B Table 310.15(B)(16) pg. 150
 Table 310.15(B)(3)(a) pg. 148

Size 10 AWG THHN ampacity (before derating) = 40 amperes
40 amps x 50% (adjustment factor for 20 wires) = 20 amperes

29. D 348.12(1) pg. 199

30. D 250.178 pg. 128

31. C 410.130(G)(1)(2)&(3) pg. 273

32. D	725.48(B)(1)	pg. 609
	300.3(C)(1)	pg. 134
33. B	210.60(B)	pg. 66
34. C	Table 430.250	pg. 322
	430.24(1)&(2)	pg. 303

10 hp - FLC = 30.8 amps x 125% = 38.5 amperes
7½ hp - FLC = 24.2 amps x 100% = <u>24.2 amperes</u>
TOTAL = 62.7 amperes

35. B	300.20(A)	pg. 141
36. A	410.68	pg. 271
	Table 310.104(A)	pg. 167
37. D	800.53	pg. 640
38. B	410.62(C)(1)	pg. 271
39. A	424.36	pg. 283
40. A	680.26(B)(2)	pg. 549
41. D	230.24(B)(4)	pg. 86
42. C	680.41	pg. 551
43. D	553.7(B)	pg. 481
44. A	230.95	pg. 91
45. C	555.17(B)	pg. 484
46. D	Table 430.22(E)	pg. 303
47. A	370.10(1)	pgs. 217 & 218
48. C	690.7	pg. 560
49. D	518.1	pg. 435
50. C	Table 310.15(B)(16)	pg. 150
	Table 310.15(B)(2)(a)	pg. 147

$$\frac{200 \text{ amperes (load)}}{.75 \text{ (temp. correction)}} = 266.6 \text{ amperes}$$

*NOTE: Size 300 kcmil conductors with an allowable ampacity of 285 amperes
should be selected.

51. A Table 300.5, Note 2 pg. 137

52. C 800.44(A)(4) pg. 639

53. D 362.30(A) pg. 213

54. B 400.22 & 22(F) pgs. 250 & 251

55. A 225.27 pg. 80

56. B 250.190(C)(1) pg. 131

57. B Chapter 9, Table 4 pg. 680
 Chapter 9, Table 5 pg. 685
 Note 7 to Chapter 9 Tables pg. 679

$$\frac{0.897 \text{ sq. in. (conduit)}}{0.0824 \text{ sq. in. (wire)}} = 10.8 = 11 \text{ wires}$$

58. D Table 310.15(B)(16) pg. 150

59. D 410.136(B) pg. 274

60. C 334.116(B) pg. 193

61. B 400.31(A) pg. 251

62. B 406.9(B)(1) pg. 261

63. C 240.21(B)(2)(1) pg. 96

800 amperes ÷ 3 = 266.6 amperes
*NOTE: Size 300 kcmil THW conductors with an allowable ampacity of 285
 amperes should be selected.

64. A 422.12 pg. 277

65. A 220.84(C)(3)(a) pg. 76
 Table 220.84 pg. 76

8 kW x 12 = 96 kW x 41% (demand) = 39.36 kW

66. D 645.4(5) pg. 526

67. C 505.7(A) pg. 377

68. B 520.41(A) pg. 438

69. D 314.16(B)(4) pg. 176

70. A 727.8 pg. 618

71. A	320.10(1)	pg. 182
	320.12(1)&(5)	pg. 182
72. B	332.108	pg. 190
73. C	300.4(E)	pg. 135
74. D	Article 100 Definitions	pg. 39
75. C	` Single-phase Current Formula	
	310.15(B)(7)(1)	pg. 149
	Table 310.15(B)(16)	pg. 150

I = VA ÷ E I = 42,000 VA ÷ 240 volts = 175 amperes
175 amperes x .83 = 145.25 amperes

Size 3/0 AWG XHHW 75ºC rated aluminum conductors with an allowable ampacity of 155 amperes should be selected from Table 310.15(B)(16).

76. A	336.104	pg. 194
77. D	408.36, Exception 3	pg. 264
78. A	430.83(A)(1)	pg. 312
79. B	430.40	pg. 306
80. C	Article 100 Definitions	pg. 37

###

NOTES

JOURNEYMAN ELECTRICIAN'S EXAM PREP GUIDE
FINAL EXAM #2

The following questions are based on the 2017 edition of the National Electrical Code® and are typical of questions encountered on most Journeyman Electricians' Licensing Exams. On each question select the best answer from the choices given and review your answers with the answer key included in this book. A passing score on this exam is 70%, and the exam consists of 80 questions valued at 1.25 points each. You therefore must answer 56 questions correctly for a passing score. If you do not score at least 70%, try again and keep studying. GOOD LUCK.

ALLOTTED TIME: 4 hours

1. All single-phase, 125-volt 15- and 20-ampere rated receptacles located within _____ of the inside walls of a storable pool, storable spa, or storable hot tub shall be provided with GFCI protection.

A. 8 feet
B. 10 feet
C. 15 feet
D. 20 feet

2. A manufactured wiring system is a system assembled by a manufacturer, which cannot be inspected at the building site without _____.

A. a permit
B. a manufacturer's representative present
C. damage or destruction to the assembly
D. an engineer's supervision

3. Type AC cable installed horizontally through wooden or metal framing members is considered supported where support doesn't exceed _____ intervals.

A. 2 feet
B. 3 feet
C. 4½ feet
D. 6 feet

4. At least one 15- or 20-ampere, 125-volt, single-phase receptacle outlet NOT more than _____ above a balcony, deck, or porch walking surface shall be installed at each balcony, deck, or porch that is attached to and accessible from a dwelling unit.

A. 3 feet
B. 6½ feet
C. 8 feet
D. 5½ feet

5. Where raceways contain _____ or larger insulated circuit conductors and these conductors enter a raceway in a cabinet, the conductors shall be protected from abrasion by a smoothly rounded insulating surface such as a bushing.

A. 1 AWG
B. 2 AWG
C. 3 AWG
D. 4 AWG

6. The lightning protection system ground terminals shall be bonded to the building or structure grounding electrode system. The bonding shall be _____ and to all raceways, boxes, and enclosures between the cabinets or equipment and the grounding electrode.

A. insulated at both ends
B. insulated from one end
C. bonded at both ends
D. bonded at only one end

7. Where the initial protection specified in the NEC® is not sufficient for the starting current of an air-conditioner motor-compressor, the rating or setting shall be permitted to be increased, but shall NOT exceed _____ of the motor-compressor rated load current or branch circuit selection.

A. 225%
B. 175%
C. 200%
D. 125%

8. The service conductors between the terminals of the service equipment and a point usually outside the building, clear of building walls, where joined by splice or tap to the service drop or overhead service conductors are recognized as _____.

A. service-drop conductors
B. service lateral conductors
C. service entrance conductors
D. none of these

9. What is the MAXIMUM permitted ampacity (current-carrying capacity) of a size 10 AWG, THHN CU conductor when there are a total of four (4) current-carrying conductors in a raceway? Assume all terminations are rated 75°C.

A. 40 amperes
B. 32 amperes
C. 28 amperes
D. 30 amperes

10. Additional services shall be permitted for a single building or other structure sufficiently large to make two (2) or more services necessary if permitted by _____.

A. the registered design professional
B. qualified personnel
C. the engineer of record
D. special permission

11. Branch circuits that supply electric signs shall be considered _____ loads for the purposes of calculations.

A. continuous
B. non-continuous
C. full-current
D. readily accessible

12. Where a ground ring is used as a grounding electrode consisting of a size 2 AWG bare copper conductor encircling a building, buried 36 in. deep, in direct contact with the earth, the conductor is required to have a MINIMUM length of _____.

A. 15 feet
B. 20 feet
C. 25 feet
D. 50 feet

13. For low voltage lighting systems operating at 30 volts or less, the output circuits of the power supply are to be rated for NOT more than _____ under all load conditions.

A. 15 amperes
B. 20 amperes
C. 25 amperes
D. 30 amperes

14. Any connections or splices in an underground installation shall be approved for such locations, and the NEC® defines an underground installation, such as the interior surface of enclosures or raceways that are installed underground are considered a _____ location.

A. wet
B. damp
C. dry
D. approved

15. What is the horsepower of a single-phase, 120-volt ac motor that draws 9.8 amperes of current?

A. 1 hp
B. ¾ hp
C. ¼ hp
D. ½ hp

16. For installations of resistors and reactors, a thermal barrier shall be required if the space between them and any combustible material is LESS than _____.

A. 2 inches
B. 3 inches
C. 6 inches
D. 12 inches

17. Given: A trade size 3 in. electrical metallic tubing (EMT) will enter the bottom of a pull box and a trade size 3 in. flexible metal conduit (FMC) will enter the side of the box; the raceways will contain conductors of size 4 AWG or larger. What MINIMUM size pull box is required for this installation?

A. 12 in. x 12 in.
B. 18 in. x 18 in.
C. 24 in. x 30 in.
D. 24 in. x 18 in.

18. A trade size 1 in. listed liquidtight flexible metal conduit (LFMC) is approved as a type of equipment grounding conductor, where the circuit conductors contained in the LFMC are protected by overcurrent devices rated NOT more than _____.

A. 20 amperes
B. 30 amperes
C. 60 amperes
D. 80 amperes

19. Individual unit equipment for legally required standby illumination systems are permitted to have flexible cord-and-plug connections, provided the flexible cord does NOT exceed _____ in length.

A. 2 feet
B. 3 feet
C. 4 feet
D. 6 feet

20. A size 10 AWG flexible SJ cord shall be permitted for:

A. locations where oil-resistant insulation is required.
B. wet and damp locations.
C. a maximum of 600 volts.
D. a maximum of 300 volts.

21. All hydromassage bathtub metal piping systems and all grounded metal parts in contact with the circulating water associated with the bathtub shall be bonded together using a solid copper bonding jumper NOT smaller than _____.

A. 10 AWG
B. 6 AWG
C. 8 AWG
D. 12 AWG

22. Where a 125-volt, single-phase, 20-ampere receptacle is install in a residential laundry area, designated for the washing machine, the receptacle must be provided with _____.

A. AFCI protection only
B. GFCI protection only
C. neither AFCI nor GFCI protection
D. both AFCI and GFCI protection

23. According to the NEC® the required MINIMUM burial depth of a direct burial cable run of a GFCI protected, 15-ampere, 120-volt circuit, where the cable passes directly under the residential driveway is _____.

A. 12 inches
B. 16 inches
C. 18 inches
D. 24 inches

24. Where practical, conductors of dissimilar metals shall:

A. be listed.
B. be marked.
C. not be intermixed.
D. be for current-carrying conductors only.

25. Branch circuits that supply electric signs, other than neon signs, shall be rated NOT to exceed _____ .

A. 15 amperes
B. 30 amperes
C. 20 amperes
D. 40 amperes

26. Where the design and operation of a generator does not prevent overloading, the ampacity of the conductors from the generator terminals to the first overcurrent protection device shall NOT be less than _____ of the nameplate rating of the generator.

A. 115 percent
B. 125 percent
C. 130 percent
D. 150 percent

27. What is the primary full-load current rating of a 3-phase, 75 kVA, transformer that is 90% efficient, with a 480-volt primary and a 208Y/120-volt secondary?

A. 156.3 amperes
B. 208.3 amperes
C. 100.2 amperes
D. 360.6 amperes

28. Cable splices are permitted in a cable tray, provided _____.

A. the splices are contained in a junction box
B. the splices are accessible
C. the conductors are size 1/0 AWG or larger
D. the splices are made with compression type fittings

29. Where conduit or tubing nipples having length NOT to exceed 24 inches between boxes or enclosures, the nipples shall be permitted to be filled to _____ of their total cross-sectional area.

A. 53 percent
B. 31 percent
C. 40 percent
D. 60 percent

30. Polyvinyl chloride conduit (PVC) larger than trade size _____ shall not be used.

A. 4 inches
B. 5 inches
C. 4½ inches
D. 6 inches

31. Given: A 100 kVA, dry-type transformer with a 4,160-volt primary, which may be subject to be close to combustible material, is to be installed indoors. The transformer must have a clearance of at LEAST _____ from the combustible material.

A. 12 inches
B. 18 inches
C. 20 inches
D. 24 inches

32. Underground service conductors that are not encased in concrete and are buried 18 inches or more below grade shall have their location identified by a warning ribbon placed at LEAST _____ above the underground installation.

A. 6 inches
B. 12 inches
C. 10 inches
D. 8 inches

33. Electric signs shall be at LEAST _____ above areas accessible to vehicles unless protected from physical damage.

A. 12 feet
B. 14 feet
C. 16 feet
D. 18 feet

34. For continuous-duty motors in a general application, the motor nameplate current rating is used to size the _____.

A. disconnecting means
B. branch circuit conductors
C. overload protection
D. overcurrent protection

35. Unless adequate protection such as a steel plate is provided, where a cable or raceway is installed through bored holes in wood members, holes shall be bored so that the edge of the hole is NOT less than _____ from the nearest edge of the wood member.

A. 1 inch
B. 1½ inches
C. 1¾ inches
D. 1¼ inches

36. Where a conduit longer than 24 inches contains two (2) ungrounded conductors, one (1) grounded conductor and one (1) equipment grounding conductor, the conduit may be filled to a MAXIMUM of _____ of its cross-sectional area.

A. 40 percent
B. 31 percent
C. 53 percent
D. 40 percent

37. Given: Four (4) size 2/0 AWG conductors contained in a trade size 2 in. conduit enter a pull box on the "east" side. The conductors then make a U turn and exit in a trade size 2½ in. conduit on the same side. What is the MINIMUM distance required, in inches, from the "east" side of the box to the opposite "west" side of the box?

A. 12 inches
B. 15 inches
C. 17 inches
D. 18 inches

38. At LEAST _____ of free conductor, measured from the point in the box where it emerges from its raceway, shall be left at each junction box for splices or connection to devices.

A. 4 inches
B. 6 inches
C. 8 inches
D. 12 inches

39. For the purpose of determining conductor fill in a device box, a three-way switch is counted as equal to _____ conductor(s), based on the largest conductor connected to the switch.

A. none
B. one
C. two
D. three

40. A metal underground water pipe is permitted for use as a grounding electrode where the water pipe is in direct contact with the earth for at LEAST _____ or more.

A. 5 feet
B. 8 feet
C. 20 feet
D. 10 feet

41. Overhead spans of open conductors of not over 300 volts to ground shall have a clearance of NOT less than _____ over residential driveways.

A. 12 feet
B. 10 feet
C. 15 feet
D. 18 feet

42. Single-phase, 125-volt, 15- and 20-ampere, receptacle outlets installed in floors of dwelling units shall not be counted as part of the required number of receptacle outlets, if they are MORE than _____ from the wall.

A. 18 inches
B. 12 inches
C. 30 inches
D. 24 inches

43. Where applying the general method of calculation for dwelling units, the load for household electric clothes dryer shall be a MINIMUM of _____ or the nameplate rating, whichever is larger, for each dryer served.

A. 4000 watts
B. 5000 watts
C. 7000 watts
D. 6000 watts

44. A transformer vault is required to be provided with a door sill or curb with a height of NOT less than _____.

A. 6 inches
B. 8 inches
C. 2 inches
D. 4 inches

45. A hazardous location where easily ignitible fibers or materials producing combustible flyings are handled, manufactured, or used, but where they are not likely to be in suspension in the air in quantities sufficient to produce ignitible mixtures is a _____ location.

A. Class I
B. Class II
C. Class III
D. Class IV

46. Given: A dairy farm with a 120/240-volt, single-phase electrical system will have the following three (3) loads supplied by a common service: one 18,000 VA, one 16,000 VA and one 10,000 VA. What is the demand load, in amperes, on the ungrounded (phase) service-entrance conductors?

A. 183 amperes
B. 152 amperes
C. 304 amperes
D. 114 amperes

47. What is the MINIMUM general lighting demand load, in VA, of a building consisting of four (4) offices having a floor space of 20 feet x 30 feet each?

A. 8,400 VA
B. 7,200 VA
C. 4,800 VA
D. 10,500 VA

48. A circuit breaker protecting a single non-motor-operated appliance shall not exceed 20 amperes if the overcurrent rating is not marked and the appliance is rated _____ or less.

A. 13.3 amperes
B. 15.3 amperes
C. 16.0 amperes
D. 14.3 amperes

49. Where two (2) or more single-phase household electric ranges used in an instructional program, are supplied by a 3-phase, 4-wire feeder or service, the total load shall be calculated on the basis of _____ the MAXIMUM number connected between any two (2) phases.

A. one-third
B. twice
C. one-half
D. three times

50. As a general rule, receptacle outlets provided for the small appliance countertop circuits in the kitchen of a dwelling, shall be located above the countertop or work surface, but NOT more than _____ above the countertop or work surface.

A. 6 inches
B. 12 inches
C. 20 inches
D. 18 inches

51. Outside open overhead individual conductors over 1000 volts shall be a MINIMUM size of _____ copper where not supported by a messenger wire when the conductor span is 60 feet in length.

A. 10 AWG
B. 8 AWG
C. 6 AWG
D. 4 AWG

52. A hermetic motor-compressor that is protected against overloads by an inverse-time circuit breaker, shall be rated at NOT more than _____ of the motor-compressor full-load current.

A. 80%
B. 110%
C. 115%
D. 125%

53. What is the MAXIMUM standard size inverse-time circuit breaker that may be used for overcurrent protection for a branch-circuit supplying a 4.5 kW, 240-volt, single phase, 30 gallon storage-type water heater?

A. 40 amperes
B. 25 amperes
C. 30 amperes
D. 20 amperes

54. For 120-volt, 15- and 20-ampere branch circuits, the rating of any one (1) cord-and-plug connected utilization equipment not fastened in place shall NOT exceed _____ of the branch circuit ampere rating.

A. 80 percent
B. 70 percent
C. 60 percent
D. 50 percent

55. Generally, where installed on the outside of a raceway, the length of the equipment bonding jumper shall NOT exceed _____ and shall be routed with the raceway.

A. 4 feet
B. 6 feet
C. 5 feet
D. 8 feet

56. Where abandoned communications cables are identified for future use with a tag, the tag shall be _____.

A. red in color
B. orange in color
C. located outside of the junction box
D. of sufficient durability to withstand the environment involved

57. When exceptions to the NEC® are not a consideration, battery back-up exit luminaires (unit equipment) of emergency systems shall receive power from _____.

A. the branch circuit that supplies normal power circuits
B. a separate dedicated lighting branch circuit
C. a 3 ft. pig-tail fed from the emergency circuit
D. the same branch circuit serving the normal lighting in the area

58. Unless approved for a higher voltage, surface nonmetallic raceways are NOT approved for use where the voltage is _____ or more between conductors.

A. 300 volts
B. 240 volts
C. 125 volts
D. 150 volts

59. Circuit breakers shall be permitted to be connected in parallel _____.

A. never
B. where factory assembled
C. where the load to be supplied is not greater than 100 amperes
D. where the nominal voltage to ground is not more than 300 volts

60. The service disconnecting means for each service shall consist of NOT more than _____ switches or circuit breakers.

A. one
B. two
C. four
D. six

61. Where a device box having dimensions of 3 in. x 2 in. x 2¾ in. contains a receptacle outlet, how may size 12 AWG conductors are permitted to be installed in the box?

A. six
B. five
C. four
D. seven

62. Given: An underground run of PVC with size 6 AWG conductors is the wiring method to be used to supply an air-conditioning unit that is protected by an overcurrent protective device rated 60 amperes. What is the MINIMUM size copper equipment grounding conductor that must be installed in the conduit?

A. 10 AWG
B. 12 AWG
C. 6 AWG
D. 8 AWG

63. In compliance with the NEC®, a trade size 1¼ in. electrical metallic tubing (EMT) may contain a MAXIMUM of _____ size 4 AWG copper THWN conductors where the tubing is more than 24 inches in length.

A. four
B. seven
C. six
D. ten

64. A one-family dwelling unit is to have the following fastened in place appliances installed:

 1,200 VA dishwasher
 4,000 VA water heater
 1,150 VA garbage disposer
 700 VA attic fan
 1,920 VA garage door opener

 The demand load, in VA, on the ungrounded service-entrance conductors for the listed appliances is _____ when using the general method of calculations for dwelling units.

A. 7,728 VA
B. 6,728 VA
C. 6,276 VA
D. 8,970 VA

65. Where switches or circuit breakers are used as the main disconnecting means for a building service, they shall be installed such that the center of the grip of the operating handle of the switch or circuit breaker, when in its highest position, is NOT more than _____ above the floor or working platform.

A. 6 feet
B. 7 feet
C. 6 feet, 6 inches
D. 6 feet, 7 inches

66. A single-phase, 125-volt, 15- or 20-ampere receptacle outlet shall be installed at each residential kitchen countertop and work surface that is at LEAST _____ or wider.

A. 12 inches
B. 24 inches
C. 36 inches
D. 20 inches

67. What is the MAXIMUM standard size overcurrent protection permitted for the protection of resistance-type electric space heating equipment?

A. 40 amperes
B. 50 amperes
C. 60 amperes
D. 70 amperes

68. Where exceptions are not a consideration, a multiwire branch circuit may supply only _____

A. 3-phase loads
B. line to line loads
C. line to ground
D. line to neutral

69. Which of the following is NOT a requirement for an intersystem bonding termination?

A. Consist of not less than three terminals.
B. Connected to the meter enclosure only with a minimum size 8 AWG conductor.
C. Terminals shall be listed for grounding and bonding.
D. Be accessible for connection and inspection.

70. The service equipment for a mobile home shall have an ampere rating of NOT less than _____ at 120/240-volts, single-phase.

A. 100 amperes
B. 50 amperes
C. 60 amperes
D. 150 amperes

71. Given: A commercial building provided with a 208Y/120-volt, 3-phase, electrical system has a calculated demand load of 72,000 VA; the ungrounded service-entrance conductors must have an ampacity of at LEAST _____.

A. 200 amperes
B. 350 amperes
C. 300 amperes
D. 250 amperes

72. For emergency systems, where internal combustion engines are used as the prime mover, an on-site fuel supply shall be provided with an on-premises fuel supply sufficient for NOT less than _____ full-demand operation of the system.

A. 8 hours
B. 4 hours
C. 6 hours
D. 2 hours

73. Which one of the following wiring methods is NOT approved for use in assembly locations, unless encased in concrete?

A. EMT
B. Schedule 80 PVC
C. Type MC cable
D. Type AC cable

74. In an industrial establishment, what is the MAXIMUM length of 200 ampere rated busway that may be tapped to 600 ampere rated busway, without additional overcurrent protection?

A. 10 feet
B. 25 feet
C. 50 feet
D. 75 feet

75. For a one-family dwelling unit, the service disconnecting means shall have a rating of NOT less than _____ when provided with a 120/240-volt, single-phase electrical system.

A. 60 amperes
B. 100 amperes
C. 150 amperes
D. 200 amperes

76. As applied to hazardous (classified) locations, a circuit in which any spark or thermal effect is incapable of causing ignition of a mixture of flammable or combustible material in air under prescribed test conditions, is known as a _____ circuit in the NEC®.

A. low voltage
B. low impedance
C. no-load
D. intrinsically safe

77. Where the heating, air-conditioning or refrigeration equipment is installed on the roof of a commercial, industrial, or an apartment building, a single-phase, 125-volt, 15- or 20-ampere receptacle outlet _____.

A. is required to be within at least 100 ft. from the equipment
B. may be connected to the line side of the equipment disconnecting means, provided the receptacle is of the GFCI type
C. shall be located on the same level and within 25 ft. of the equipment
D. is permitted to be connected to the load side of the equipment disconnecting means, if within 10 ft. of the equipment and GFCI protected.

78. In Class II, Division 1 locations, where pendant mounted luminaires are suspended by rigid metal conduit (RMC) or intermediate metal conduit (IMC) and a means for flexibility is not provided, the conduit stems shall have a length of NOT more than _____.

A. 12 inches
B. 18 inches
C. 24 inches
D. 30 inches

79. In a dwelling unit bedroom, any wall space that is at LEAST _____ or more in width must be provided with a general-use 15- or 20-ampere, 125-volt, single-phase receptacle outlet.

A. 2 feet
B. 4 feet
C. 6 feet
D. 10 feet

80. A hazardous location where combustible dust is in the air under normal operating conditions in quantities sufficient to produce explosive or ignitable mixtures is a _____ location.

A. Class IV
B. Class III
C. Class I
D. Class II

END OF JOURNEYMAN FINAL EXAM #2

JOURNEYMAN ELECTRICIAN'S EXAM PREP GUIDE
FINAL EXAM #2
ANSWER KEY

ANSWER	REFERENCE	NEC PG. #
1. D	680.32	pg. 551
2. C	604.2	pg. 494
3. C	320.30(C)	pg. 183
4. B	210.52(E)(3)	pg. 66
5. D	300.4(G)	pg. 136
6. C	250.64(E)(1)	pg. 115
	250.106	pg. 120
7. A	440.22(A)	pg. 327
8. C	Article 100 – Definitions	pg. 41
9. B	110.14(C)	pg. 45
	Table 310.15(B)(16)	pg. 150
	Table 310.15(B)(3)(a)	pg. 148

10 AWG THHN ampacity before derating = 40 amperes
40 amperes x .8 (adj. factor) = 32 amperes allowable ampacity
However, according to 240.4(D)(7) the overcurrent protection is limited to 30 amperes.

10. D	230.2(B)(2)	pg. 84
11. A	600.5(B)	pg. 488
12. B	250.52(A)(4)	pg. 112
13. C	411.3(A)	pg. 275
14. A	300.5(B)	pg. 136
15. D	Table 430.248	pg. 321
16. D	470.3	pg. 340

17. B 314.28(A)(2) pg. 180

3 inches (raceway) x 6 = 18 inches

18. C 250.118(6)(c) pg. 122

19. B 701.12(G)(b) pg. 589

20. D Table 400.4 pg. 244

21. C 680.74(B) pg. 555

22. D 210.8(A)(10) pg. 59
 210.12(A) pg. 60

23. A Table 300.5, Column 4 pg. 137

24. C 110.14 pg. 45

25. C 600.5(B)(2) pg. 488

26. A 445.13(A) pg. 330

27. C Three-phase current formula

$$\frac{75\ kVA \times 1,000}{480 \times 1.732 \times .9} = \frac{75,000}{748.22} = 100.2\ amperes$$

28. B 392.56 pg. 232

29. D Chapter 9, Note 4 pg. 679

30. D 352.20(B) pg. 202

31. A 450.21(A) pg. 335

32. B 300.5(D)(3) pg. 136

33. B 600.9(A) pg. 490

34. C 430.6(A)(2) pg. 298

35. D 300.4(A)(1) pg. 135

36. A Chapter 9, Table 1 pg. 679

37. C 314.28(A)(2) pg. 180

2.5 in. (largest conduit) x 6 = 15 in. + 2 in. (additional conduit) = 17 inches

38. B 300.14 pg. 135

39. C	314.16(B)(4)	pg. 176
40. D	250.52(A)(1)	pg. 112
41. A	225.18(2)	pg. 80
42. A	210.52(A)(3)	pg. 64
43. B	220.54	pg. 73
44. D	450.43(B)	pg. 337
45. C	500.5(D)	pg. 351
46. B	220.103 Table 220.103 Single phase current formula	pg. 78 pg. 78

18,000 VA x 100% = 18,000 VA
16,000 VA x 75% = 12,000 VA
10,000 VA x 65% = 6,500 VA
 Total = 36,500 VA

$$I = VA \div volts \quad I = \frac{36,500}{240} = 152 \text{ amperes}$$

47. D	Table 220.12 230.42(A)(1)	pg. 71 pg. 87

20 ft. x 30 ft. = 600 sq. ft. per office x 3.5 VA = 2,100 VA
2,100 VA x 4 offices = 8,400 VA x 125% = 10,500 VA demand load

48. A	422.11(E)(2)	pg. 277
49. B	220.55	pg. 73
50. C	210.52(C)(5)	pg. 65
51. C	225.6(A)(2)	pg. 78
52. D	440.52(A)(3)	pg. 328
53. C	422.11(E)(3) Table 240.6(A) Single-phase current formula $I = P \div E$	pg. 277 pg. 95

$$I = \frac{4.5 \text{ kW} \times 1000}{240 \text{ volts}} \quad I = \frac{4,500}{240} = 18.75 \text{ amperes} \times 150\% = 28 \text{ amperes}$$

The next standard size OCP with a rating of 30 amperes should be selected.

54. A 210.23(A)(1) pg. 63

55. B 250.102(E)(2) pg. 119

56. D 800.25 pg. 639

57. D 700.12(F)(2)(3) pg. 585

58. A 388.12(3) pg. 227

59. B 240.8 pg. 95

60. D 230.71(A) pg. 89

61. C 314.16(B)(4) pg. 176
 Table 314.16(A) pg. 176

 6 size 12 AWG permitted in the box – 2 (device) = 4 size 12 AWG permitted

62. A 250.122(A) pg. 123
 Table 250.122 pg. 125

63. B Table C.1 of Annex C pg. 714

64. B 220.53 pg. 73

 1,200 VA dishwasher
 4,000 VA water heater
 1,150 VA garbage disposer
 700 VA attic fan
 1,920 VA garage door opener
 8,970 VA connected load x 75% (demand factor) = 6,728 VA demand load

65. D 240.24(A) pg. 98
 404.8(A) pg. 255

66. A 210.52(C)(1) pg. 65

67. C 424.22(B) pg. 282

68. D 210.4(C) pg. 57

69. B 250.94 (1)-(6) pg. 117

70. A 550.32(C) pg. 461

71. A 3-phase current formula
 I = VA ÷ E x 1.732

 I = $\underline{72,000}$ I = $\underline{72,000}$ I = 200 amperes

208 x 1.732 360.25

72. D	700.12(B)(2)	pg. 585
73. B	518.4(A)	pg. 435
74. C	368.17(B), Exception	pg. 216

$$\frac{600 \text{ amperes}}{3} = 200 \text{ amperes}$$

Therefore, the length of the 200 ampere busway may be 50 feet.

75. B	230.79(C)	pg. 90
76. D	504.2	pg. 371
77. C	210.63	pg. 66
78. A	502.130(B)(4)	pg. 367
79. A	210.52(A)(2)(1)	pg. 64
80. D	500.5(C)	pg. 351

###

NOTES

Glossary

Adjustable-trip circuit breakers: Circuit breakers whose trip setting can be changed by adjusting the ampere rating, trip time characteristics, or both, within a particular range.

Aluminum wire: An electrical conductor composed of aluminum metal.

Ambient temperature: The surrounding temperature present in a specific area.

American Wire Gauge (AWG): Standard used to identify the size of a wire.

Ampacity: The maximum current, in amperes that a conductor can carry continuously, under the conditions of use without exceeding its temperature rating.

Ampere: The unit of current measurement. The amount of current that will flow through a one ohm resistor when one volt is applied.

Appliance: Utilization equipment, installed to perform one or more functions, such as clothes washing, air conditioning, cooking, etc.

Appliance branch circuit: A branch circuit that supplies energy to one or more outlets to which appliances are to be connected.

Arc-Fault Circuit Interrupter (AFCI): A device intended to provide protection from the effects of arc faults by recognizing characteristics unique to arcing and by functioning to de-energize the circuit when an arc fault is detected.

Automatic: Performing a function without the necessity of human intervention.

Balanced load: The load of an electrical system, in which two or more branches are balanced and symmetrical with respect to voltage and intensity of current.

Ballast: An electrical circuit component used with discharge lighting luminaires to provide the voltage necessary to strike the mercury arc within the lamp, and then to limit the amount of current that flows through the lamp. (Examples of discharge lighting luminaires are fluorescent and HID lighting fixtures.)

Bare conductor: A conductor with no insulation or covering of any type.

Bonded (Bonding): Connected to establish electrical continuity and conductivity.

Bonding conductor: The conductor that connects the non-current carrying parts of electrical equipment, cable raceways or other enclosures to the approved system ground conductor.

Bonding jumper: A conductor used to assure the required electrical connection between metal parts of an electrical system.

Bonding jumper, System: The connection between the grounded circuit conductor and the supply-side bonding jumper, or the equipment grounding conductor, or both, at a separately derived system.

Box: A metallic or nonmetallic electrical enclosure used to house utilization equipment and devices, the support of luminaires and pulling or terminating conductors.

Branch circuit: That portion of a wiring system beyond the final overcurrent protection device protecting the circuit and the outlet(s).

Branch circuit, Multiwire: A branch circuit that consists of two or more ungrounded conductors that have a voltage between them, and a grounded conductor that has equal voltage between it and each ungrounded conductor of the circuit and that is connected to the neutral or grounded conductor of the system.

Branch-circuit rating: The ampere rating or setting of the overcurrent device protecting the conductors.

Building: A stand-alone structure or a structure which is separated from adjoining structures by fire walls.

Buried cable: A cable laid directly in the ground without being enclosed or protected in an electrical conduit.

Bus: A conductor, or group of conductors, that serve as a common connection for two or more circuits.

Busway: A sheet metal enclosure that contains factory assembled aluminum or copper busbars which are supported on insulators.

Cable: One or more insulated or non-insulated wires used to conduct electrical current.

Cable assembly: A flexible assembly containing multiconductors with a protective outer sheath.

Cablebus: An assembly of insulated conductors and terminations in an enclosed, ventilated protective metal housing.

Cable tray system: An assembly of sections and associated fittings which form a rigid structural system used to support cables and raceways.

Carrying capacity: The MAXIMUM current strength, in amperes, that a conductor can safely carry continuously. (See ampacity)

Celsius: A unit of measurement, in degrees, for temperature at which the freezing point is 0° and the boiling point is 100°. It is commonly represented by the letter "C".

Circuit: A complete path over which an electric current can flow.

Circuit breaker: A device which opens and closes circuits by nonautomatic means and opens circuits automatically when a predetermined overcurrent exists.

Circuit voltage: The greatest effective difference of potential between any two conductors in a given circuit.

Circular mil (CM): A measurement of the cross-sectional area of a conductor. The area of one circular mil equals .001 inches in diameter.

Circular mil foot: A unit of conductor size, equal to a portion of the conductor having a cross-sectional area of one circular mil and length of one foot.

Clamp: A device intended to secure raceways, tubing or cables.

Commercial equipment: Equipment intended to be used on commercial, industrial or institutional premises, such as schools, hotels, office buildings, manufacturing facilities, libraries and other public buildings.

Computer: An electronic machine which, by means of stored instructions and information, performs rapid, often complex calculations or compiles, correlates and selects data.

Conductor: A wire that is used to transmit the flow of electrons in an electrical circuit. Copper wire is the most common used today in the electrical industry.

Conduit: A metallic or nonmetallic pipe or tubing used to enclosed conductors.

Connected load: The sum of the rating(s) of the load consuming equipment, connected to an electrical system or any part thereof.

Contactor: An electrically operated switch, usually by a coil or solenoid. The switch contains one or more sets of contacts which controls one or more circuits.

Continuous duty: Operation at a substantially constant load for an indefinitely long time.

Continuous load: A load in which the MAXIMUM current may continue for three hours or more.

Controller: A device, or group of devices, which serves to govern in some predetermined manner the electric power delivered to the apparatus to which it is connected.

Control panel: A panel containing switches and other protective, controlling and measuring devices for electrical equipment, motors, and/or machinery.

Copper: A brownish-red, malleable, ductile, metallic element that is an excellent conductor of electricity and heat. The most common element used for conductors in the electrical industry.

Copper Wire: An electrical conductor composed of copper metal.

Cord: A small cable, very flexible, and substantially insulated to withstand wear. There is no sharp dividing line in respect to size between a cord and a cable, and likewise no sharp dividing line in respect to the character of insulation between a cord and a stranded wire.

Cord-and-plug connected appliance: An appliance to be connected to the power source by means of a supply cord.

Cord-connected unit: A unit intended for connection to the power source by means of a supply cord to prevent vibration or enable the unit to be moved.

Cross-section: A cutting or piece of something cut off at right angles to an axis. The cross-sectional area is 100% of the cross-section.

Current: The flow of electricity in a circuit, measured in amperes. Represented by the letter "I" or "A".

Current transformer (CT): An instrument transformer with a primary winding in series with a current-carrying conductor and secondary winding connected to a meter or device which is actuated by conductor current and current changes.

Demand factor: The ratio of the MAXIMUM demand of a system, or part of a system, to the total connected load of a system or the part of the system under consideration. All the loads of a system are usually never used all at the same time due to the many uses of the power.

Device box: A box which houses an electrical device(s), such as receptacles and switches.

Device: Electrical components, such as receptacles, switches and dimmers, that are designed to carry and/or control electric energy as its principle function, but not use electricity.

Disconnecting means: A device, or group of devices, by which the circuit conductors are disconnected from their source of supply.

Double pole: Switch or device connected to both lines of a circuit or controlling both lines of a circuit.

Dry location: A location not normally subject to dampness or wetness. A location classified as dry may be temporarily subject to dampness or wetness, as in the case of a building under construction.

Duty cycle: The time interval occupied by a device on intermittent duty in starting, running, stopping and idling.

Dwelling: A structure that contains eating, living and sleeping space and permanent provisions for cooking and sanitation.

Dwelling unit: A dwelling with one or more rooms used by one or more people for housekeeping.

Effectively grounded: Grounded with sufficient low impedance and current-carrying capacity to prevent hazardous voltage build-ups.

Efficiency: The ratio of output power to input power, expressed as a percentage.

Electrical discharge luminaire: A luminaire (lighting fixture) that utilizes a ballast for the operation of the lamp.

Electrical metallic tubing (EMT): A lightweight tubular steel raceway used to enclosed conductors.

Electric circuit: The complete path of an electric current.

Electric power production and distribution network: Power production, distribution, and utilization equipment and facilities, such as electric utility systems that deliver electric power to the connected loads, that are external to and not controlled by an interactive system.

Electric sign: A fixed, stationary, or portable self-contained, electrically illuminated, utilization equipment with words or symbols designed to convey information or attract attention.

Electrode: A conducting substance through which electric current enters or leaves.

Enclosed: Surrounded by a case, housing, fence or walls which will prevent persons from accidentally contacting energized parts.

Enclosure: The case or housing of equipment or other apparatus which provides protection from live or energized parts.

Equipment: A general term including devices, luminaires, appliances, materials, machinery, apparatus, etc. used in conjunction with electrical installations.

Equipment bonding jumper: A conductor that connects two or more parts of the equipment grounding conductor.

Equipment grounding conductor: An electrical conductor that provides a low-impedance path between electrical equipment and enclosures and the system grounded conductor and grounding electrode conductor.

Explosionproof equipment: Equipment enclosed in a case that is capable of withstanding an explosion of a specified gas or vapor that may occur within it and of preventing the ignition of a specified gas or vapor surrounding the enclosure by sparks, flashes, or explosion of the gas or vapor within, and that operated at such an external temperature that a surrounding flammable atmosphere will not be ignited thereby.

Fahrenheit: A unit of measurement, in degrees, for temperature at which the freezing point is 32° and the boiling point is 212°. It is commonly represented by the letter "F".

Fault: An electrical defect.

Fault current: Any current that travels an unwanted path, other than the normal operating path of an electrical system.

Feeder: All circuit conductors between the service equipment or the source of a separately derived system and the final branch circuit overcurrent device.

Feeder neutral load: The maximum unbalanced load between any of the ungrounded conductors and the grounded conductor of a feeder.

Fished: A means of installing electrical wiring in existing inaccessible hollow spaces of buildings with a minimum damage to the building finish.

Fixed appliance: An appliance which is fastened in place or otherwise secured at a specific location.

Fixed equipment: Equipment intended to be permanently connected electrically and not easily moved.

Flexible cord: An assembly of two or more insulated conductors, with or without braids, contained within an overall outer covering and used for the connection of equipment to a power source.

Flexible metal conduit (FMC): A raceway consisting of metal strips which are formed into a circular cross-sectional raceway, which is used to enclose conductors.

Fluorescent light: A method of lighting which makes use of ultraviolet energy to activate a fluorescent material coated inside of the bulb's surface.

Full-load amperes (FLA): The amount of current, in amperes, in an electrical circuit when the load is operating in a full-capacity condition.

Full-load current (FLC): The current required by a motor to produce the full-load torque at the motor's rated speed.

Fuse: A protective device with a fusible element that opens the circuit by melting when subjected to excessive current.

Galvanizing: The process of coating metals with zinc to prevent corrosion.

Ganged switch box: A box containing more than one switch.

General lighting: Lighting designed to provide a substantially uniform level of illumination throughout an area, exclusive of any provision for special local requirements.

General-purpose branch circuit: A branch circuit that supplies a number of outlets for lighting and appliances.

General-use snap switch: A form of general-use switch constructed so that it can be installed in device and/or outlet boxes.

General-use switch: A switch for use in general distribution and branch circuits. The ampere rated switch is capable of interrupting its rated current at its rated voltage.

General-use receptacle: 125-volt, single-phase, 15-or-20 ampere receptacles connected to a branch-circuit supplying two or more receptacles provided for the purpose of supplying cord-and-plug connected loads. Not provided for specific loads such as small appliances or laundry equipment.

Generator: A device that is used to convert mechanical energy to electrical energy.

Grade: The final level or elevation of the earth at a given location.

Ground: A conducting connection between electrical circuits or equipment and the earth.

Grounded (Grounding): Connected to the earth or a conducting body connected to the earth.

Grounded circuit: A circuit in which one conductor or point (usually the neutral) is intentionally grounded, either solidly or through a grounding device.

Grounded conductor: A conductor that has been intentionally grounded.

Ground-fault: An unintentional connection between an ungrounded conductor and any grounded raceway, box, enclosure, fitting, etc.

Ground-fault circuit interrupter: An electrical device which protects personnel by detecting hazardous ground faults and quickly disconnects power from the circuit.

Grounding: The connection of all exposed non-current carrying metal parts to the earth.

Grounding conductor: A conductor used to connect equipment or the grounded circuit of a wiring system to a grounding electrode or electrodes.

Grounding electrode: A conducting object through which a direct connection to earth is established.

Grounding electrode conductor: The conductor used to connect the system grounded conductor and/or the equipment to a grounding electrode or to a point on the grounding electrode system.

Handhole enclosure: An enclosure for use in underground systems, provided with an open or closed bottom, and sized to allow personnel to reach into, but not enter, for the purpose of installing, operating, or maintaining equipment or wiring or both.

Health care facility: A location, either a building or a portion of a building, which contains occupancies such as, hospitals, nursing homes, limited or supervisory care facilities, clinics, medical and dental offices and either ambulatory facilities.

Hermetic refrigerant motor-compressor: A combination of a compressor and motor enclosed in the same housing, having no external shaft or shaft seals, with the motor operating in the refrigerant.

Hickey (fitting): A fitting used to mount a lighting fixture in an outlet box or on a pipe or stud. It has openings through which fixture wires may be brought out of the fixture stem.

HID lamp: A high-intensity discharge lamp.

High-intensity discharge (HID) luminaire: A luminaire (lighting fixture) that generates light from an arc lamp contained within an outer tube.

Horsepower (hp): A unit of power equal to 746 watts that describes the output of electric motors.

Hybrid system: A system comprised of multiple power sources. These power sources may include photovoltaic, wind, micro-hydro generators, engine-driven generators, and others, but do not include electrical production and distribution network systems. Energy storage systems, such as batteries, do not constitute a power source for the purpose of this definition.

Identified: Recognized as suitable for the use, purpose, etc.

Illumination: The supplying of light or lighting up a given area. The density of light flux projected on a surface, measured in footcandles (FC).

Impedance: The total opposition to the flow of current in an ac circuit.

Incandescent lamp: A lamp in which the light is produced by a filament of conducting material contained in a vacuum and heated to incandescence by an electric current.

Individual branch circuit: A branch circuit that supplies only one unit of utilization equipment.

Induction: The process by which an electrical conductor becomes electrified when near a charged body and becomes magnetized.

Information Technology Equipment (ITE): Equipment and systems rated 600 volts or less, normally found in offices or other business establishments and similar environments classified as ordinary locations that are used for creation and manipulation of data, voice, video, and similar signals that are not communications equipment as defined in the NEC®.

Instantaneous: A qualifying term used in giving properties and characteristics of apparatus indicating that no delay is purposely introduced in its action. Done in an instant.

Instantaneous-trip circuit breakers: Circuit breakers with no delay between the fault or overload sensing element and the tripping action of the device.

Insulated: Separated from other conducting surfaces by a dielectric substance or air space permanently offering a high resistance to the passage of current and to disruptive discharge through the substance or space.

Insulated conductor: A conductor covered with a material identified as electrical insulation.

Intensity of current: The strength of an electric current. It is the quantity of electricity that flows past any point in a circuit in one second, and is measured by a unit called the ampere. Represented by the letter "I".

Interactive system: A solar photovoltaic system that operates in parallel with and may deliver power to an electrical production and distribution network. For the purpose of this definition, an energy storage subsystem of a solar photovoltaic system, such as a battery, is not another electrical production source.

Intermittent duty: Operation for alternate intervals of (1) load and no load; or (2) load and rest; or (3) load, no load, and rest. A requirement of operation or service consisting of alternate periods of load and rest so apportioned and regulated that the temperature rise at no time exceeds that specified for the particular class of apparatus under consideration.

Intermittent load: A load in which the MAXIMUM current does not continue for three hours.

Interrupt: To stop a process in such a way that it can be resumed.

Interrupting rating: The maximum rating, in amperes, of an overcurrent protective device (OCPD).

Intersystem bonding termination: A device that provides a means for connecting bonding conductors for communications systems to the grounding electrode system.

Inverse-time circuit breakers: Circuit breakers with an intentional delay between the time when the fault or overload is sensed and the time when the circuit breaker operates. The greater the overload the less time the circuit breaker takes to trip. Conversely, the smaller the overload the more time the circuit breaker takes to trip.

Inverter: Equipment that is used to change voltage level or waveform, or both, of electrical energy. Commonly, an inverter [also known as a power conditioning unit (PCU) or power conversion system (PCS)] is a device that changes dc input to an ac output. Inverters may also function as battery chargers that use alternating current from another source and convert it into direct current for charging batteries.

Junction box: A box in which splices, taps or terminations are made.

kcmil: One thousand circular mils. Conductor sizes from 250 kcmil through 2,000 kcmil are expressed in this manner.

Kilo: A prefix often used with a physical unit to designate a quantity one thousand times as great. Designated by the letter "K".

Kilo-volt amperes (kva): One thousand (1,000) volt amperes.

Kilowatt (kw): One thousand (1,000) watts.

Lamp: A light source. Reference is to a light bulb, rather than a lamp.

Lampholders: Devices designed to accommodate a lamp for the purpose of illumination.

Lighting outlet: An outlet intended for the direct connection of a lampholder, a lighting fixture (luminaire) or pendant cord terminating in a lampholder.

Lighting outlets: Outlets that provide power for lighting fixtures (luminaires).

Lighting track: An assembly consisting of an energized track and luminaire units which can be positioned along the track.

Liquidtight flexible metal conduit (LFMC): A flexible metal raceway of circular cross-section with an outer liquidtight, non metallic, sunlight-resistant jacket over an inner helically-wound metal strip.

Liquidtight flexible nonmetallic conduit (LFNC): A flexible nonmetallic raceway of circular cross-section with an outer jacket which is resistant to oil, water, sunlight, corrosion, etc. The inner core varies based on intended use.

Load: The amount of electric power used by any electrical unit or appliance at any given moment.

Location, damp: Partially protected locations under canopies, marquees, roofed open porches and like locations and interior locations subject to moderate degrees of moisture, such as some basements, barns and cold storage warehouses.

Location, dry: A location not normally subject to dampness or wetness. A location classified as dry may be temporarily subject to dampness or wetness, as in the case of a building under construction.

Location, wet: Installations underground or in concrete slabs or masonry, in direct contact with the earth and locations subject to saturation with water or other liquids, such as vehicle washing areas and locations exposed to weather and unprotected.

Locked rotor: The condition when a motor is loaded so heavily that the shaft can not turn.

Locked rotor current: The steady-state current taken from the line with the rotor locked and with rated voltage applied to the motor.

Luminaire: A complete lighting fixture consisting of the lamp or lamps, reflector or other parts to distribute the light, lamp guards and lamp power supply.

Main bonding jumper: The connection at the service equipment that bonds together the equipment grounding conductor, the grounded conductor and the grounding electrode conductor.

MAXIMUM: The greatest value in any given group. A value greater than any which precedes or follows it in succession of values.

Metal wireway: A sheet metal raceway with a hinged or removable cover that houses and protects wires and cables laid in place after the wireway has been installed.

Mil: One thousandths of an inch (0.001").

Mobil home: A transportable factory assembled structure or structures constructed on a permanent chassis for use as a dwelling. A mobile home is not constructed on a permanent foundation but is connected to the required utilities. The term "mobile home" does not include manufactured homes.

Module: A complete, environmentally protected unit consisting of solar cells, optics, and other components, exclusive of tracker, designed to generate dc power when exposed to sunlight.

Motor: A device for converting electrical energy into mechanical energy.

Motor branch circuit: The point from the last fuse or circuit breaker in the motor circuit out to the motor.

Motor control center: An assembly of one or more enclosed sections with a common power bus and primarily containing motor control units.

Motor Efficiency: The effectiveness of a motor to convert electrical energy in to mechanical energy. The more efficient a motor is the less current it draws. Conversely, the less efficient a motor is the more current it draws.

Motor starter: An electrically operated switch (contactor) that includes overload protection.

Multiconductor cable: It consists of a number of individually insulated wires, either solid or stranded, which may or may not be grouped together within an outer covering. Sometimes an outer sheath of aluminum or steel is placed over the cable.

Multifamily dwelling: A dwelling with three or more dwelling units.

Multioutlet assembly: A metal raceway with factory-installed conductors and attachment plug receptacles. Usually surface mounted.

Multiwire branch-circuit: A branch circuit with two or more ungrounded conductors having a potential difference between them, and is connected to the neutral or grounded conductor of the system.

Nameplate: A plaque giving the manufacturer's name, current rating and voltage of a transformer, generator, motor, appliance, etc.

Neutral: Neither positive nor negative; having zero potential; having electrical potential intermediate between the potentials of other associated parts of the circuit, positive with reference to some parts, negative with reference to others.

Nipple: A short piece of conduit or tubing having a length not exceeding 24 inches.

Noncoincidental loads: Loads that are not on at the same time.

Nonlinear load: A load where the wave shape of the steady-state current does not follow the wave shape of the applied voltage. Examples of nonlinear loads are electronic equipment, such as computers and HID and fluorescent lighting.

Nonmetallic-sheathed cable (NM): A factory assembly of two or more insulated conductors having an outer sheath of moisture-resistant, flame-retardant, non-metallic material.

Non-time delay fuses: Fuses that may detect an overcurrent and open the circuit without any delay.

Ohm: The unit of measurement of electrical resistance. One ohm of resistance will allow one ampere of current to flow through a pressure of one volt.

Ohm's Law: A law which describes the mathematical relationship between voltage, current and resistance.

One-family dwelling: A dwelling with one dwelling unit.

Outlet: Any point in the electrical system where current supplies utilization equipment.

Overcurrent: Any current in excess of that for which the conductor or equipment is rated. It may result from overload, short circuit, or ground fault.

Overload: Operation of equipment in excess of normal, full-load rating, or of a conductor in excess of its rated ampacity that, when it persists for a sufficient length of time, would cause damage or dangerous overheating. A fault, such as a short circuit or ground fault, is not an overload.

Overload protection: A device that prevents overloading a circuit or motor such as a fuse or circuit breaker.

Panelboard: A single panel or group of assembled panels with buses and overcurrent devices, which may have switches to control light, heat or power circuits.

Parallel conductors: Two or more conductors that are electrically connected at both ends to form a single conductor.

Pendants: Hanging luminaires (lighting fixtures), that use flexible cords to support the lampholder.

Permanently-connected appliance: A hard-wired appliance that is not cord-and-plug connected.

Permanently installed swimming pool: A pool constructed in ground or partially above ground and designed to hold over 42 inches of water and all indoor pools regardless of depth.

Phase: Used in ac terminology, refers basically to time. Usually the phase position is defined by specifying the number of electrical degrees between the phase and the reference position. The number of electrical degrees that two quantities are out of phase is called the phase angle.

Phase conductor: The conductors other than the neutral conductor.

Phase converter: An electrical device that converts single-phase power to three-phase power.

Phase-to-ground voltage: The maximum voltage between any two phases of an electrical distribution system.

Portable appliance: An appliance which is actually moved or can be easily moved from one place to another in normal use.

Power (watts): A basic unit of electrical energy, measured in watts. Power is usually expressed as the letter "P" or "W".

Power (volt- amperes): The apparent power in an ac circuit or electrical system. Represented by the letters "VA".

Power factor: The ratio of the voltage and current, or volt-amperes that do useful work in an ac circuit or equipment, to the total voltage and current, volt-amperes, flowing in the circuit. Power factor is usually expressed as "pf."

Premises wiring: Basically all interior and exterior wiring installed on the load side of the service point or the source of a separately derived system.

Primary: The part of a motor or transformer having windings that are connected to the power supply line.

Primary current: The current in the primary of a transformer.

Primary winding: The coil of a transformer which is energized from a source of alternating voltage and current. The input side.

Pull box: A box used as a point to pull or feed electrical conductors in the raceway system.

Rated current: The load, in amperes, that a circuit breaker is intended to carry continuously without opening of the circuit.

Raceway: A metal or nonmetallic channel for enclosing and protecting conductors.

Receptacle outlets: Outlets that provide power for cord-and-plug connected equipment.

Recreational vehicle: A vehicular type unit which is self-propelled or is mounted on or pulled by another vehicle and is primarily designed as temporary living quarters for camping, travel or recreational use.

Resistance: That property of a conductor by which it opposes the flow of an electric current, resulting in the generation of heat in the conducting material. Usually measured in ohms. Resistance is usually represented by the letter "R".

Rigid metal conduit (RMC): A conduit used to enclose conductors, made of metal with a galvanized protective coating.

Rigid nonmetallic conduit (RNC): A conduit made of materials other than metal, usually polyvinyl chloride (PVC).

Secondary current: The current induced in the secondary of a transformer or induction coil.

Separately derived system: A premises wiring system whose power is derived from a source of electric energy or equipment other than a service. Examples of separately derived systems are transformers, generators and storage batteries. Such systems have no direct connection from circuit conductors of one system to circuit conductors of another system, other than connections through the earth, metal enclosures, metallic raceways, or equipment grounding conductors.

Series circuit: A circuit supplying energy to a number of loads connected in series. The same current passes through each load in completing its path to the source of supply.

Service: The conductors and equipment for delivering electric energy from the serving utility to the wiring system of the premises served.

Service conductors: The conductors from the service point or other source of power to the service disconnecting means.

Service drop: The overhead service conductors that extend from the last pole of the utility supply system to the service-entrance conductors at the building or structure.

Service-entrance cable (SE): A single or multiconductor assembly with or without an overall covering.

Service-entrance conductors: Conductors that connect the service equipment for the building or structure with the electrical utility supply conductors.

Service equipment: All of the necessary equipment to control the supply of electrical power to a building or a structure.

Service lateral: The underground service conductors that connect the utility's electrical distribution system with the service-entrance conductors.

Service mast: An assembly consisting of a service raceway, guy wires or braces, service head and any fittings necessary for the support of service drop conductors.

Sheath: The final outer protective coating applied to a cable.

Short circuit: The unintentional connection of two ungrounded conductors that have a potential difference between them. The condition that occurs when two ungrounded conductors (hot wires), or an ungrounded and grounded conductor of a circuit, come in contact with each other.

Short circuit protection: Any automatic current-limiting system that enables a power supply to continue operating at a limited current. and without damage, into any output overload including short-circuits.

Show window: Any window used or designed to be used for the display of goods, products, services, or advertising material. Usually visible by the general public from street or floor level.

Single phase: A term applied to a simple alternating current of uniform frequency as distinguished from polyphase currents.

Single-phase circuit: An ac circuit consisting of two or three intentionally interrelated conductors.

Solar cell: The basic photovoltaic device that generates electricity when exposed to light.

Solar photovoltaic system: The total components and subsystems that, in combination, convert solar energy into electric energy suitable for connection to a utilization load.

Spa (hot tub): An indoor or outdoor hydromassage pool or tub that is not designed to have the water discharged after each use.

Special permission: The written approval of the authority having jurisdiction.

Splice: A joint used for connecting conductors together.

Stationary appliance: A cord-connected appliance that is intended to be fastened in place or located in a dedicated space.

Switch: A device, with a current and voltage rating, used to open or close an electrical circuit.

Switchboard: A single panel or group of assembled panels with buses, overcurrent devices and instruments.

Temperature rise: The amount of heat that an electrical component produces above the ambient temperature.

Thermal protection: Refers to an electrical device which has inherent protection from overheating. Typically in the form of a bimetal strip which bends when heated to a certain point.

Three-phase circuit: a combination of circuits energized by ac that differ in phase by one third of a cycle, which is 120 degrees.

Three-phase power: A combination of three alternating currents (usually denoted as a, b and c) in a circuit with their voltages displaced 120 degrees or one third of a cycle.

Three-phase transformer: A combination in one unit of three single phase transformers with separate electric circuits, but having certain magnetic circuits in common. There are three magnetic circuits through the core and the fluxes in the various circuits are displaced in phase.

Time delay fuse: Fuses designed to provide a time interval upon detection of an overload, before blowing. This type of fuse is used primarily for overcurrent protection for motors.

Transformer: An electrical device that contains no moving parts, which converts or "transforms" electrical power at one voltage or current to another voltage or current.

Transformer vault: An isolated enclosure either above or below ground, with fire-resistant walls, ceiling and floor, for unattended transformers.

True power: The actual power used in an electrical circuit measured in watts or kilowatts. Represented by the letter "P" or the letter "W".

Unfinished basement: The portion of area of a basement which is not intended as a habitable room, but is limited to storage areas, work areas, etc.

Ungrounded: A system, circuit or apparatus without an intentional connection to ground except through potential indicating or measuring devices or other very high impedance devices.

Uninterruptible power supply: A power supply used to provide alternating current power to a load for some period of time in the event of a power failure.

Utilization equipment: Any electrical equipment which uses electrical energy for electronic, mechanical, heating, lighting, or similar purposes.

Ventilated: Provided with a means to permit circulation of air sufficient to remove an excess of heat, fumes or vapors.

Volt: The practical unit of electric pressure. The pressure which will produce a current of one ampere against a resistance of one ohm.

Voltage: The greatest root-mean-square (effective) difference of potential between any two conductors or the circuit concerned.

Voltage drop: The drop of pressure in an electric circuit due to the resistance of the conductor. This loss exists in every circuit. It is directly proportional to the length of the conductor, and is inversely proportional to its cross-sectional area.

Voltage, nominal: A nominal value assigned to a circuit or system for the purpose of conveniently designating its voltage class (e.g., 120/240-volts, 480Y/277-volts, 600- volts). The actual voltage at which a circuit operates can vary from the nominal within a range that permits satisfactory operation of equipment.

Voltage-to-ground: The difference of potential between a given conductor and ground.

Volt-ampere: the volt-ampere is the apparent power in an ac circuit. Represented by the letters "VA".

Wall mounted oven: An oven for cooking purposes designed for mounting in or on a wall or other surface and consisting of one or more heating elements.

Watt: The practical unit of power, being the amount of energy expended per second by an unvarying current of one ampere under a pressure of one volt.

Weatherproof: So constructed or protected that exposure to the weather will not interfere with successful operation.

Wireway: A metallic or nonmetallic trough with a hinged or removable cover designed to house and protect conductors and cables.

Wye connection: A connection that has one end of each coil connected together and the other end of each coil left open for external connections.

APPENDIX A
State Licensing Offices

Alabama
Electrical Contractors Board
2777 Zelda Road
Montgomery, AL 36106
(344) 420-7232

Alaska
Division of Occupational Licensing
Construction Contractor Section
P.O. Box 110806
Juneau, AK 99811-0806
(907)465-2550

Arizona
Registrar of Contractors
1700 W Washington Street, Suite 105
Phoenix, AZ 85007-2812
(602) 542-1525

Arkansas
Board of Electrical Examiners
10421 W Markham Street
Little Rock, AR 72205
(501) 682-4549
Fax (501) 682-1765

California
Department of Consumer Affairs
Contractors State License Board
9821 Business Park Drive
Sacramento, CA 95827
(800) 321-2752
Fax (916) 255-3900

Colorado
State Electrical Board
1560 Broadway, Suite 110
Denver, CO 80202
(303) 894-7855
Fax (303) 894-7885

Connecticut
Department of Consumer
Protection License Services
165 Capital Avenue, Room 147
Hartford, CT 06106
(860) 713-7240

Delaware
Division of Professional Regulation
Board of Electrical Examiners
861 Silver Lake Blvd., Suite 203
Dover, DE 19904
(302) 744-4500
Fax (302) 739-2711

Florida
Dept. of Business and Professional
Regulation
Electrical Contractors' Licensing Board
1940 North Monroe Street
Tallahassee, FL 32399-0071
(850)487-1395
Fax (850) 488-8748

Georgia
State Construction Industry
Licensing Board
Division of Electrical Contractors
237 Coliseum Drive
Macon, GA 31217-3858
(478) 207-2440
Fax (478) 207-1425

Hawaii
Department of Commerce and
Consumer Affairs
Board of Electricians and Plumbers
Division of Professional and Vocational
Licensing
P.O. Box 3469
Honolulu, HI 96801
(808) 586-3000

Idaho
Division of Building Safety
Electrical Bureau, Licensing Section
1090 E Watertower
Meridian, ID 83642
(208) 334-3950
Fax (877) 810-2840

Illinois
The State of Illinois does not issue
State Contractor's Licenses. Licensing is
done on a local level. Look in the
telephone directory under "Town of,"
"City of," or "County of."

Indiana
The State of Indiana does not issue
State Contractor's Licenses. Licensing is
done on a local level. Look in the
telephone directory under "Town of,"
"City of," or "County of."

Kansas
The State of Kansas does not issue State
Contractor's Licenses. Licensing is done on
a local level. Look in the telephone
directory under "Town of," "City of," or
"County of."

Kentucky
Department of Housing, Buildings and
Construction
Electrical Licensing
101 Sea Hero Road, Suite 100
Frankfort, KY 40601
(502) 573-2002

Louisiana
Licensing Board of Contractors
2525 Quail Drive
Baton Rouge, LA 70808
(225) 765-2301, (800) 256-1392

Maine
Electricians' Examining Board
35 State House Station
Augusta, ME 04333-0035
(207) 624-8603
Fax (207) 624-8637

Maryland
Board of Master Electricians
500 N Calvert Street, Room 302
Baltimore, MD 21202
(410) 230-6270

Massachusetts
Division of Professional Licensure
Board of State Examiners
Of Electricians
1000 Washington Street, Suite 710
Boston, MA 02118
(617) 727-9931

Iowa

Must be registered with the state. Licensing is done on a local level. Look in the telephone directory under "Town of," "City of," or "County of."

Michigan

Department of Labor
Electrical Administrative Board
7150 Harris Dr.
P.O. Box 30254
Lansing, MI 48909
(517) 241-9320
Fax (517) 241-9308

Minnesota

Electrical Licensing and Inspection
443 Lafayette Rd N.
St. Paul, MN 55155
(651) 284-5005
Fax (651) 284-5743

Mississippi

Contractor Licensing Board
2679 Crane Ridge Dr., Suite C
Jackson, MS 39216
(601) 354-6161

Missouri

The State of Missouri does not issue State Contractor's Licenses. Licensing is done on a local level. Look in the telephone directory under "Town of," "City of," or "County of."

Nevada

State Contractors Board
2310 Corporate Circle, Suite 200
Henderson, NV 89074
(702) 486-1100 Fax (702) 486-1190

New Hampshire

Electricians' Licensing Board
Office of the State Fire Marshal
110 Smokey Bear Blvd.
Concord, NH 03301-0646
(603) 223-4289

New Jersey

Board of Examiners of Electrical Contractors
124 Halsey Street, 6th Floor
P.O. Box 45006
Newark, NJ 07101
(973) 504-6401

New Mexico

Construction Industries Division
2550 Cerillos Rd., 3rd Floor
Santa Fe, NM 87505
(505) 476-4700
Fax (505) 476-4685

Montana

State Electrical Board
301 South Park, 4th Floor
P.O. Box 200513
Helena, MT 59620-0513
(406) 841-2309

Nebraska

State Electrical Division
800 S 13th Street, Suite 100
P.O. Box 95066
Lincoln, NE 68509-5066
(402) 471-3550
Fax (402) 471-4297

North Dakota

State Electrical Board
1929 N. Washington Street, Suite A-1
Bismarck, ND 58507
(701) 328-9522
Fax (701) 328-9524

Ohio

Construction Industry Licensing Board
6606 Tussing Road
P.O. Box 4009
Reynoldsburg, OH 43068-9009
(614) 644- 2223
Fax (614) 644-2618

Oklahoma

Occupational Licensing Service
Electrical Division
2401 NW 23rd St., Suite 2F
Oklahoma City, OK 73107-1299
(405) 521-6550

New York

The State of New York does not issue State Contractor's Licenses. Licensing is done on a local level. Look in the telephone directory under "Town of," "City of," or "County of."

North Carolina

State Board of Examiners of Electrical Contractors
3101 Industrial Dr., Suite 206
P.O. Box 18727
Raleigh NC 27619
(919) 733-9042, (800) 392-6102
Fax (800) 691-8399

South Carolina

Contractors Licensing Board
P.O. Box 11329
Columbia, SC 29211
(803) 896-4300

South Dakota

State Electrical Commission
308 S. Pierre Street
Pierre, SD 57501
(605) 773-3573, (800)233-7765
Fax (605) 773-6213

Tennessee

Board of Licensing Contractors
500 James Robertson Parkway
4th Floor
Nashville, TN 37243
(615) 741-8307
Fax (615) 532-2868

Oregon

Department of Consumer and
Business Services
Building Codes Division-Licensing
1535 Edgewater Street, N.W.
Salem, OR 97304
(503) 378-4133
Fax (503) 378-2322

Pennsylvania

The State of Pennsylvania does not
Issue State Contractor's Licenses.
Licensing is done on a local level.
Look in the telephone directory
Under "Town of," "City of," or "County of."

Rhode Island

Department of Labor & Training
Division of Professional Regulation
1511 Pontiac Avenue
P.O. Box 20247
Cranston, RI 02920-0943
(401) 462-8000
Fax (401) 462-8872

Virginia

Board for Contractors
9960 Maryland Dr., Suite 400
Richmond, VA 23233-1066
(804) 367-8511
Fax (804) 430-1033

West Virginia

State Fire Marshal
Electrician's Licensing Section
1207 Quarrier Street, 2nd Floor
Charleston, WV 25301
(304) 558-2191
Fax (304) 558-2537

Wyoming

Department of Fire Prevention
And Electrical Safety
Herschler Bldg., 122 W. 25th St.,
1-West
Cheyenne, WY 82002
(307) 777-7288
Fax (307) 777-7119

Texas

Department of Licensing and Regulation
P.O. Box 12157
Austin, TX 78711
(800) 803-9202 (TX)
Fax (512) 463-9468 (no applications)

Utah

Division of Occupational and Professional
Licensing
160 East 300 South
P.O. Box 146741
Salt Lake City, UT 84114-6741
(801) 530-6628
Fax (801) 530-6511

Vermont

State Electricians Licensing Board
1311 US Route 302, Suite 600
Barre, VT 05641
(802) 479-7561

Washington

Department of Labor and Industries
Electrical Section
P.O. Box 44000
Olympia, WA 98504-4000
(360) 902-5800

Wisconsin

Safety and Building Division
201 West Washington Avenue
P.O. Box 7970
Madison, WI 53707-7970
(608) 266-1018

APPENDIX B

NEMA Classifications

NEMA 1 – Enclosures constructed for indoor use to provide a degree of protection to personnel against incidental contact with the enclosed equipment and to provide a degree of protection against falling dirt.

NEMA 2 – Same as NEMA 1 including protection against dripping and light splashing of liquids.

NEMA 3 – Enclosures constructed for either indoor or outdoor use to provide a degree of protection to personnel against incidental contact with the enclosed equipment; to provide a degree of protection against falling dirt, rain, sleet, snow, and windblown dust; and that will be undamaged by the external formation of the ice on the enclosures.

NEMA 3R – Same as NEMA 3 excluding protection against windblown dust.

NEMA 3S – Enclosures constructed for either indoor or outdoor use to provide a degree of protection to personnel against incidental contact with the enclosed equipment; to provide a degree of protection against falling dirt, rain, sleet, snow, and windblown dust; and in which the external mechanism(s) remain operable when ice laden.

NEMA 4 – Enclosures constructed for either indoor or outdoor use to provide a degree of protection to personnel against incidental contact with the enclosed equipment; to provide a degree of protection against falling dirt, rain, sleet, snow, windblown dust, splashing water, and hose-directed water; and that will be undamaged by the external formation of ice on the enclosure.

NEMA 4X – Same as NEMA 4 including protection against corrosion.

NEMA 5 – Enclosures constructed for indoor use to provide a degree of protection to personnel against incidental contact with the enclosed equipment; to provide a degree of protection against falling dirt; against settling airborne dust, lint, fibers, and flyings; and to provide a degree of protection against dripping and light splashing of liquids.

NEMA 6 – Enclosures constructed for either indoor or outdoor use to provide a degree of protection to personnel against incidental contact with the enclosed equipment; to provide a degree of protection against falling dirt; against hose-directed water and the entry of water during occasional temporary submersion at a limited depth; and that will be undamaged by the external formation of ice on the enclosure.

NEMA 6P – Same as NEMA 6 including protection against the entry of water during prolonged submersion at a limited depth.

NEMA 7 – Enclosures are for indoor use in locations classified as Class I, Groups A, B, C, or D, and shall be capable of withstanding the pressures resulting from an internal explosion of specified gases, and contain such an explosion sufficiently that an explosive gas-air mixture existing in the atmosphere surrounding the enclosure will not be ignited. Enclosed heat generating devices shall not cause external surfaces to reach temperatures capable of igniting explosive gas-air mixtures in the surrounding atmosphere. Enclosures shall meet explosion, hydro-static, and temperature design tests.

NEMA 9 – Enclosures are intended for indoor use in locations classified as Class II, Groups E, F, or G, and shall be capable of preventing the entrance of dust. Enclosed heat generating devices shall not cause external surfaces to reach temperatures capable of igniting or discoloring dust on the enclosure or igniting dust-air mixtures in the surrounding atmospheres. Enclosures shall meet dust penetration and temperature design test, an aging of gaskets (if used).

NEMA 12 – Enclosures constructed (without knockouts) for indoor use to provide a degree of protection to personnel against incidental contact with the enclosed equipment; to provide a degree of protection against falling dirt; against circulating dust, lint, fibers, and flyings; and against dripping and light splashing of liquids.

NEMA 12K – Same as NEMA 12 including enclosures constructed with knockouts.

NEMA 13 - Enclosures constructed for indoor use to provide a degree of protection to personnel against incidental contact with the enclosed equipment; to provide a degree of protection against falling dirt; against circulating dust, lint, fibers, and flyings; and against the spraying, splashing, and seepage of water, oil, and non-corrosive coolants.

Hazardous Location Basics

<u>Definitions:</u>

Hazardous location [NEC®-500] – An area where the possibility of explosion and fire is created by the presence of flammable gases, vapors, dusts, fibers or flyings.

Class I [NEC®-500.5(B)] – Those areas in which flammable gases or vapors are or may be present in the air in qualities sufficient to produce explosive or ignitible mixtures.

Class II [NEC®-500.5(C)] – Those areas made hazardous by the presence of combustible dust.

Class III [NEC®-500.5(D)] – Those areas that are hazardous because of the presence of easily ignitable fibers or flyings, but in which such fibers or flyers are not likely to be in suspension in the air in quantities sufficient to produce ignitible mixtures.

Division 1 [NEC®-500.5(B)(1), 500.5(C)(1), 500.5(D)(1)] – Division One in the normal situation, the hazard would be expected to be present in everyday production operations or during frequent repair and maintenance activity.

Division 2 [NEC®- 500.5(B)(2), 500.5(C)(2), 500.5(D)(2)] – Division Two in the abnormal situation, material is expected to be confined within closed containers or closed systems and will be present only through accidental rupture, breakage, or unusual faculty operation.

Groups [NEC®-500.6(A)(1,2,3,4) & 500.6(B)(1,2,3)] – The gases of vapors of Class I locations are broken into four groups by the code. A, B, C, and D. These materials are grouped according to the ignition temperature of the substance, its explosion pressure and other flammable characteristics.

Class II – dust locations – groups E, F, and G. These groups are classified according to the ignition temperature and the conductivity of the hazardous substance.

Seals [NEC®-501.15 & 502.15] – Special fittings that are required either to prevent the passage of hot gasses in the case of an explosion in a Class I area or the passage of combustible dust, fibers, or flyings in a Class II or III area.

Articles 500 through 504 (2011 NEC®) – Explains in detail the requirements for the installation of wiring of electrical equipment in hazardous locations. These articles along with other applicable regulations, local governing inspection authorities, insurance representatives, and qualified engineering/technical assistance should be your guides to the installation of wiring or electrical equipment in any hazardous or potentially hazardous location.

Typical Class I Locations:

- Petroleum refineries, and gasoline storages and dispensing areas.
- Industrial firms that are flammable liquids in dip tanks for parts cleaning or other operations.
- Petrochemicals companies that manufacture chemicals from gas and oil.
- Dry cleaning plants where vapors from cleaning fluids can be present.
- Companies that have spraying areas where they coat products with paint or plastics.
- Aircraft hangars and fuel servicing areas.
- Utility gas plants and operations involving storage and handling of liquefied petroleum gas or natural gas.

Typical Class II Locations:

- Grain elevators, flour and feed mills.
- Plants that manufacture, use, or store magnesium or aluminum powders.
- Plants that have chemical or metallurgical processes of plastics, medicines, and fireworks, etc.
- Producers of starch or candies.
- Spice-grinding plants, sugar plants, and cocoa plants.
- Coal preparation plants and other carbon-handling or processing areas.

Typical Class III Locations:

- Textile mills, cotton gins, cotton seed mills, and flax processing plants.
- Any plant that shapes, pulverizes, or cuts wood and creates sawdust or flyings.

Note: Fibers and flyings are not likely to be suspended in the air, but can collect around machinery or on lighting fixtures and where heat, a spark, or hot metal can ignite them.

NOTES

Made in the USA
Coppell, TX
02 February 2020